INSIDE THE GENDER JIHAD

Islam in the Twenty-First Century

Series Editor: Omid Safi

Also in this series:

Sexual Ethics and Islam, Kecia Ali
Progressive Muslims, Ed. Omid Safi

Inside the Gender Jihad

Women's Reform in Islam

Amina Wadud

ONEWORLD

OXFORD

INSIDE THE GENDER JIHAD

Oneworld Publications
185 Banbury Road
Oxford OX2 7AR
England
http://www.oneworld-publications.com

ISBN-10: 1–85168–463–8
ISBN-13: 978-1-85168-463-2

Typeset by Forewords, Oxford

Cover design by E-digital Design

Printed and bound by The Maple-Vail Book Manufacturing Group,
Braintree, MA, USA

Learn more about Oneworld. Join our mailing list to
find out about our latest titles and special offers at:

www.oneworld-publications.com

Contents

Foreword

Khaled Abou El Fadl, UCLA School of Law[*]

The author of this book became internationally famous as the woman who led a mixed-gender congregation in prayers in March, 2005. Her act raised a firestorm of heated exchanges all over the Muslim and non-Muslim world, but the author remained silent throughout the controversy except for an appearance on the Al Jazeera television channel. It is not an exaggeration to say that from Egypt, Malaysia, Nigeria, Saudi Arabia, South Africa, and the Ivory Coast to England, Italy, and China, hundreds of journals and television shows not only debated the permissibility of women leading men in prayer but also inappropriately analyzed or attacked the author's character and motivation. For many Wahhabi spokesmen, slandering the author became a favored pastime, and the very influential Islamic activist, Shaykh Yusuf al-Qaradawi, dedicated an hour-long episode of his twice-weekly program on Al Jazeera to attacking the author and branding her actions as clearly un-Islamic and thus heretical. On the other hand, the Islamic scholar Gamal al-Banna, the young brother of Hasan al-Banna, the founder of the Muslim Brotherhood, wrote a short book arguing that the author's actions are well supported by Islamic sources and thus entirely orthodox. Although I suspect the author is not all too happy

[*] Professor of Islamic Law and Jurisprudence. He also teaches International Law, Human Rights, and Comparative Law as well as National Security, Immigration, and Political Asylum Law. Professor Abou El Fadl is the author of many publications on Islamic law and jurisprudence; his latest books are *The Great Theft: Wrestling Islam from the Extremists* (2005) and *The Search for Beauty in Islams* (2006).

about this, her act gained a symbolic value that, depending on one's perspective, could be characterized as positive or negative.

Towards the end of *Inside the Gender Jihad*, the author does address this incident but I think whether one supports or opposes the author's position on women-led prayers, this ought not be the reason for reading this book. This book is about much more than that, and the author's formidable intellectual output and her long history of thoughtful activism ultimately cannot be reduced to a single event or set of events regardless of how meaningful such events are or should be. The author has spent a lifetime waging a very courageous struggle against gender prejudice, and in part, this book should be read because it is an incisive condemnation of the various institutions of patriarchy within Islam. The title of this book indicates that it is about the gender *jihad* in Islam, and this is certainly true, but even this does not quite describe it – this book is about more.

Readers of *Inside the Gender Jihad* will be taken on an intellectually rigorous and truly thrilling journey not just through the problems that confront Muslims today, or the many gender injustices that plague contemporary articulations of the Islamic faith, but also through the many forms of intolerable oppression, including racism, bigotry, religious intolerance, and economic exploitation – all of which have become interminable causes of human suffering in our world. As I say intellectually rigorous, I hasten to add that this is an accessible book written to reach a broad audience and that it can be engaged by any serious reader who cares about Islam or simply human beings.

What makes this book particularly accessible is that it is semi-autobiographical – with remarkable candor and transparency the author walks the reader through her own intellectual and ethical struggles as a woman, as a mother, as an African-American, as an academic, as a Muslim, and, most importantly, as a human being. Yet because of her awe-inspiring honesty, this is one author who resists categorization or any form of reductionism. Professor Wadud cannot comfortably be fitted with a label such as feminist, progressive, liberal, or Islamist. The author does wage a *jihad* against gender prejudices and other injustices, including what she describes as the erasure of human beings and their dignity. But with a level of frankness, conscientiousness, and self-consciousness that is rarely found, she is simultaneously critical not just of conservative or traditional Islam, but also of progressive Muslims, feminism, and even, when need be, herself. The author's transparency and ability to engage and interrogate Islamic texts, and her fellow Muslims, as well as interrogate her own thought and intellectual development allows the reader to gain unique insight into the very real challenges that confront modern Muslims.

As a Muslim reading this book, I felt at different times variously engaged, enriched, enthralled, excited, upset, angered, and enraged. At times, I found myself strongly disagreeing with some of the author's arguments about Islamic law, but at all times I could not but feel a deep sense of respect for the author's integrity, courage, and honesty. This is hardly surprising in a book written by an author who does not mince words, engage in double-talk, or hide in ambiguities. But even more, I believe that this is an author who would not be happy with an uncritical and complacent reader, and would be flattered by disagreement if it were the result of a serious and engaged reading of her text. Professor Wadud is the living embodiment of someone who takes to heart the Qur'anic command to bear witness for God's sake in justice even if it is against her loved ones or herself. In essence, this is a scholar who practices what she believes and preaches, and instead of theorizing from the cushioned safety of an ivory tower, she is down in the trenches fighting for what she believes, and suffering enormously for it. Professor Wadud does share with the reader some of her experiences from this frontline, but she does not emphasize the extent to which she has consistently suffered, and has been ostracized, attacked, and even persecuted for taking her religion very seriously – in fact, more seriously than most Muslims. Consequently, the author is better positioned than most scholars to understand and explain the realities of Islam as lived and experienced by its adherents. And, indeed, Professor Wadud's book avoids the essentialisms, stereotypes, prejudices, apologetics, and sheer fantasies that fill so much of the literature on Islam that crowds the shelves of so many bookstores.

The author continues to wage a gender *jihad* from the trenches against an entrenched and stubborn patriarchy, and, in part, this book is a faithful record of that moral struggle. But, unlike so much of the sensationalistic, and at times Islamophobic, writings that are published these days, this is not a book about the trouble with Islam, what went wrong with Islam, why Islam is a problem, or why Islam is some type of implicitly failed religion. Sadly, there are too many readers in the West today who hope to find a self-hating Muslim blathering or spewing venom about the countless evils inflicted upon the author's poor suffering Muslim soul by a religion he or she supposedly chooses to follow. These types of ugly gyrations by self-declared Muslims who prostitute their own religious tradition in order to appease bigots or who clamor to serve certain vested political interests have become all too common. Of course, as to these self-hating confessional writers, one cannot help but wonder why, if Islam torments them so, they continue to associate themselves with the Islamic faith. Whatever their personal motivations, however, the reality is that there is a vast difference between those who gaze inwards while standing on a firm grounding of knowledge and those who do so while swimming in a sea of ignorance. There is also a vast difference between those who critically engage the Islamic tradition while believing that Islam is a problem and those who do so while believing that Islam is the solution. Unfortunately, particularly in the West, works by pretenders who pretentiously act out the role of reconstructionists have considerably obfuscated that critical line that differentiates learned reformers from ignorant sensationalists who are motivated by nothing more than the most prurient interests.

Those readers who are searching for the tormented soul of a self-hating Muslim or the gyrations of a sensationalist eager to please Islamophobes had better leave this book alone. On the other hand, readers who are seeking to engage in a journey of conscientious struggle and learning will find this book nothing short of enlightening. For this author, it is Islam that nourishes her struggle for justice, that forces her to be uncompromising in her honesty with others and with herself, and ultimately, that motivates her to stand steadfastly in the trenches discharging her duties as a fully autonomous moral agent. Significantly, Professor Wadud does so in the context of critically analyzing Islamic theology and reconceptualizing the relationship between a Muslim and her God. The author carefully constructs what she calls a Tawhidic paradigm – a paradigm not only of pure monotheism but of a sincere and total submission to God.

According to the author's paradigm, a person who makes the commitment to surrender to God accepts a covenant of conscientious moral and autonomous agency. The divine covenant offered by God to human beings entails an unwavering commitment to justice, integrity, truthfulness, and resistance to all forms of dominance and oppression. Injustice as well as all forms of dominance and oppression undermine and at times completely obliterate a human being's moral agency – they rob people of their autonomy – of their ability to be responsible before God for their own moral judgments and actions. Surrendering to God, however, is laden with challenges – meaningful surrender means that one must be vigilant in waging a relentless *jihad* against human weaknesses such as vanity, cowardliness, apathy, mindless conformity, self-deception, dishonesty, arrogance, and acquiescence in ignorance. Further complicating the challenge to surrender is the sheer magnanimity, limitlessness, and omnipotence of the Divine. The Divine cannot be constrained or fully represented by a text, a code of law, creation, or the actions or thoughts of created beings. In order for human agency to be a true exercise in autonomy and for the surrender to be meaningful, it is imperative that Muslims critically interrogate their texts, laws, customs, and thoughts. This critical stance vis-à-vis the divine text or law is not done for its own sake; it is an essential component of the Muslim covenant with God, as it is a critical part of the ongoing struggle to surrender meaningfully by gaining mastery and autonomy over oneself, and as it is a necessary part of the persistent quest for justice.

One cannot fully surrender what one does not own, but self-ownership, or, more precisely, self-mastery, has many impediments. Those impediments include everything that compromises the self and renders its surrender to God false, artificial, or spurious. Upon reflection, most Muslims will agree with the above statements, and they are likely to recall the oft-repeated Islamic polemic that only through sincere submission to God does one attain true liberty. But what is often overlooked or intentionally ignored is the difficulty of this surrender. Consequently, Professor Wadud's insightful and painfully honest discourse on the struggle to surrender is not just precisely the point but is also inspirational. What many Muslims fail to realize is the extent to which the exploitation of human beings, oppression, authoritarianism, and despotism are truly potent impediments – impediments that render the whole human dynamic with the Divine covenant plagued with falsehood, insincerity, and hypocrisy. As the author recognizes, despotism and oppression take many forms and are perpetuated under a variety of guises. From a theological point of view, the worst forms are when human beings usurp the role of God, and exploit the name of the Divine in the process of erasing the autonomy and will of other human beings. Professor Wadud perceptively describes the many ways by which the Divine authority, text, or law are transformed into instruments exploited by those in power in order to erase the other. This, in turn, brings us full circle to the necessity of interrogating the tools or instruments that are used to commit the religious and moral offense of erasing other human beings in God's name.

This brings me to the most important contribution of this book. Unfortunately, an inordinate number of Muslim men, and also women, fail to recognize the many ways that patriarchy is an offense against morality and Islam. Too many Muslims and non-Muslims are not sufficiently sensitized to the fact that patriarchy is despotism and that it is a morally offensive condition. As an institution, patriarchy feeds on the eradication of women's moral agency; it erases and marginalizes women; and, most significantly, it negates the possibility of true surrender to God. Likewise, an inordinate number of Muslims fail to reflect upon the extent to which patriarchy exploits the instruments of religious authority but ends up displacing God's authority altogether. Professor Wadud's frank and generous narrative about the many ways in which Muslim women, including the author, experience erasure in their various respective communities is compelling evidence of this lack of sensitivity, reflection, and awareness. Often erasure is purposeful and sinister, as when it is the result of willful animosity to women, but what is more challenging and also endemic is when erasure is subtle, inconspicuous, and nearly imperceptible because it is the outcome of moral ambivalence, or a well-theorized and well-fortified act of self-deception. After all, what could be more potent and dangerous than the seemingly endless ability of human beings to deceive themselves into believing that those who are erased are actually being affirmed, that the oppressed are actually in the process of being liberated, that the marginalized are well sheltered and protected, and that, ultimately, they like it this way?

Centuries ago the Qur'an warned human beings against the psychology of ambivalence – the dealing with moral failures through escapist strategies of displacement and projection. The Qur'an warned that the psychology of ambivalence creates people who are oblivious to the true nature of their conduct – such people corrupt the earth while insisting that they are doers of good. Corrupting the earth is a Qur'anic expression that refers to conduct that fundamentally undermines and tears apart the fabric of God's creation. The Qur'an gives several examples of such conduct, including: oppression, exploitation, duress and compulsion (*al-istid'af wa al-istibdad wa al-ikrah*), destroying life in all its forms, the attempt to annihilate the richness and diversity of human societies and their ability to intercourse with one another and reach greater understanding (*al-ta'aruf*), impeding reflection and thought, and the pursuit of knowledge (*al-tafakkur wa talab al-'ilm*), preventing people from worshipping and supplicating God each according to his or her particular way and *shari'ah* (*likulin shir'atan wa minhaja*), planting the seeds of acrimony, friction, and warfare, the destruction of places of worship, including temples, churches, and mosques, the spreading of fear, insecurity, and terror (*al-khawf wa al-irhab*), and robbing people of their sense of safety, serenity, and tranquility (*al-aman wa al-mann wa al-salwa*), and usurping people of their livelihood and properties (*al-ma'ash wa al-'amlak*). However, the quintessential act of corruption is, whether intentionally or obliviously, to perpetuate conditions that rob humans of their agency and thus their ability to partake in God's covenant in any meaningful way. A part of this corruption is to attempt to erase the Divine presence, to replace God's role by usurping and claiming the authority of the Divine as one's own, to arrogantly and pretentiously stand ready to issue judgments about God's will without due diligence, critical moral reflection, or conscientious pursuit of learning. It is the psychology of ambivalence that is responsible for the virtual flood in self-designated so-called experts indulging in *ijtihad*-talk and simultaneously spewing a plethora of ill-informed *fatwas*. Speaking one's mind is an exercise in autonomy and agency, but the practice of *ijtihad* has its own equally compelling ethics, the most essential and basic of which is well embodied by the meaning of the word itself, which is: to exert and exhaust oneself in the pursuit of thought and knowledge in search of the Divine will. Without question, Muslims ought to be free to speak their minds and voice their opinions, but it is a different thing altogether to pretend to speak the mind of the Divine and, instead of humbly voicing one's opinions, presump-tuously endowing oneself with the voice of God. I think the current state of affairs in the Muslim world is a living proof of the chaos and confusion that is borne when people lose their sense of self-respect, which is the only real barrier against people speaking out of ignorance. Perhaps it is this widespread condition of ambivalence that is responsible for the fact that so many Muslims have forgotten that learning, reflection, investigation, and invention are integral parts of the covenant to civilize the earth and spread justice throughout its corners. Perhaps it is this widespread condition of ambivalence that has made so many Muslims forget the Prophet Muhammad's teachings about the nature of piety – piety as a struggle to understand, as the pursuit of learning, and as an ethic of humble reserve in which the process of seeking enlightenment is considered far more deserving of respect than the claim of having become enlightened. I suspect that it is the psychology of ambivalence that erased and marginalized the Prophet's tradition that once uplifted Muslims into understanding that learning is a never-ending process of *jihad*, and that, taught that in the sight of God, it is far more honorable to read and think than to speak.

Ultimately, ambivalence does not only lead to a thoroughly compro-mised self, but also to the injustice of compromising others. Because of the moral offenses committed while in this condition, the Qur'an likens people who allow themselves to slip into this state of being to those who persistently forget God and so eventually God relinquishes them to their own charge – after having afforded them full autonomy and agency, and given them one opportunity after another, God leaves them to their own self-abandonment. In the Qur'anic expression, having forgotten God, ultimately God lets them forget themselves. In my view, it is this state of ethical and moral ambivalence, willful ignorance as well as well-fortified self-deceptions that precludes Muslims from critically confronting a whole host of dangerous challenges that haunt them today – evils such as patriarchy, despotism, fanaticism, puritanism, and the latest vintage brand of foreign domination and imperialism. I fear that both the moral obliviousness and ambiguity found in confronting these evils – both of which grow from the widespread condition of moral ambivalence – are directly responsible for the vastly compromised sense of dignity that so many Muslims feel today. The very least that can be said about Professor Wadud's work is that, besides articulating a resounding wake up call to Muslims, her integrity, thought, and methodology provide a much-needed and effective antidote to many problems that plague Muslims today. In his final pilgrimage and sermon, after reminding Muslims of their ethical and moral obligations, the Prophet, standing on a mountain top, called out: "God, bear witness that I have discharged my duties and warned my people!" The clear implication of the Prophet's sermon was that after Muslims have been duly warned, as fully autonomous agents it was now up to them to assume full responsibility for their own conduct and hopefully heed the Prophet's teachings. After Professor Wadud's valiant *jihad* in writing this insightful book, she has earned the right to say that she has discharged her duties, and may God bear witness that she has warned!

Acknowledgments

Over the many years that I have gathered research, participated actively, and simply prayed on each word, for each page, for each chapter, for this book, there have been countless others who have benefited me in the process. Although I will mention several specific people here, may Allah bless them all and all those who prayed, supported, encouraged, and challenged my transformations as well as all those who listened at conferences and workshops, asked questions, disagreed, and even directly humiliated me. Praise to Allah under all circumstances.

First I acknowledge institutional support. Virginia Commonwealth University first extended its support by way of a V.C.U. Grant in Aid, in 1996, to begin collecting data on "Alternative Concepts on Islam." The V.C.U. summer workshop, "Survival in the Electronic Classroom," brought me up to speed, from my dinosaur days, with the ever-expanding technology that has played multiple roles in the work I have been able to do on the gender *jihad* worldwide. It still remains a challenge. Finally, I received two academic research leaves, fall 2004 and part of summer 2005, which I used explicitly for actually writing the manuscript. In 1997–1998, I appreciated the challenge of being Research Associate and Visiting Lecturer in the Women's Studies in Religion Program, at Harvard Divinity School, in helping me to continue my work further with resources and time to investigate "Alternative Concepts of Family and Muslim Personal Law Codes."

While at the Divinity School, I was especially fortunate to create a bond that has sustained itself in love, faith, intellect, honesty, and laughter, with Dr. Susan Shapiro, a conservative Jewish Scholar currently at the University of Massachusetts also working diligently on the research project she had worked on there, to be published soon along with a second book. Thank you Susan for the grace, stamina, and wisdom of your advice and friendship; both have sustained me in faith and love.

Of my religious studies colleagues at V.C.U., I wish to acknowledge the integrity of the collective, but especially to indicate my lifelong debt to Dr. Clifford Edwards, as mentor, confidante, art museum companion, and a soul at the center of the universe, whose very presence could remind me to keep my own center, and whose professional advice surely kept me sane in an insane world (or was it insane in a sane world?). I agreed to come to V.C.U. on his example alone, as reflected in his person and his personal office, a living museum in its own right with the esthetics of one who can find and see the beauty of God in everything. I also especially wish to thank Rev. Dr. Lynda Weaver-Williams, whose lists of achievements go from the sublime to the silly. I would never have survived without the presence of these two friends and colleagues, whose consistent support, advice, and companionship helped remind me of the limitlessness in the grace of God.

Other V.C.U. colleagues whom I wish to thank for their friendship and advice, on and off campus, are Dr. Kathryn Murphy-Judy and Dr. Njeri Jackson from my earliest years on campus. And Mrs. Stephanie Yarborough Freeman for just 'being there!' May the words we shared impact the good of the planet, in the ways they were so honestly expressed.

In the larger arena of Islamic Studies I wholeheartedly thank Dr. Omid Safi for continuing to include me in his Progressive Islam projects, assisting me in finding a publisher for this book, reading through the manuscript to help strengthen its presentation and final edits, and introducing me to his family. Hold on to the rope, even when only bare-threaded. Dr. Aminah McCloud, my true sister in multiple aspects of these struggles for nearly thirty years: thank you for letting me borrow your husband Frederick Thufurrideen whenever testosterone alone would suffice to move out of the trench. Safiyah Godlas, artist, graphic designer, and dear friend: thank you, for not only reminding me to stop and smell the roses, but also for teaching me to revel in esthetic appreciation of variant hues, compositions, foreground, shapes, sizes, and the subtle variety of smells from each rose itself. Salbiah Ahmad, the first human being on the planet that Allah blessed me with to open my eyes to the delicate yet necessary balance between theory and practice: thank you for your constant presence, endearing friendship, and earnest advise for almost two decades now. Dr. Gisela Webb and Dr. Mohja Kahf, for surviving academia without being soiled by its muck and mire. Na'eem Jeenah for years of honest discourse and deep reflections. Dr. Ebrahim Moosa I mention specifically because he confirmed for me that the eloquence of articulation is nothing against the passion of direct experience. I am grateful to Allah for passion as its experiences helped shape my greater goals in life. Zainah Anwar, Executive Director of Sisters in Islam, for countless opportunities to share my work in public, with her and with love and humor. Dr. Khaled Abou-Fadl for the spirit and the substance of his work and his direct support in times of trouble. Dr. Ziba Mir-Husseini for mirroring the struggles in making the discourse real to the lives of women and men. Sh. Noorudeen Durkee, his wife Hajjah Noura Durkee, and their daughter Saeeda Durkee for many encounters of spirit and brave faith, even sometimes over a cup of coffee, surrounded by books. My Richmond sisters of brave faith, Aminah Jennah Qadir, I will miss you the most, Latifah Abdus-Sabur for your patience, Zenobia for your vision, Hanan and Khadijah for sharing the outside world away from my retreat in the trees.

Several younger Muslim women inspired, respected, and encouraged me in my work and I admit more than most will know: they are the ones to whom this book is most specifically addressed. Shahidah Kalam-I-Din and Sham-e Ali al-Jamil were both readers of earlier chapters and still struggle in many ways toward greater justice and well-being. Aliyah Bilal was a personal research assistant in the summer of 2003 who not only helped me review resources for this book, but also read earlier drafts of chapters. She is still seeking knowledge, even as far away as China.

Several Muslim men associated with the L.B.G.T.Q. Muslim organizations became friends and co-strugglers for greater tolerance, faith, and freedom. Thank you for helping me in my continued learning process as an ally: Daayiee, Siraj, Faisal, and el-Farouk.

Special thanks and adoration for my loving and wise teacher, Shaykh Ahmed Abdur-Rashid, who more than once saved my soul from the fires of hell that surrounded it and still kept the twinkle in his eye and the smile on his face while adhering to the formulas and wisdom of the *tariqah* in the deepest spirit.

Of course the last acknowledgment belongs to my children from whom I have learned more about the struggle to believe and practice Islam than through any of the various other gifts from Allah, over a period of thirty years as an active single parent with little or no support. My prayer is that one day they will come to understand the struggles of my life which made loving and caring for them even more difficult because I sometimes had work for Allah outside the home that did not allow me enough time to do the work for Allah that they might have wanted me to do for them inside the house; for that is the foundation of my gender *jihad*.

January 2006

Introduction

Inside the Gender *Jihad*, Reform in Islam

The scarcity of works that challenge the underlying paradigmatic basis of Islamic thought for the absence of gender, *as a principle category of Islamic thought* and as an aspect of analysis in the articulation of Islamic ideals, could not be more glaring.[1]

In the last decade, when humankind entered into the twenty-first century, Muslim women and men were already fervently engaged in discourses, activities, and developments in a struggle for greater justice in Islam and Islamic thought. The terms of this "greater justice" imply a belief that Islam, as an historical movement starting over fourteen centuries ago, was intended to establish and sustain a just social order. At different times throughout its past, it was successful in meeting that intention in many ways. It also met some failures. From both its successes and failures we learn that neither justice nor Islam is static.

Consistently, the Islamic justice tradition refers to two predetermined sources, the Qur'an, as revelation from God, and the *sunnah*, normative practices of the Prophet Muhammad who received that revelation. These have been the foundation for continued debate, interpretation, re-interpretation, contestation, and implementation. Their continuity as references does not keep even these sources static. To continue with successful advancement and progress toward competing ideas that have developed about justice through this complex time in human history also requires thorough and ongoing re-examination of ideas of justice and their manifest forms as understood by engaging meaningfully with the Islamic intellectual tradition. This must be done in concert with ongoing interpretation of the two predetermined sources along with modern global discourse and civilizational movements. Gender justice is but one, albeit significant, aspect of that re-examination. Some would assert that the very idea of gender justice, as first conceived and exerted as crucial to society, along with particular practices of gender inclusiveness and mainstreaming, as well as the essential integration of gender as a category of thought, are Western ideals in juxtaposition to certain central ideas and practices throughout Islamic history. Others have rushed to conclude that gender justice is impossible in Islam itself, on the grounds that feminism originates in the West and is therefore incongruent with Islam. Meanwhile many think all strategies and methods of reform must stem from outside the religious framework. Yet many other thinking believers in Islam have engaged in a struggle to demonstrate a correlation between Islamic ideas of justice and more recent global developments about the potential of women as full human beings in light of more gender-explicit analysis. One of my objectives here is to demonstrate part of how to transform Islam through its own egalitarian tendencies, principles, articulations, and implications into a dynamic system with practices that fulfill its goals of justice, by first admitting that concepts of Islam and concepts of justice have always been relative to actual historical and cultural situations. Our current global communalism requires more rigorous examinations and analyses into the basic sources of our tradition, then requires strategies to apply critical analysis to reform movements congruent with the Islamic core even – or especially – when occasionally it appears starkly different from some recent historical manifestations. In short, Islam, which is nothing unless lived by the people, must be lived by its people today, people who are no longer isolated from the pluralistic chaos and consequences of modernity and the after-effects of colonialism.

My life experiences as a believing Muslim woman, and Islamic studies professor, have been intimately connected with Islamic reforms. As a participant in these reforms, I struggle to knit together intellectual discourse, strategic activism, and holistic spirituality. I did not enter Islam with my eyes closed against structures and personal experiences of injustice that continue to exist. In my "personal transition,"[2] most often called conversion, however, I focused with hope and idealism to find greater access to Allah as *al-Wadud*, the Loving God of Justice. For many years and in many ways I have worked to keep that hope confirmed. While my experiences of verification form the core motivation for this book, many aspects of the

Muslim world seem to be continually spiraling away from the ideals that have inspired me and I must look thoroughly at the work needed toward arriving at renewed hope. This book negotiates between the center and the margins shared with Muslim women working, hoping, and attempting to have meaningful lives despite experiences of utter dismay and humiliation in the name of Islam. I have experienced first hand the despair and anguish, joy and exhilarations of being a Muslim woman. This work has been achieved in my own U.S. context, in the Middle East, both Northern and Southern Africa, East and Western Europe, but especially in Southeast Asia. This is a look at issues of gender justice in Islam as written from an insider perspective.

I entered Islam with a heart and mind trusting that divine justice could be achieved on the planet and throughout the universe. Not two years after I entered Islam I moved to Libya, a North African Arab country, for two years. There I found myself in the middle of a struggle for more gender-egalitarian concepts of Islamic identity and practice. I began to seek out recent ideas and behaviors that address women's marginalization in the historical development of the Islamic intellectual legacy and to Islamically empower women's consciousness about the reality of our full human dignity as a divine right. My initial theoretical focus was soon entwined with Muslim women's networks in the context of existing Muslim organizations, whether male and female, or whether exclusively female. Later I worked with government and non-government organizations, in academic circles, with non-Muslim national and international human rights and interfaith institutions, as well as with other women's groups. Coincidently, I entered Islam during the important second-wave feminist movement in the West.[3] Muslim women's engagement with issues of concern to women's well-being in Muslim societies continues to increase. Now there is a greater percentage of participants than at any other time in human history, even though still a minority against the male hegemony and privilege in Islamic reform discourse, a new critique that runs throughout this book as well as being addressed directly in chapter 7. The increased participation of women in these activities indicates a movement toward a critical mass building a variegated movement of gender empowerment, mainstreaming, and reform, including consciousness-raising, increased levels of education, promotion and protection of the rights of girls and women, movements to protect and eradicate violence against women, affirmations of women's bodily integrity, policy reforms, political empowerment and representation, religious authority, and personal spiritual wholeness.

I present some ideas about Islam and about social justice in Islamic thought and praxis with a few references to Muslim women's experiences, including my own. Primarily I reference subtle and not so subtle constructs of gender across a broad spectrum of epistemological possibilities and through formulations of fundamental ideas about the ontology of being in Islam. I look at recent historical perspectives and strategies in the struggle for gender equality, particularly during the latter part of the twentieth century and the early twenty-first century.

Some stories have a single moment of origin. Subsequent moments build upon that origin or offer supplementary stories that continue to shape the original and to help formulate ways perhaps even more significant than that original moment. For me, the origin of three decades of work on Islam, justice, and gender was the awesome light of belief that I inherited from my father, a man of faith and a Methodist minister who was born and died poor, black, and oppressed in the context of racist America. Growing under the umbrella of his love, guidance, and faith, I was never taught and therefore did not recognize any contradiction between the realities of subjective historical experience and transcendence of faith. The inner and the outer coexist and mutually affect each other. I was raised not only to link conceptions of the divine with justice, but also to link notions of justice with the divine. The development of my moral awareness started during the height of the American civil rights movement under the leadership of Dr. Martin Luther King, Jr. Of course, being the daughter of a minister who followed closely and participated personally in that struggle for justice with its strong articulation through a religious leader left its influence on me. Now, as a Muslim, wherever injustice, discrimination, and oppression occur, I am immediately conscious of explicit and repeated articulations in the Qur'an that "Allah does not oppress (*do zulm*)."[4] *Zulm* is real in historically subjective terms, but its practices cannot claim divine inspiration or values. This reasoning causes me to consider myself a believing Muslim who works for justice *on the basis of my faith*. I consider myself a pro-faith, pro-feminist Muslim woman.

Standing up for justice inspired by belief in the Ultimate, or in the divine, *Allah* in Arabic, may seem unnecessarily overstated. Yet this is an imperative at the outset to emphasize my disagreement with those who resist my positions on Islam and gender justice by hurling charges of blasphemy or heresy. Sometimes such charges push people out of the pro-faith perspective and oblige them to take up secular Western articulations of human rights or social justice. As a Muslim woman struggling for gender justice in Islam, I have not only been accused of working from outside Islam doing whatever I want, but also rejected as anti-Islamic. I will show later that efforts to push progressive Muslim women and men outside of predetermined parameters of Islam actually result from matters of definition or particular interpretation. The implication is that for any who wish to be accepted as truly Muslim, their struggles cannot go beyond established patriarchy or male authorities, otherwise they face the potential consequence of being labeled outsiders to Islam. Many sincere women and men accept the choice to stay in Islam as authoritatively defined by Muslim neo-conservative specialists or laypersons, sometimes erroneously called "fun- damentalist," so they simply choose silence. This is precisely why female voices and female-inclusive definitions of key terminology are central to the development of this work. This book offers a look at some of that terminology and at the implications behind the pragmatic inclusion of alternative definitions in the developments of all aspects of Islamic reform.

Islam is not a monolith. It has a plethora of meanings and experiences. For that reason I begin with constructions of the term Islam, not only as I have experienced them as a woman and a Muslim, but also because those who struggle for gender justice are continually confronted with contested meanings. Indeed, just as Americans were presented with a horrible affront to their sense of integrity and security by the events of September 11, 2001, when a dozen or so Muslim men laid claim to "Islam" as justification for their vehemence and violence, so too are babies born and women and men surrender in peace and harmony to a claim of "Islam." Which is the true picture, the face of evil and destruction or the face of love and life? How does any one author, believer, or audience negotiate between complex and contradictory meanings of Islam?

Recently, I have acknowledged intellectually that full honesty in struggling with the girth of possible meanings and uses of the term Islam is crucial to the development of my personal identity as a Muslim. For while I do not identify with suicide bombers or acts of violence, I cannot ignore that they occur within the ranks of that vast community of Islam. Despite their presence amongst us, I still care deeply to be Muslim. Multiple, contested, and coexisting meanings of Islam are integral to the struggles for justice in Islamic reform today, which is one of the main points that this book will demonstrate.

Early after my transition into Islam, I held an ideal of perfect Islam as both a utopian aspiration and a potential reality. This aspiration shielded me from the discordance between the utopian ideal and the realities of experience across the Muslim world and sometimes developed historically within the Islamic intellectual legacy. I reduced these to errors of interpretation or incompetent practices influenced by the diversity of cultures that make up the Muslim world. It is just as easy for liberal Muslims to dismiss Muslim terrorists by saying they are not "true" to Islam. When I engaged in such oversimplification and reductionist claims, I inadvertently implied I actually had the power to express and possess the "true" Islam. The arrogance of this claim allowed me to remove myself from the responsibility of standing against certain evils performed in the name of Islam. A painful experience at the Second International Muslim Leadership Conference on H.I.V./A.I.D.S.[5] resulted in an important transformation in this reductionist tendency. Some Muslims in the audience vehemently disagreed with the ideas and beliefs I presented in an effort to help fulfill the quest for justice for those most vulnerable to the spread of the pandemic: women and children. Those who opposed my analysis boisterously hurled their opposition directly in my face, claimed certain of my comments were blasphemous, according to their interpretations of Islam, and eventually named me a "devil in *hijab*" (head-covering).[6] At the time I was utterly stunned in the presence of such insolence from other Muslims. Since that experience, however, I have moved toward a new, albeit uncomfortable, reflection: neither their "Islam" nor my "Islam" has ultimate privilege. We are all part of a complex whole, in constant motion and manifestation throughout the history of multifaceted but totally human constructions of "Islam." I will discuss at length some of these construction in the next chapter and give justification within an Islamic framework for Muslims to struggle toward an egalitarian, humanistic, pluralistic Islam for the future.

Curiously enough, relinquishing the idea that there exists a perfect thing called Islam devoid of the consequences of human interactions allowed me to relinquish my own self-agonizing expectation that I could one day become a perfect Muslim. This book is also born out of recent transformations in my life as a Muslim, thinker, activist, and woman, allowing me to accept my flaws without sacrificing my dreams and aspirations. Indeed upon the pages that follow is a lifelong battle with my own identity as a Muslim seeking to reflect the beauty of Allah's vast dominion in all its wonder and glory while admitting to the many ways that I and other Muslims have failed to establish a believing community that mirrors that beauty without constant trials of insufficiency and trails of frailty. Thus, Islam is no longer the goal, but a process. One must continuously engage in this process, as I have done for more than three decades, including wrestling with the relationship between meanings and experiences.

The essays that follow will be expressed in the variety of ways to reflect my engagement in that process. Some essays are more idealistic than others. Some essays are more complex, abstract, and analytical than others. Some essays easily express their commonality with the stories and struggles of other writers, thinkers, and participants, especially women, in Islam, whether living or dead. Others essays stand starkly in the margins of thought and form, as a consequence of recent discourse, developments, discoveries, and disappointments. By negotiating between these structural inconsistencies as elements of my whole experience within the struggle for gender justice, I hope to show my engagement in the process to find full voice and to contribute to the meanings of being Muslim and woman. That whole experience and full voice both grows from my meager transformations and includes understanding multiple meanings of the term "Islam." The first chapter explicitly examines these multiple meanings, and provides female-inclusive meanings of foundational and key terms that are used throughout this book.

In particular my contribution remains faithful to the imperative that Muslim women appropriate Islamic primary sources, especially the Qur'an. It is indispensable to women's empowerment that they apply their experiences to interpretations of the sources when they participate in the development and reform of Muslim politics – especially in the context of ongoing deliberations of *shari'ah* (Islamic law).[7] More female-inclusive interpretations raise the legitimacy of women's claims to authority within the intellectual tradition and bear upon the practical implementation of that tradition. Although my research focus has been particularly on Qur'anic reinterpretation, simple analogies can and on occasion will be made between this reinterpretive methodology and similar applications, especially to *shari'ah*. References must be made to the scarcity of existing research reinterpreting *ahadith* (plural of *hadith*, oral report), from the Prophet, or about *sunnah*, which I encourage others to direct more attention to, to form gender-inclusive perspectives.

I used to feel that my goal in this struggle was to experience well-being in both the public and private domains of human existence through interaction with Islamic historical developments, intellectual and practical, and in the context of change and challenge. I have come to ascertain that well-being is a spiritual consequence of the process and participation. It is not the goal. Indeed, when it becomes the goal, it is often lost.[8] The Qur'an does not promise us a life of ease, while it does give indications of how to live a life of struggle and surrender in order to achieve peace and beauty here on earth as a movement toward the Ultimate.

In a later chapter of this book I will acknowledge and partially validate the recent attacks on Muslim feminists' interpretive methodologies proposed by a few male progressive thinkers.[9] However, this book demonstrates how and why these methods remain a significant part of the quest for legitimacy and efficacy for the more than 50% of the Muslim population who happen to be female. In our struggles, women continue to be either marginalized or excluded because Muslim men, including many of those who consider themselves progressive, assume and maintain authority not only based on their interpretation of those sources, but also because the conception of the public domain of an Islamic paradigm still focuses upon a fixed center in public space as predominately defined and inhabited by men. The origins of today's Muslim women's movements for greater empowerment and inclusion were heavily influenced by Western theoretical developments on women's rights and social justice.[10] Despite this larger global connection, this book will point to many ruptures between this Western origin and the need for an indigenous Muslim theoretical and practical reconstruction in the human rights discourse more appropriate to our own Islamic theoretical origins.

The benefits of this pro-Western basis lost critical ground in the frenzied accelerated reassertion of patriarchal-based interpretations of the sources, which were intertwined with authoritative abuses and random selectivity.[11] Muslim women and men began to reappropriate the primary source texts as evidence in support of their ideas and objectives to create indigenous Islamic reforms. Women were still the last ones to use textual reappropriation as a fundamental strategy of empowerment. Now we have come to address the primary sources directly and pushed for greater interpretive inclusion, not only as an act of equality against a history of near-exclusive male authority over texts, but also as a means for better self-understanding of those sources to fortify both our identity in Islam and the Islamic authenticity of our claims for reform.

At the more personal level, the following edited quote[12] gives witness to my personal identity within the context of developing Islamic thought as it led toward the struggle for gender justice:

Each of us can decide to follow the holy quest in a manner which makes our lives meaningful and which allows us the persistence and stamina to see it through the hard times.

My door into Islam was accidental. During my freshman and sophomore years in college, I began to change my lifestyle. I wore only long clothes, cut my already natural hair very short, and eventually kept it covered (in mostly African styles and wraps). I also became more conscientious about my diet: with no meat and more wholesome foods. These things I began in celebration of the honor of my being. Life is a gift that we must live with honor – not by random standards imposed on us by an exploitative environment.

Once I visited a mosque around the corner from my mother's house in a Washington, D.C. neighborhood. I think the brothers assumed from my modest attire that I "understood" all about Islam. They were anxious to increase the number of females within the ranks. They offered little information, but just said that if I believed that there is no god but Allah and Muhammad was the Prophet, I should take *shahadah*, the witness or declaration to faith and first pillar of Islam.

I pronounced my *shahadah* on Thanksgiving Day, 1972. A few months after the declaration of my Islam, another accident occurred which proved important: a non-Muslim woman from my old neighborhood, near the mosque where I took *shahadah*, gave me a copy of the Qur'an (given to her by local Muslim brothers searching out female converts). In reading the Qur'an, I relived my childhood sense of worlds of meaning through words. Sometimes, very simple statements moved me to tears and awe.

Sometimes the complexities quenched my thirst for deeper understanding. I come away from the Qur'an – to which I have dedicated all of my professional energies up to the Ph.D. in learning to interpret – with the sense that all the questions I have asked can be clarified therein. Not literally "answered," as some would say, implying that the Qur'an has the (only) Truth, or that all Truth is in it. Rather, the Qur'an establishes a true vision of the world and beyond, with meanings and possibilities of self that lead to certainty and peace.

I owe my full embrace of Islam to the Qur'an, although other reasons for sticking closely to the method of female-inclusive interpretations, especially as they relate to public policy reforms, will be unveiled throughout this book. In chapter 6, "Qur'an, Gender, and Interpretive Possibilities," I return directly to matters of text and female-inclusive interpretation, and tentatively respond to recent expressions of privileged male reformists still claiming authority in evaluating women's inclusion and justifying the sufficiency or appropriateness in women's role in justice reform.

The Qur'an inspired my participation in what has been a continual process of makeover in the Islamic intellectual legacy. In particular, it was my main source of inspiration to transform historical practices of gender asymmetry. That inspiration confirmed the idea that gender justice is essential to the divine order of the universe. Since the end of colonialism, Muslims and non-Muslims, women and men have united their recognition of gender injustice with multiple efforts to improve the status of women. These efforts are part of what could be termed a "gender *jihad*."[13] The pejorative meanings sometimes attached to the word *jihad* by both Muslim extremists and Western conservatives are intentionally overlooked here. Instead *jihad* refers to "effort" or "exertion"[14] and is translated here as "struggle." The gender *jihad* is a struggle to establish gender justice in Muslim thought and praxis. At it simplest level, gender justice is gender mainstreaming – the inclusion of women in *all* aspects of Muslim practice, performance, policy construction, and in both political and religious leadership. Although this book will focus specifically on the struggle for gender justice, it simultaneously contributes to a corpus of literature aimed at eradicating all practices, public and private, of injustice to women's full humanity in the name of Islam. Similar exclusionary and dehumanizing practices are directed toward non-Muslims and increasingly more toward non-heterosexual Muslims.

As a Muslim woman living and working with other Muslim women worldwide, I have encountered enough to understand how many seek to find their identity and full voice through continued struggle in the gender *jihad*, whether consciously or coincidentally. This book, at the dawn of the twenty-first century, joins a concert of resounding voices creating and learning songs about what "Islam" means with full inclusion of real Muslim women. Hear our song, and when the words become familiar, sing along, for ours has too often been the silence that sustained and nurtured the background. Today we need to see how esthetic balance and harmony can only result from equal integration of that background with the foreground of local, national, international, and universal recognition.

Chapter Outlines

The Introduction, "Inside the Gender Jihad, Reform in Islam," locates both my research and my personal identity within the larger framework of modern thought and practice for greater justice within an indigenous Islamic worldview rather than as a mere by-product of or reaction to Western and secular developments, practices, and experiences of justice since the Enlightenment, not as a by-product reacting to Islamist discourse. It also briefly outlines the remaining chapters of the book.

The first chapter, "What's in a Name?," identifies both the significance of definitions and the power dynamics, legitimacy, and authority accompanying those who define. The particular terms chosen here are crucial to gender inclusion of some overarching concepts. The first term discussed is "Islam," pointing out its random but authoritative abuses. Other key concepts like *tawhid*, *khilafah*, and *taqwa* are combined with some considerations of justice, *shari'ah*, and there is a short consideration of power as an ethical term used in distinct ways yielding distinct results. All terms are explored within the framework of the particular nuances of gender-inclusive reading of the Qur'an and other texts to justify legitimacy and authority, and to promote greater efficacy crucial to a paradigm shift in Islamic thought.

Chapter 2, "The Challenges of Teaching and Learning in the Creation of Muslim Women's Studies," includes both pedagogical matters and personal narrative affecting new objectives as an academic. This is more than mere objective pedagogy and discourse hierarchies; it is my reality as teacher and scholar. Thus the narratives are integral to what fuels, motivates, justifies, and legitimates actions for rethinking the role of academe in relation to Islamic reform, Islamic activism, and to having control over gender theory. It includes some consideration of the history of Muslim women's studies to suggest possibilities for more interdisciplinary corroborations and coherent theory development by prioritizing Islamic studies.

That is one reason why chapter 3, "Muslim Women's Collectives, Organizations, and Islamic Reform," follows. It attends to the relationship between theory and practice to situate women's networks within the framework of women's full human agency. Special attention is given to African-American Muslim women's networks, usually formed at the grassroots level and focused away from controversy in an attempt to "establish what is good." This is true for many grassroots organizations, and Muslim women globally are contributing to community care-giving in this context. There is a discussion of Sisters in Islam Malaysia, as it developed through various stages, to demonstrate how women's organizations evolve from the grassroots or personal collectives to the level of international acclaim, especially as granted extensive funding as well as government support.

Chapter 4, "A New Hajar Paradigm: Motherhood and Family," is the heart and soul of my life as a Muslim woman. It expands on a single thread that runs through the heart of my gender *jihad*. It discusses motherhood, marriage, and "family" as the birthplace of gender inequalities, and situ-ates the life of Hajar as an archetype for the consequences of unexamined applications of laws based on concepts insufficient to include meaningful connections to the realities of single female heads of household in the African-American Muslim community.

Chapter 5, "Public Ritual Leadership and Gender Inclusiveness," is based on an important event in South Africa in 1994 with a woman as *khatibah*, delivering a sermon in the still primarily male role, in an attempt to challenge status quo. It also, however, points to contradictions and missing comprehensive collective theory dealing with the strategic impli-cation that women are still used as objects of utility rather than fully human identities. It shows how the hybrid of activities can break stasis without reconstructing or building bridges for long-term collective forums and insti-tutional transformation. Ultimately it introduces some radical ideas about removing gender asymmetries in Islamic ritual practices – especially in leadership. Very little research has been focused on a female perspective of Islamic ritual leadership in the haste to articulate other more political opportunities for leadership.

Chapter 6, "Qur'an, Gender, and Interpretive Possibilities," context-ualizes the developments from the radical originality initiated in my book, *Qur'an and Woman*, as female-voice-inclusive, and the contradictory–complementary nature of text and interpretation. My own research has continued into the major challenge of textual hermeneutics, epistemology, and historiography over the past decade in further developments of textual analysis and implementation in more recent progressive discourse. While I have come to newer articulations of some of my contributions to textual analysis two decades ago, I juxtapose these developments to the historical continuum while simultaneously maintaining the necessity of more female-inclusive analysis.

Chapter 7, "Stories from the Trenches," provides an opportunity to discuss a few areas that have become central to considerations of gender in Islam, like *hijab*, an essay about 9/11, and explanations and responses to some public controversies as they have impacted my identity formations and feelings of belonging in community. Selective persons or arguments have constructed the gender *jihad* as an exclusion from modern Islamic realities, rather than as an indication of the failures of inclusive diversity and practices. A short rendition of the paper presented at the International Muslim Leaders' Council on H.I.V./A.I.D.S. in 2002 in Malaysia provides proof of the continued male sanctions of gender inequities of sexuality.

My concluding chapter, "Why Fight the Gender *Jihad*?," juxtaposes spirituality as an essential qualification for just actions and public policy reforms. I return, after a long journey, to my original motivation to stand up and rejuvenate faith by "spiritual activism," that is, to augment the abstract epistemology of reform discourse over revelation and human meaning toward acts of kindness and good, by joining them into a single process – change of heart, body, and soul for participants hoping to create a meaningful alternative in governing Islamic affairs worldwide. Ultimately, it is the divine gift of spirit in agency that mandates service toward building a reformed Islam to replace the chaos and corruptions, including gender oppression currently at the forefront and on the rise.

1 What's in a Name?

What's in a name?
That which we call a rose,
by any other name would smell as sweet.
– Shakespeare, *Romeo and Juliet*, II.ii.1–2

My interest in language grew from my childhood love of reading. "I was not [then] fascinated so much with the story lines: saved damsels and handsome heroes, as I was intrigued with words which could unfold images and meaning. Worlds of words. Meanings through naming."[1] Throughout this book, several key theoretical or conceptual ideals continually surface. Here they are defined in detail as foundational to a paradigm shift in the movement to attain social justice for all Muslims. In addition, these definitions are critical for understanding and appropriately applying them as they are referred to in this book. The definitions themselves were drawn directly from female-inclusive readings, especially of fundamental Qur'anic themes like *tawhid* (the unicity of God), *khalifah* (moral agent), and *taqwa* (moral consciousness). In my earliest research, Fazlur Rahman's scholarship inspired me to consider terms and their relationships to a Qur'anic worldview. He insisted that "There is no doubt that a central aim of the Qur'an is to establish a viable social order on earth that will be just and ethically based."[2] Later, I would use these terms in transforming and reconstructing an understanding of human nature in Islam. I conclude that the notion of what it means to be human is built upon a dynamic relationship between *tawhid* and *khilafah* (agency). *Taqwa* is essential to the moral attitude of the agent both as an individual as well as as a member of society in Islam. Activating the *tawhidic* principle as a matter of personal practice and in the definitions, establishment, and sustenance of a just social order – the primary responsibility of being human – is the means for practicing a more egalitarian, humanistic, and pluralist Islam today. Injustice (*zulm*), on the other hand, signals neglect of these conceptual developments. Such *zulm* has been directed toward women not only throughout Islamic history, but also with new and more vicious consequences today.

> Whether ultimately it is the individual that is significant and society merely the instrument of his [*sic*] creation or vice versa is academic, for individual and society appear to be correlates. There is no such thing as a society less individual. Certainly the concepts of human action we have discussed, particularly that of *taqwa*, are meaningful only within a social context.[3]

Despite the utility of *tawhid* and *khalifah* as fundamental aspects of social justice, I admit that theory alone is insufficient to end patriarchy and gender asymmetry.[4] To acknowledge a crucial interplay between theory and praxis, however, emphasizes the belief in certain ideals, principles, and values as they lead to practical implementation of gender justice. Advocating the inclusion of female experiences to alternative Qur'anic interpretation was one of the first radical yet simple justifications demonstrating the facility and necessity of gender mainstreaming within intra-Islamic theory as fundamental to the means and methods of actually implementing that justice. Admittedly, we achieve little or nothing from the Qur'an alone except in the pragmatic sense of those who claim allegiance to its mandates, values, and virtues to implement justice. These Qur'anic values and virtues inspire persistence in the struggle and resistance to the limitations put on women's full human dignity. Too many claim authority and legitimacy on the basis of literal, narrow, reductionist, and static interpretations of justice, Islam, Islamic sources, and gender. As much as this was pervasive in the patriarchal history of Muslim society, the proactive inclusion of women's experiences and interpretations is crucial to transforming gender status toward its higher egalitarian potential.

Semantics

Although it may seem simple enough to challenge patriarchal perspectives by re-reading and radically interpreting the same sources to which Muslim neo-conservatives refer as authorities, only in the last two decades have Muslim women most effectively used this particular strategy for participating in practical reforms at a comprehensive level. As early as the first century of Islam one might find random references to women who disputed on a Qur'anic basis, but this was not the norm. The development of a female inclusive theory based on interpretative authority as central to a basic paradigmatic core of what is considered "Islam" began only in the latter part of the twentieth century. Its efficacy as a form of legitimacy has helped reconstruct the exclusively male control over who determines what "Islam" means. It was also not developed initially as a direct consequence of already existing discourse over Qur'anic interpretation by male liberal and reformist scholars.

This chapter does not intend to overlook what this book demonstrates throughout; the challenge to women's full human dignity is not limited to mere rhetorical debates over theory and interpretation. The ultimate intention is to achieve living experiences of justice for as many Muslim women and men as possible, as part of what it means to be human. The premise of my preoccupation with the development of theoretical considerations and analysis of intra-Islamic ideas is that a theory is only as good as its practical implementation. Furthermore, my motivation has always been pro-faith in perspective. Any comparative analysis with secular Western theories or strategies for mainstreaming women in all aspects of human development and governance is coincidental and secondary. I have recognized how essential it is to construct underlying theoretical frameworks through many opportunities to work with women and men on the real experiences of lived Islam – from personal faith, to family structures, in the context of conflicts and resolution, and onto the larger arena of policy and legal reforms in national and international political and economic environments. Examining the terms as I have expressed these definitions and nuances inclines one toward potential pragmatic goals. Semantics is part of developing liberative theory. It contributes to a paradigm shift that can help Muslims build a theology of care, or an ethics of compassion, where nurturing and compassion are ultimate determining characteristics of true "Islam." As it stands, women in families are the best exemplars of this care. This is why my definitions emphasize female inclusion in reading Islamic primary sources and in defining certain key terms. These definitions and ideas demonstrate their utility in creating actual change in Muslim societies while yielding mechanisms to integrate lived Islam into global pluralism.

Isuzu makes a "technical distinction between . . . 'basic' meaning and 'relational' meaning, as one major methodological concepts of semantics . . . Each individual word, taken separately, has its own basic meaning or conceptual content on which it will keep its hold even if we take the word out of its Koranic [*sic*] context." He does not assert that this will "exhaust the meaning of the word." In the Qur'anic context, words assume an "unusual importance as the sign of a very particular religious concept surrounded by a halo of sanctity . . . In this context, the word stands in a very close relationship to Divine revelation" and "acquires a lot of new semantic elements arising out of this particular situation, and also out of the various relations it is made to bear to other major concepts of that system . . . The new elements tend gravely to affect and even modify essentially the original meaning structure of the word." Concepts "do not stand alone and in isolation but are always highly organized into a system or systems."[5] Part of my discussion helps organize a structure or system of social justice for Islam – especially inclusive of the full range of women's lives and potentialities as contributors – relevant to today's global pluralistic complexities. It is a partial attempt to establish a modern universal understanding of human rights that can be fairly and uniformly implemented across various cultural and historical differences.

To Define Islam Is to Have Power Over It

Of all the terms in this chapter, the multiple and complex use of the word "Islam" as offered by various participants in public discourse requires first review. The following list refers to many of the definitions commonly used (in no particular order).

1. Islam is everything.
2. Islam means engaged surrender: consciously accepting to surrender to the will of Allah as an exemplification of the human status as both agent (*khalifah*) and servant (*'abd*).
3. Islam means peace: from its S-L-M root form, and as a reflection of the peace achieved when one lives in harmony with the greater cosmic or divine order.
4. Islam means terrorism and, conversely, terrorism means Islam.
5. Islam is the name of a religious tradition.
6. Islam is whatever any Muslim does, no matter how extreme or how mainstream.
7. Islam is a reflection of the primary sources: Qur'an and *sunnah*.

8. Islam is the most recent descendent of the three Abrahamic faiths.
9. Islam means following the *shari'ah*, usually said without distinction from *fiqh*, historical jurisprudence. (In other words, *shari'ah* itself has more than one definition.)
10. Islam is culture.
11. Islam is used to delineate one of many cultures, with the notable exclusion of Western cultures.
12. Islam is the history, culture, esthetics, and the political, intellectual, and spiritual developments of Muslims.
13. Islam is a set of fixed prescriptions or codes.
14. Islam is whatever I do or my culture does.
15. Islam is in the heart.
16. Islam is an Arab religion pre-eminent and exclusive to Arabic culture and history.
17. Islam is *din*, "a way of life."
18. Islam is "other," deviant, an aberration of true religion.
19. Islam is irrelevant to anything in the real world.

In the politics of working to reform Islam, some definitions can be used to limit gender justice and others to liberate. Definitions are the heart of interpretation and part of the path for gender-inclusive implementation. Therefore, the use and abuse of the word "Islam" is politically charged. People attach the word "Islam" onto their arguments to acquire definitive authority and to authoritatively construct limits on discourse. Abou El Fadl[6] gives an example of this using the Qur'anic passage "*No one can know* the soldiers of God except God" (74:31) (emphasis mine). After elaborating on some interpretations given to this passage, he admits: "I have always understood this Qur'anic verse to be a negation of the authoritarian – *it denied any human being the claim* that he or she is a soldier of God endowed with God's authority" (emphasis mine). Despite this, such claims are pervasive and persuasive.

In particular, interpretations of Islam's primary sources, or even the very claim that what one is espousing *is* "Islam," continues to be one of the most effective tools to silence oppositional voices, inhibiting a large majority of Muslims in their intent and claim to honor the Islamic tradition, either with an obscure, reductionist, out of context quotation or without reference to a specific source text in defense of their arguments. At another level, discourse between those more familiar with the Islamic intellectual tradition and sources of the debates becomes more elaborate in the use of

"Islam," but the meaning and use of the word is indispensable to the conclusions drawn, sometimes despite consensus over other definitions. Finally, political regimes or opposing political parties corroborate with certain definitions provided by their own experts incorporated in ministries, advisory councils, or think tanks specifically set up to determine religious legitimacy. Many Muslim governments support these specific usages of the term "Islam" and the users have the coercive legal force to threaten and restrict discourse and disqualify certain discussants. Hopefully greater freedom from authoritative abuses will result from a general rise in education and institutions of learning. Unfortunately, even in higher learning only fragmented concepts are provided, depending upon larger agendas and ulterior motives of control and authority. This again points to manipulative intents in using the word "Islam" or its derivatives to narrow the space for genuinely free and open dialogue. There are endless implications behind multiple ways Muslims and non-Muslims consistently or inconsistently use the term "Islam."

Anyone writing, reading, or speaking about "Islam" has some meaning in mind. Clear articulation about meaning(s) is therefore an imperative prerequisite to the clarity of discussion. Likewise, it is obligatory that there is consistency between stated definitions and subsequent uses. Confusion arises when multiple meanings are used in the absence of clear definitions, or when using meanings that differ from the one initially provided. There does not have to be a single or consistent meaning throughout one's discussion, but at the very least, if an author begins by defining a particular meaning, he or she must either supply new ones wherever the term is used differently, or remain consistent to that initial definition.

Some definitions seem impartial, like using "Islam" as one of three Abrahamic traditions. It merely distinguishes it from the history, development, and dogma of the other traditions, especially considering the unlimited distinctions and similarities between them. This is Islam as a historically based faith movement. Its utility is best demonstrated when teaching at the undergraduate level. To even engage those distinctions and similarities requires a handle term to indicate the reference to Islam in particular. Islam is the name of a religion, which students in that course will be considering through a complete learning process.

At the level of the average Muslim man or woman on the street, Islam is whatever they have inherited, culturally and ethnically. Since they are Muslim, they do Islam. When my youngest daughter goes to a mosque or community function she is enthusiastic about the opportunity to eat

"Muslim food." Here, her Islam is somehow essential to basmati rice, curried meats and vegetables, certain seasonings or Mediterranean delicacies, and chapatti bread. Fatima Mernissi[7] elaborates on what might be called Islam by birth in Arab culture in her chapters "The need to be Arab" and "The need to be Muslim":

> By affirming its claim to be Arab and Muslim, Morocco expresses a view of the world based on specific aspirations and drawing its ideology from specific sources. Islam *is not merely a religion*. It is a holistic approach to the world characterized by a "unique" insistence upon itself as a coherent and closed system, a sociological and legally and even politically organized system in the mundane world. (emphasis mine)

Leila Ahmed also refers in her memoirs[8] to her inheritance of Islam as the upbringing by Muslim parents or in a Muslim cultural context. Here the emphasis is shifted to undefined qualities resulting from cultural experience whether or not they include aspects of volition regarding acceptance of definitions given to methods or conclusions of historical study. Cultural affiliations may not even be related to observation of religious rituals. She once told me she had been asked, "Are you a practicing Muslim?" Being "in the West" – with its conspicuous community of Muslims, including those who transit into Islam (converts, reverts, born-againers); those who are transnational (immigrants from cultural and ethnic communities with a long history of Islam) and their descendents; those with various orientations toward Islam, such as neo-traditionalists, recently formed clusters of reformist (still not always clearly identified against Muslim liberals) progressives; those who reject Islam; as well as secularist Muslims – she faces an unprecedented set of criteria used to determine status in Islam. Within the female space of her cultural upbringing, which created its own self-identity distinct even from practices and perspectives dictated in mosque discourse, she was exempted from such concerns over identity as Muslims. Consequently, her diverse position within this amalgam qualifies her and others to remain *within* the boundaries of Islam in the ways most meaningful to their personal identity and the methods and motivations used to determine the boundaries of Islam.

Within the context of definitions and conceptions of "Islam," I also began evaluations of gender and was led ultimately to justify the need for extensive reform in Muslim thought and praxis. My first question was how are women treated in "Islam"? The answer to this question I presumed would primarily be based on how women were treated as individuals, in families, and as members of Muslim societies, all of them patriarchal. The resulting research and observation primarily showed grave inequalities. I learned and began to teach the significant distinction between "Islam" and "what Muslims do." The main way Western media uses the term "Islam" is based on whatever Muslims do. If they treat women cruelly despite its incoherence from a long intellectual tradition of Islamic principles, ideals, and values, the resulting reform is insufficient because it is incomprehensive. With such a definition Islam is the reason for Muslims who are abusive and therefore only the full destruction of Islam is mandated. While this book focuses on the need for reforms, it provides some theoretical justifications from a theological perspective, and looks at strategies toward constructing such reforms from within the framework of my primary use of the word "Islam," as premised upon the conceptual framework that Muslims either choose engaged surrender to Allah's will or justify deviation from it by selective inclusions and omissions within the broad possibilities for naming "Islam."

The more years I have lived as a Muslim woman, the more inequality I have discovered between women and men. My initial theoretical concern was to determine if the cause of women's inequality was because of "Islam" itself. I did not fully grasp how this question not only presumed a uniform understanding of "Islam," but also presumed that all Muslims used that definition to do whatever they do. It did not take long to identify how certain definitions of Islam were condoned or condensed exclusively by male authority, by various ideologies, as well as by culture, history, and by the sheer privilege of presumption – even up to the present time.

Despite numerous definitions, historical and current, whether explained or not, knowingly or unknowingly, each user assumes some authority that justifies him or her to determine when others would be considered adherents to their understandings, practice, and limitations of "Islam." From the multiple parameters of these understandings of "Islam," the discussions with diverse presumptions, the social-cultural climate, and the positions of authority, others could be accused of heresy, deviance, or even blasphemy or *kufr*, disbelief or infidelity to Islam. Meanwhile, if one intends to work from "an Islamic perspective," he or she does not want to forfeit Islamic legitimacy. One of the most intimidating strategies used to deter women from working openly on reforms within an Islamic framework is the powerful force of techniques that accuse others of denying or going against "Islam." So as Muslims learn about developments in Islamic thought, either for themselves as believers or as potential and actual participants in establishing and maintaining a reformed "Islam," they either become skeptical of themselves or of the intent of certain references used negatively to accuse them of "going against Islam." Eventually, this skepticism has led many to question whether the solution to establishing a just society or human rights lay within "Islam" at all.

I reclaim the right for all Muslims to accept their own identity as Muslim while holding a vast diversity of opinions and experiences. While I accept their identification as Muslims, I also expect their acceptance of others who identity as Muslims. Over time, my concept of "Islam" has gone through several transformations. In the earliest days of my research, I agreed wholly with Fazlur Rahman, that the best way to determine what is or is not Islam is on the basis of the primary sources.[9] "I welcome the phenomenological approach with the provision that its users recognize the Qur'an and the *sunnah* as normative criteria-referents for all expressions and understandings of Islam."[10] While Muslim scholars and laity who claim to articulate "an Islamic position" refer to these sources, the various conclusions drawn from their claims lead to an important caveat. As they analyze the same sources, their diverse conclusions indicate that what is basic to "Islam" results from only the human interaction with those texts – an interpretive process. Ultimately textual meaning is neither fixed nor static. Hermeneutics, as core to the act of interpretation, must be emphasized, since a single source can and has led to diverse conclusions.[11] This historical and current method of interpretive reference mostly excludes women and women's experiences. Therefore interpretations of the textual sources, and application of those interpretations when constructing laws to govern personal and private Islamic affairs and to construct public policies and institutions to control Islamic policies and authority, are based upon male interpretive privilege.

Using the Qur'anic text to define "Islam" has the same potential pitfalls as claiming certain definitions of "Islam." The patriarchal norms of seventh-century Arabia left its mark upon the nature of the Qur'anic articulation and continued to do so for centuries with interpretation and implementation. Furthermore, narrow minds point to even more narrow interpretive potential of textual references. Hopefully, reformists will not only point to more liberative and egalitarian references, they will also elaborate on those references to free the text from the potential snares in some of its own particular utterances. This fortunately lends support to accepting human agency as a critical resource for establishing and maintaining dynamism between a linguistically articulated text, of divine origin, addressed at a fixed time while simultaneously intending to provide eternal guidance, as well as for understanding the meanings of Islam.[12]

Islam as Engaged Surrender

Most introductory textbooks and courses on "Islam" equate Islam with the word submission. "Islam means submission to God's will." Since "God's will" is a complex conceptual assertion too – for example, one that equates "God's will" with the historically developed legal system through *shari'ah*, because it was explicitly derived by the use of divine sources – then the meaning of "God," "Allah," as well as of "God's will" also requires clarification or definition. After some thought, I departed from one norm by rejecting the word submission. I prefer to use Islam as "engaged surrender." Although subtle, the idiosyncrasy between submission and surrender is significant. I understand the word submission as involuntary, coerced externally and limited to a prescribed set of required duties. Many Muslims actually confess that a Muslim *must submit* to their understandings of a prescribed set of required duties as if there is no choice. Submission is enforcement situated completely outside of the one who submits. However, if such a coercive construction really existed, then the extensive and continual failure of Muslims to submit – as evident throughout Muslim history and in the present – would be impossible. Islam would be universally sanctified and religiously exemplary. Muslims disobey Allah's will obviously because they *can* exercise choice.

In this respect, engaged surrender emphasizes the requisite role of human agency. It is conscious recognition of choice and exercising that choice as an agent, not a puppet. For example, even if a woman is under duress, say at knifepoint, to submit her purse, she still has choice. She could choose to resist the command, accepting responsibility for the potential perils and even catastrophic consequences of her resistance. Ultimately her choice might not save her purse or her person from the one with the knife. However, she still has the agency of choice in facing the situation and ultimately shares responsibility in the consequences. In choosing the term "engaged surrender" for Islam, the outcome shows greater agency exercised through personal conscientious participation.

No definition has been as significant to my identity and work as a Muslim woman in the gender *jihad* as has Islam as "engaged surrender."[13] The combination implies the acknowledgment of some standard idea of

Islam that includes Allah's power over His creation with simultaneous free will in the human response. The form of submission or surrender to His will, that is human obedience, calls attention to the significance of the human response at his or her discretion as agent. Meanwhile it takes nothing away from the ultimate power of Allah's will. It simply constructs its availability in the mundane realm through voluntary human action or interaction and renders to Islam a much more dynamic formula by recognizing what human surrender means vis-à-vis Allah's will. This is confirmed by the Qur'anic identification of the human being as 'abd, or servant. Surrender is mutually accepting human volition while recognizing Allah's ultimate authority. As a servant one must act in accordance with how one understands Allah's will. It is abundantly evident that most people on the planet do not surrender to Allah's will; they surrender to greed, ego, desires, and whims.

The term "engaged" confirms human volition. A human can surrender but only through the autonomy of full consciousness. One can choose not to surrender. This makes it easier to understand Allah's unique gift to humans as morally free beings. Engaged surrender binds human agency and divine will into the dynamic and enduring relationship that is always being exercised from one moment to the next whether in public or private human actions. Often tension arises between the divine will and human agency, so Islam is the voluntary choice of surrender. Emphasis is placed upon the agent for the choice he or she makes to surrender to Allah's will. That should be taken for granted, not as blame for the chaos and destruction human civilizations have chosen to create, be they Muslims or not.[14] I will return to look at agency in more detail after my discussion of *tawhid*.

The Tawhidic Paradigm

Tawhid is the principle theoretical or foundational term underlying my use of the term Islam to claim that it does not oppress women. I have developed what I call the *tawhidic paradigm*. There were many experiences of being a woman engaged in the gender *jihad* that influences my thinking and drives my research. This book will include selective references to some of these experiences integral to my journey and theoretical conclusions. As the *tawhidic* paradigm is discussed here, it is unequivocal and fundamental to my work on gender. It began with experiences of Muslim gender "double-talk" that presumes that "woman is *not* to man as man is to woman."

For example, I once attended a *halaqah*, a religious study circle, in a local mosque. The *halaqah* is a confessional community function geared to the level of general membership and hardly the place to offer or expect challenging ideas about Islamic studies or reform. This can sometimes be frustrating, but even after completing my Ph.D. in Islamic studies, I would occasionally attend these as part of my need for community life. That day the topic was Muslim family life. Generally, this means telling women and men their rightful place in traditional patriarchal family. Although perhaps unintended by the (male) instructor, I learned something else. For while the speaker started by stating "men and women are equal in Islam," he followed with a Qur'anic quote, "and the rights due to women are similar to the rights against them with regard *ma'ruf* (a well-known or established idea of justice) but men have a degree over them" (2:228). Normally, I am opposed to the use of this second half of the verse without the context of the whole verse, because it is not a universal discussion but rather a particular discussion related to the institution of divorce.

As confirmed in Islamic law, divorce is clearly unequal between women and men. Men have the unilateral right of repudiation while women can only obtain divorce after the intervention of the courts. I have argued elsewhere[15] that this inequality reflects the circumstances of marriage of subjugation that existed at the time of the revelation. A woman would never have any hope of divorce, besides the one initiated by the husband, unless she had the court guarantee the protection of her choice.[16] It remains, however, that men have a degree of advantage over women: they need only say "I divorce you" to initiate the termination of the marriage contracted, agreed upon by the husband and wife, and witnessed by honorable members of the community. They also have the circumstantial advantage as well as physical power to force women to break the *iddah*, a required three-month waiting period of sexual abstinence which, at the time of revelation, was the only means to determine paternity if a divorced woman entered another marriage. Still, the verse announces that rights against women are the same as the rights owed to them, specifically with regard to *ma'ruf*.

The day of the *halaqah*, I did not object to the omission of the full text. The fine slice of Muslim double-talk consciously disturbed me over male–female equality. Double-talk refers to multivalent linguistic obscurities in meaning. Language can be intentionally ambiguous. One can use rhetoric to manipulate double or variant meanings. While "double-talk" demonstrates the power of language to yield multiple meanings, it can be intentionally evoked as a powerful mechanism of interpretation. Take the opening statement, "women and men are equal," and add the quoted verse "men have a degree over them." Visualize a vertical line between two spheres. Man, in the upper sphere, is *said* to be equal to woman, located in the lower sphere, *only* as a matter of linguistic ambiguity or double-talk. The line of relationship between the man's upper location and the woman's lower is held in place only if there is no potential of actual reciprocity. The relationship is static and prevents equality. The positions are not inter-changeable. If for any reason, theoretical or practical, a woman is located in the upper sphere, the male hierarchy actually intended by this rhetoric is disrupted, as is the line that connects them. This may be one reason why equality talk seems threatening to many Muslim men. Their statement "women and men are equal" is linguistically un-examined. Despite how grand the statement sounds, some men are insulted by talk of women's parity with men because the words are meaningless against actual practice. Men have to give up something in order for women to be on the same plane they consider themselves to occupy. The relationship that is maintained between women and men is paired, but not reciprocal.

Here was an incentive to search for horizontal reciprocity. When women and men share perhaps distinct yet *horizontal* spheres, then the exchange of one for the other does not upset any hierarchy, because none exists. What is more, the following illustration of horizontal equality allows and also presumes mutual input, significance, and dynamism. The female is in the lower place on a direct line to the male both to facilitate and to be the foundation upon which male dominance stands. It is not reciprocally dynamic. It is Muslim male double-talk to reflect and maintain male legit-imacy and hierarchical privilege over women. Woman is not to man as man is to woman.

Too much double-talk occurs to counter articulations of genuine equality between women and men. Another encounter with this linguistic double-talk occurred in a response given by a neo-conservative Pakistani professor at the International Islamic University in Malaysia regarding the election of Benazhir Bhutto as a female prime minister to Pakistan. He calmly pointed out that "Men and women are equal in Islam. Islam has nothing against anyone becoming a leader. Whether they are 5 feet tall and weigh 95 pounds, or 6 feet 4 weighing 200 pounds. Whether they are male or female, if they are capable of being leaders, they can lead. *Women simply cannot lead.*" Did I miss something here, Aristotle? Here are two syllogisms to help illustrate the points:

A	B
All men are humans.	All humans can be leaders.
Ahmad is a man.	Women are human.
Ahmad is a human.	Women cannot be leaders.

Column B is obviously not a correct syllogism. It is double-talk, dependent upon syllogism in column A, which is only technically correct as articulated. The fact that Fatimah, for example, is also human but not a man is hidden in the first syllogism. To ascribe humanity to a man overlooks women's humanity. Both syllogisms stand upon a fundamental logical error. The double-talk discourse housed within the rhetoric of human equality disguises the intention of legitimate exclusion or inconsistencies that keep women inferior. As housed this way, however, a woman's objection would seem both irrational and un-Islamic.

Like the man from the *halaqah* who began speaking about male–female equality only to follow it with "men have a degree over women," there is no simple mechanism to correct the self-contradiction. It's a set up. While actual inequality cannot be corrected by language alone, at least examining the language used to create imbalance is useful in proposing a theory to create and sustain balance. The following theoretical question motivated my search: how can relations between women and men be maintained along a horizontal axis of equality and reciprocity?

Only a few of the most arrogant Muslim men would openly express their underlying belief that men are and must remain superior to women. Instead it is more common to contribute to the victimization of women and other men by the ambiguity of double-talk. In the end, it is also intended to impress upon the woman that if she is truly Muslim, she must remain satisfied with her rightful status – even if actually second-class. The use of the word "equal" in accordance to a definition that keeps men superior simultaneously confirms male superiority and silences analysis and opposition.

"Islam" among neo-traditionalists, neo-conservatives, extremists, and some Islamists[17] is selective use of primary sources and the Muslim intellectual legacy for the purpose of exclusion. Islamist discussion of the vertical rhetoric of equality extensively employs the word complementarity. Each person, male or female, plays significant yet gender-specific roles. All roles are necessary and good; however, their distinctions must remain beneficial to each other only within the stasis of particular determinations of "natural complementarity." This is tantamount to saying that women's roles complement men's nature. This is not only harmonious and organic, such thinking asserts, it is divine. But such complementarity has an unequal power dimension. A woman can complement a man like a tie complements a suit. The relative value of men's roles and women's roles in this fixed system says nothing about values attributed to those roles in the larger context of gender relations in family, community, and ultimately in geopolitics. It rhetorically and actually constructs an unequal relationship which, if disrupted, destroys something inherent to "Islam." Thus complementarity discourse is a direct by-product of double-talk. While positively stressing relationships, it keeps their inequality central, by evaluating each player on a separate and unequal standard, leaving the relative power and privilege to men and male roles. It further concludes with the consequence and significance of the relationship as a whole by establishing it as fundamental to family bonds and community continuity. Particular roles played by members in the family are unevaluated, especially women's morally voluntary contributions as nurturers and care-takers. Women continue with the double burden of supporting men's autonomy as a means for honor in the patriarchal family.[18]

No matter how Islam is defined, it foundation is *tawhid*. More than mere monotheism, the many nuances of *tawhid* have been and continue to be subjects of Islamic discourses.[19] In unique ways, many modern Muslim thinkers have also contributed toward a greater understanding of the significance of *tawhid* as a major cornerstone of Islamic reform.[20] Yet all articulations point toward the same essence. *Tawhid* is the operating principle of equilibrium and cosmic harmony. It operates between the metaphysical and physical realities of the created universe, as well as within them both. On a theological level, *tawhid* relates to the transcendent and yet eminent divinity or ultimate reality, the "unicity" of Allah. Allah is not only one and unique, Allah is uniform, and unites existing multiplicities or seeming dualities in both the corporeal and the metaphysical realm.

As an ethical term, *tawhid* relates to relationships and developments within the social and political realm, emphasizing the unity of all human creatures beneath one Creator. If experienced as a reality in everyday Islamic terms, humanity would be a single global community without distinction for reasons of race, class, gender, religious tradition, national origin, sexual orientation or other arbitrary, voluntary, and involuntary aspects of human distinction. Their only distinction would be on the basis on *taqwa* (49:13). *Taqwa* is moral consciousness, not accessible for external human judgment, although I will show that external results or consequences are palpable.

Because of *tawhid*, Islam exists along the lines of the irrefutable and unconditional notion of Allah's oneness. Indeed the Qur'an states unequivocally that *all* sins can be forgiven, except *shirk* (the opposite of *tawhid*) (4:116). God is not only one. God is indivisible. By means of indivisibility God acts upon all creation to bring peace, harmony, and unity. That which emanates from Allah participates in this unity. Ultimate separation between creature (self) and Creator (Allah) is an illusion. Separation between one person and another is literal, but metaphorically or internally an illusion, causing prejudice. Allah is one and in our true state of surrender we are all at one with Allah. Obviously, human preoccupation with their materiality keeps them from realizing, acting upon, and constructing systems to reflect their essential unity. In actuality, there is no basis for schism in the duality of "self" and "other," since ontologically they are co-dependent according to the statement, "And from all things we have created the pair," *min kulli shay' khalaqnaa zawjayn* (51:49). The one cannot exist without the other since both were integral to this Qur'anic cosmology.

Thus, the overarching concept *tawhid*, or the unicity of Allah, forms a trajectory organizing Islamic social, economic, moral, spiritual, and political systems. All are under a single divine reality. Indeed, all of nature is interconnected under the rubric of *tawhid*. At the transcendent level Allah is the tension that holds the opposites in juxtaposition. Opposites are the illusion of separation between self and other.

Other ways of emphasizing this mutual existence include the golden rule of reciprocity,[21] which has been articulated in all religious and moral systems as the highest universal ideal of human relationality. There are many indicators in Islam[22] stressing this basic principle of reciprocity – for example, at a pragmatic level, the Prophetic *hadith*, "One of you does not believe until he/she loves for the other what is loved for self."[23]

In looking at Islamic cosmology and eschatology according to the Qur'an, the notion of reciprocity and *tawhid* is obvious. Starting with the passage, "*Laysa ka mithlihi shay'un*" (there is no-thing like It) (42:11), the Qur'an removes any similitude between the limited creation and the divine Ultimate. This statement stresses Allah's incomparability or *Jalal* attributes. Although the *Jalal* attributes point to Allah as remote, distant, and incomprehensible, Allah also has Her domain of love, mercy, and concern for all creation, which is best described by the *Jamal* attributes.[24] Ali, the fourth caliph, said, "God is outside of things, but not in the sense of being alien to them; and He is inside things, but not in the sense of being identical with them."[25] The full understanding of the divine/ human relationships is a paradox beyond the restrictions that mental reasoning places upon conceptions of Allah. Yet we would be less than human beings endowed with wisdom were we not to exert the limits of our reasoning in deciphering the mysteries of this paradox.

In the Qur'an, all *shay'* (things) are part of a system of dualism, divisible and necessarily contingent. Like male and female pairs in humankind, some of these pairs coexist as complementary and contingent equals. Other pairs, like night and day, in and out, up and down, are drawn into mutually necessary opposition. All of creation, according to the Qur'an, is interconnected in this way, except Allah, described as not like *shay'*. In this way, Allah can be seen as the tension holding the pairs in balance and harmony.

This Qur'anic system of correlated and contingent pairs at the metaphysical level is further emphasized on the material level, especially in social-moral terms, by another passage. Whenever two persons come together, Allah is the third among them (58:7). To illustrate, each and every human-to-human relation can be represented as a triad formed with Allah as a supranatural component. Allah, the Ultimate, is in a transcendent place supporting and sustaining the horizontal juxtaposition between any two human beings or any human group. The presence of Allah maintains the "I–Thou" proposal of Martin Buber.[26]

> Buber indicates that 'the primary word I–Thou can only be spoken with the whole being.' In other words this combination forms a unit that implies the relationship of reciprocity. Otherwise, '(t)he primary word I–It can never be spoken with the whole being.' One aspect in this relationship is asymmetrical and reduced to a state of less than wholeness.[27]

This relational paradigm looks like this triad:

Allah

I   Thou

Each two persons are sustained on the horizontal axis because the highest moral point is always occupied metaphysically by Allah. The real center of this metaphysical occupation coincidently is the heart. So only when two people reflect through the clear mirror of each other's heart can they avoid violation of *tawhid*. Then the vertical diagram:

I

(no existential symbol of balance, harmony, and reciprocity)

It

can appear only if Allah is absent from the formula. If Allah is present in any way, a new horizontal plane is created since Allah operates at the highest point. What appears as hierarchical between the two humans on the physical plane:

I

Allah

Thou

would not be hierarchical in reality because Allah, the highest point in the composition, constructs a new horizontal axis that sustains parity between the I and the Thou. In fact one must think in terms of a sphere, or in three-dimensional terms, to put this diagram in its fullest conceptual framework.

The continual awareness and active reflection of Allah's presence – the metaphysical component of all human-to-human relations – creates a means for understanding that there can only be parity on a horizontal basis between any two persons or any two collectives. To keep Allah present in all our encounters on the corporeal level a certain moral consciousness is required. That moral consciousness is *taqwa,* according to the Qur'anic worldview. Yet *taqwa* is a volitional function of our *khilafah* or agency. If consciousness of Allah is absent, it is possible to think of others on the vertical plane of inequity and transgression, leading to oppression, abuse, and transgression.

This linguistic reference to a triad does not mean that Allah is a physical thing, an object, let alone a person. She or He is not separate from the creation, especially from the human creature. St. Augustine's articulation to consider God as a circle, the center of which is everywhere and the circumference of which is nowhere, reflects the metaphysical reality of the universe, which I agree with, provided it is considered at the level of the three-dimensional sphere. The *tawhidic* paradigm is more than our physical make up. We live in a complex universe. Within each person is an essence (*dhat*) reflecting our union with the cosmic design and the harmony in all creation. We can acknowledge this transcendent reality, in ourselves and all others – and act upon it – or we can ignore it, to emphasize our superiority over others, rather than our relational reciprocity. That is a significant idea underlying the diagram above. When a person seeks to place him or her self "above" another, it either means the divine presence is removed or ignored, or that the person who imagines his or her self above others suffers from the egoism of *shirk*.

At the metaphysical level of reality, Allah is present in all circumstances; then at the level of human free will, Allah's presence must be acknowledged. This way of conceptualizing the Buberan formula provides a means for understanding the sacred union between self and other, so the I–Thou relationship of horizontal reciprocity is sustained. Continual application of this transcendent component gives superiority only in Allah. To experience the metaphysical reality of this three-dimensional relationship of wholeness, the two-dimensional human relationship must reflect awareness, remembrance, and participation in the presence of Allah within and between them. The basic construction of humankind is composed of its male and female pair. The *tawhidic* paradigm becomes the inspiration for removing gender stratification from all levels of social interaction: public and private, ritual and political. Not only does it mean that I and Thou are equal, but also it means that I and Thou *are one within the oneness of Allah*. Social, liturgical, and political functions become determined by the capacity of both women and men in a larger realm of education, dedication, and contribution with no arbitrary exclusion of women from performing any of these functions.

Each Human is Created as a Moral Agent (khalifah) of Allah

In search of an Islamic construction of human dignity, I continue to examine certain major Qur'anic constructs. For example, I consider the Qur'anic description of an exchange between the angels – creatures of pure light without free will – and Allah, Lord of the Worlds, Master of the Universe, and Creator of all existence. In that exchange Allah announces, "Verily I will create a *khalifah*, vicegerent on the earth" (2:30).[28] The angels voiced their concern that this creature might cause havoc on the earth by way of chaos and destruction. Allah responds first from Its sovereignty with the statement, "I know what you do not know" (2:30), then completed His intention by creating the first human being. The angels readily agree that they only know what Allah gives them to know (2:32). As they submit to the superiority of Allah's knowledge they also glorify Her. As human readers, we can speculate on what Allah knows. Here, I do not. For the current analysis I make, what is more important is that human creation follows this cosmic dialogue. In my earlier analysis of the Qur'anic statement, "*Wa min kulli shay'in khalaqnaa zawjayn*," "and from all (created) things we made pairs" (51:49), there is an essential consequence relative to male–female mutual dependency in human creation. The Qur'anic statement indicates that "things" are created in pairs. I especially note that human creation is included in this system of created duality. I have discussed at length the perfection of human creation[29] and its gender inclusiveness in the Qur'anic design.[30] Here, that gender inclusiveness is taken for granted for my discussion and focus is shifted to the mutual function or role the Qur'an designates for all humankind with several important cosmological and ontological implications.

The part of the statement "on the earth" not only emphasizes that being on earth is fundamental to the Islamic conception of human destiny, it also defies any implication that the human sojourn on the earth is a type of punishment, or "fall" of an originally sinful creature. The second and more important aspect of this statement is the intent implied, "I will create a '*khalifah*'." This shows that the characteristic of *khilafah* (trusteeship or agency) is fundamental and essential to being human.

That is why the term *khalifah* is foundational to an ethics of human dignity. On a more pragmatic level, I have explored the significance of this aspect of human dignity in the context of civil society, where I use the term *khalifah* to refer to "citizen."[31] Here, my first task is to review some fundamental and perhaps universal implications of what it means to fulfill this task of *khilafah*[32] as implied by the Qur'anic term. Then I will emphasize *khilafah* in its particular relation to gender and the dignity of women.

First I will propose less archaic English translations for the terms *khalifah* and *khilafah*. These modern translations are easily borne out after examining the overall Qur'anic use of the terms and from an analysis of the meaning of the archaic term English translators tend to use: "vicegerent." A modern equivalent for *khalifah* is "trustee" or "moral agent." For the term *khilafah* a modern translation is "trusteeship" or "moral agency." I will use agent and trustee interchangeably.

Since the discussion quoted above between Allah and the angels precedes the creation of humankind, this is a statement of intent. Allah intends to create a trustee. In fulfilling that intention, humankind is created. The implications of a particular role to be fulfilled by that human creation give the statement its ontology, intent, or purpose. Human beings are created to be trustees on the earth. They are trustees of Allah. That is, human beings are charged with fulfilling a trust with Allah. Throughout the Qur'an, fulfilling the terms of this trust necessarily involves: (1) (voluntarily) obeying the will of Allah – alternatively interpreted as surrendering to the will of Allah, another term for "Islam"; and (2) participating in that obedience while here on earth. This implies responsibility: we are charged to manage our affairs on the earth in a fashion that demonstrates our surrender. Like the *hadith* (statement) of the Prophet, "would you serve Allah? Serve your fellow creatures (first)."

For some, obey "the will of Allah" has had a specific legal understanding: follow the mandates of *shari'ah*. However, historical *shari'ah* was an intellectual movement that began after the death of the Prophet, the end of revelation, and is never referred to in the Qur'an to mean a man-made legal system (45:18). Examination of the Qur'anic discussions about nature, an ahistorical, metaphysical level of human nature, and the whole of the universe, provides a more comprehensive understanding of the "will of Allah" as reference to the greater cosmic order. That is, Allah's will, *qadr* (the term for both power and measuring out), extends over the entire universe.[33] What creates the checks and balances, causes and effects, cycles and patterns from the most minute to the complex, extensive form of everything in the creation is the "will" of the Creator. Being *khalifah* is equivalent to fulfilling one's human destiny as a moral agent, whose responsibility is to participate in upholding the harmony of the universe. In respect to society, harmony means working for justice.

Furthermore, the use of "engaged surrender" corroborates the general understanding of the term *din*, which means a complete way of life, and is the closest Arabic term to the English word "religion." As a complete way of life, the Islamic intellectual tradition did not distinguish a separation between church and state, as characterizes civil society in modernity. Although not a detailed part of this book, today's idea of state, as in nation-state, did not exist during the formative discussions and is not developed here. Islamic civilization was an empire in relation to other world empires. However, if all affairs – public and private – are accountable before Allah, "Whoever does an atom's weight of good shall see it and whoever does an atom's weight of evil shall see it" (99:7–8), then all affairs are under the sovereignty of Allah's will. Muslims must not only believe that Allah's sovereignty is over all things, they must accept their responsibility as agents of Allah. Accepting Allah's sovereignty means that humans, as equal citizens, are responsible for constructing social justice and for governing all matters of state. By implication, the historical formulations of *shari'ah* are not the eternal representation of the fullest human effort to understand, articulate, and then implement Allah's sovereignty. This leads to another key concept under intense consideration in reformist Islamic discourse, the meanings and applications of *shari'ah* today.[34]

Based on the above statement of intent in the Qur'an, all humankind is created with the purpose of trusteeship for Allah on earth. This purpose is the most significant feature of the moral agent. Elsewhere in the Qur'an, humanity is charged with a trust, *amanah*,[35] or a covenant, *mithaq*,[36] between themselves and Allah. Humans accept this trust, or covenant, primordially (33:72). Between human acceptance and divine purpose for human creation rests the basic idea of Qur'anic guidance: cooperation between Allah, as Creator of all the worlds, and humankind, as creature and *khalifah* in Allah's creation, on earth.

Again these Qur'anic discussions about the notion of Islam – or being in surrender – include all of creation and not just humans. Yet, while all of nature is *muslim* without volition, by virtue of the phenomenon of free will, humanity is a special case. There have been endless and circular theological discussions about this phenomenon, which I overlook here in my attempt to bring home some particulars about Creator/creature cooperation. Instead, I presume that humans are agents possessing limited power, via free will, while Allah is all-powerful.[37] This metaphysical reality has practical implications in the circumstances of human control over all matters on the earth. For while Allah has made the earth subservient to us (22:65), having free will means we are equally capable of making choices that reflect our conscious surrender to Allah's will and our acceptance to fulfill the trust or of making choices that follow our own egos, greed, and lusts for power that violate the trust.

By agency, or *khilafah*, therefore, I mean the responsibility of each human being to establish social justice, as a representative of the divine will or cosmic harmony. Responsibility means accepting to find the motivation both to understand the divine will and then to act in accordance to that understanding. While one cannot ever come to understand completely the divine will because its totality begins and ends in transcendence and is therefore incomprehensible, the term responsibility implies at least an initiative toward understanding, followed by practices that establish that will in real-life circumstances. Everyone is invested with this responsibility. Some may acquire greater facility in understanding. Some may acquire greater facility in acting upon their understandings, as circumstances dictate. To the end of full moral responsibility, a Muslim is required to continue to seek understanding, individually and in concert with others.

Still, this responsibility includes the flexibility of changing one's perspective on any issue as humanity acquires more understanding toward a better means to fulfill that which best reflects the divine will. Therefore, one must act better as one's understanding develops. This growth in understanding and action is equally true of humanity at large as it is for the individual in terms of personal growth. That is the crux of moral responsibility.

Furthermore, as *shari'ah* developed, it helped determine the understanding that "to act" includes both personal actions of faith and ritual worship (*'ibadah*), as well as actions in the private and public spheres toward establishing what is just in society at large in terms of mutual interactions (*mu'amalat*) in accordance to the divine will. In the development of *shari'ah*, these areas of *'ibadah* and *mu'amalat* form the two central categories of focus in articulations of the law. Ultimately, only Allah can judge personal actions, the arena of one's spiritual enhancement, and one's true intentions or consciousness. However, it is my contention that one's personal spiritual development forms the cornerstone of one's activities in both the public and the private realm of society. In this regard, my analysis differs from secular articulations of social justice in that the total well-being of the human creature is not limited to the physical or material. At the end of the day, it is the moral center of one's being, or one's consciousness, that determines the nature of one's social actions and relationships. This discussion was necessary to show how being a moral agent is central to the construction of and participation in struggles for social justice.

Agency, human empowerment, is best described as responsibility. We are responsible for the choices we make at every juncture, and we will be held accountable via the ultimate judgment for all of our choices. According to the Qur'an, "Whoever does an atom's weight of good, shall see it; and whoever does an atom's weight of evil, shall see it" (99:7–8). As trustees, we are charged with the ability to make choices that facilitate the completion of our trust. To best fulfill our trust the Qur'an also describes the human being as *'abd*, or servant before Allah. The *'abd* is entrusted to complete *'ibadah* to Allah, or service in the creation. Narrowly speaking, *'ibadah* is worship, with the term *ihsan* (doing good deeds) carrying the broader meaning that every good deed is done as servants of Allah and hence also acts of worship.[38]

The agent–servant paradigm in the Qur'an sets up an understanding of both the limits of human will and the expectations on humanity for using free will toward moral service. Although humans are given a certain capacity through agency, that capacity – a gift – must be used morally in the service of Allah and of maintaining cosmic harmony, as a responsibility. Furthermore, there is a reciprocal relationship in the Qur'an between capacity and responsibility. The one with greater capacity is charged with a greater responsibility, and vice versa. Thus *at the time of revelation*, when slavery was still practiced, a slave was not charged the same recompense for certain crimes as the free person (4:25). Another example at the time of revelation was the proportions of inheritance. The male share is twice that of the female in the same position amongst the relatives in correspondence to the greater responsibility of the male, for *nafaqah*, material provisions, of the family that women did not have. Ultimately I argue against both the institution of slavery and the marriage of subjugation referenced here to show the underlying Qur'anic correlation between responsibility and agency.[39]

This focus on responsibility is intended to prevent the term "moral agency" from being read like some kind of unconditional individual privilege. I accept the *shari'ah* restrictions on full human capacity or agency for children and those with mental deficiency,[40] requiring others to act as guardians managing their affairs unless or until they reach the age of reasoning. However, nothing exists in the Qur'an or *sunnah* that restricts or limits agency – in the sense of full moral responsibility to obey the will of Allah – on the basis of race, class, or gender. This chapter is especially aimed at deconstructing assumptions that limit human agency in women. The assumption of male superiority produced by culture and circumstantial convenience are not essential to "Islam."

Ethical Theory and Justice

Adding the term "moral" as fundamental to the meaning of *khalifah* reflects the uniquely human ethical capacity through their exclusive characteristic of free will. According to Majid Fakhry,[41] "An ethical theory is a reasoned account of the nature and grounds of right actions and decisions and the principles underlying the claim that they are morally commendable or reprehensible." Such a theory then provides a "justification and appraisal of moral judgment as well as the discrimination between right and wrong actions or decisions."[42] In Islam, "we start from the premise that the [Qur'an] and the traditions embody the original core of the Islamic ethical spirit."[43] From the perspective of our discussion of moral agency: the responsibility of acting on the earth to fulfill moral agency involves acting in accordance with the guidance about right and wrong given in these two primary sources. It should not be hard to understand that the purpose of the historical construction of Islamic law or *shari'ah* was to fulfill that end: to construct a system that reflects the "justification and appraisal of moral judgment as well as the discrimination between right and wrong actions or decisions."[44]

As Fakhry has explicitly stated, although we have the Qur'an, which embodies the whole of the Islamic ethos and "around which the whole of Muslim moral, religious and social life revolves," it "contains no ethical *theories* in the strict sense."[45] Fakhry distinguishes between the Islamic ethos and Islamic ethics, which is "a reasoned account of the nature and grounds of right actions and decision and principles underling the claim that they are morally commendable or reprehensible. [With] special stress on the definition of ethical concepts . . . To be complete, an ethical system must deal adequately with these aspects of moral inquiry in an articulate and coherent way."[46]

That the Qur'an has been invoked by various ethical theorists, but has resulted in the development of theories sometimes contradictory to each other, reiterates the significance of interpretation as a process of constructing "Islam." In other words, even based upon the same primary sources, practical implications, implementations, and the development of ideas and theories will differ based upon many other factors relative to being human. The Qur'an does not develop a single uniform ethical system; it contains ethical principles and values. The development of a system must be formulated through human beings: the agents responsible for implementing and maintaining those systems in the first place.

Fakhry gives the eleventh and twelfth centuries as the starting point in the intellectual discourse of Islamic ethical theory. Prior to that time, of course ideas of morality or of right and wrong existed and were directly or indirectly based on the revelation and the practices of the Prophet, but there was no fully developed theory. There are at least two important implications in developing ethical theory. First, understanding what is ethical is relative to context. Therefore, secondly, it affects the ways we resolve new issues outside the parameters available through literal application of rules or codes established in the early development of *shari'ah* and Islamic thought. Again, these were human-made, relative to the existing civil and moral contexts, perhaps based on the Qur'an and the *sunnah*, which Muslims agree embody the original core of the Islamic ethical spirit. Not surprisingly, women did not participate in the historical development of Islamic ethics. Theories were always based upon the presumption of the male Muslim as the normative human being. For example, in a discussion of musical instruments, al-Ghazzali compares the flute as "a reference to the human [*sic*] essence, and the nine holes are a reference to the openings in the outer frame (*zahir*), which are nine, viz the (2) ears, the (2) nostrils, the (2) eyes, the mouth and the private parts."[47] That only the male human has two openings in the private parts and the female has three indicates that nine as part philosophical description used elsewhere determines what it is to be human, explicitly upon the male person. If not predicated explicitly upon the male person then, often the agent referred to is developed while obscuring and giving the "superficial appearance . . . [that] can easily lead to the impression that they are inclusive of women." However, when a gender notification is given, it not only specifies the male person, but also relegates women to "restricted opportunities" within such theories.[48]

Furthermore, the variations in the conclusions drawn about ethics guarantee that none have precedence over others. There is certainly a scarcity of scholarly effort to study the development of Islamic ethical theory and to concentrate specifically on examining what reconstructions might be constructive in progressive Islamic thought. As yet I know of no women involved specifically in this area of study, nor of any men, progressive or otherwise, who are examining ethics with gender as a category of thought. This only means that the conclusion of the matter will be the same male privilege as elsewhere.

The Qur'an exhorts, "Let there be among you a community [of people] who invite unto all that is *khayr*, good, and enjoin the doing of *ma'ruf*, a well-known or established idea of justice, and forbid the doing of *munkar*, wrong" (3:104). From a pro-faith perspective, the goal of civil society is to establish a moral order while recognizing that morality extends from an inward state of being that motivates certain frameworks for building legislation. While you cannot legislate a person to moral excellence as some narrowly constructed dogmatic Islamic institutions have tried to enforce, human agents can be raised toward moral excellence through structures of care and well-being. One principle of this ethical upbringing centers on the term *taqwa*.

Taqwa

I first mentioned *taqwa* in the discussion of agency as personal spiritual development forming the cornerstone of one's activities in both the public and private realm. I applied the word *taqwa* to that development as it emanates from within the person out into realm of actions. Although the semantic word *taqwa* was used before the Qur'anic revelation, it is in the Qur'an that it gains a certain religious meaning and moral implication, and according to Fazlur Rahman is "perhaps the most important single term in the Qur'an."[49]

Most often simply translated as "piety," I define *taqwa* as moral consciousness in the trustee of Allah. It is the motivating instinct to perform all actions as though they are transparent. The Qur'an grants free will to an agent as part of the greatest paradox in the divine–human relationship. The idea of responsibility or accountability reinforces this relationship between Allah's absolute sovereignty and absolute freedom of an agent to choose how to act. Ultimately, the agent is held accountable for all choices made.

To embrace the responsibility of agency means knowing that one is completely free to choose. Instead of deferring to escapism, leaving everything a consequence of Allah's sovereignty, the agent accepts a dynamic partnership between Allah's will and his or her choice as agent whether to follow that will or not. That is why Islam, as engaged surrender, reflects both the conscious choice to accept or reject one's surrender – a choice not granted to all of creation. The Qur'an is replete with messages that encourage the agent to exercise responsibility in making choices and performing actions that demonstrate the power to choose and the wisdom and guidance to make those choices reflect surrender to Allah's will also elaborated in the text. According to the Qur'an, however, all choices have consequences.

Since Allah is the ultimate Judge, and Allah is always watching, there should be no double standard whereby one chooses to commit an act only under the condition that it is not witnessed by another human being. Rather, one acts within moral constraints by one's own volition. One's actions are always under judgment. Islamic metaphysics reflects constant awareness of the omniscience of Allah. Allah sees the outward deed as also judged by *shari'ah*, but Allah also knows and will judge by the innermost secrets of the heart. Domestic violence research, for example, documents the increased rate of abuse in those circumstances when the abuse is unknown to anyone except the perpetrator and the victim. The victim is often silenced by the threat of further violence should the secret be revealed and by the cultural support of the idea that the domestic domain is the private realm of male dominance where women must obey. Such a disadvantage results from the split between personal Islamic identity and forces of institutional and political Islamic policy. Without comprehensive (i.e. female-inclusive) Islamic moral policies, Muslim women are continuously exposed to abuse but forced to comply by circumstances that justify their silence.[50]

At the spiritual level, *taqwa* establishes moral character based in personal and social practice that reflect moral self-constraint and self-sacrifice. Moral self-constraint forms the foundation of all human interactions, inclusive of the family and extended to public policy. Human civilization benefits from our romantic ideals about "family," no matter how crucial it is as the cornerstone of society and community life. Critical analysis of the basic oppressive nature of the patriarchal family structure, past and present, is not always integrated into discourse over policy reform. Yet, not surprisingly, gender disparity occurs first within the family. Women are oppressed *by those who love them*: their fathers, brothers, husbands, and sons who enjoy the fruits of their labor without acknowledging the full extent of that labor as a set of moral of volitional acts performed through the graciousness of female agency with indispensable moral impact on the well-being of society.[51]

This idea of the oppressed Muslim woman, mostly often characterized as the norm by Western media, is also the principal motivation for struggling in the gender *jihad*. Muslim family life is acculturated by ideas that encourage the performance of *taqwa* in women and in the raising of girls. But according to *shari'ah* women are not full, autonomous, and independent agents in the family. They are only a facility to its wholeness and well-being. They are taught to sacrifice or develop personal interests to the higher goal of family well-being. Meanwhile men and sons are encouraged to develop ideas of manhood as unlimited empowerment. Therefore, sons are raised to fulfill the view of themselves as masters, providers, and protectors in the family. Such characteristics of manhood minimize the ideals of deference in women, women's services, to children, and even between each other but this deference is not equally emphasized in the development of manhood. Instead, autonomy and independence are woven into the ideas about their Islamic responsibility as leaders in both the public and the private domain. Occasionally *taqwa* for men might be referred to through the rhetoric of a Friday *khutbah* (sermon) or in community discussions. It remains disconnected to fundamental or intimate family relationships of genuine spousal reciprocity since its discussion remains locked within the rhetorical double-talk and the language of complementarity. Furthermore, the domestic parameters of *taqwa* are never essentially integrated as a basis for public policy. The purpose of public policy has been the power of men in the male public space. Women and women's organizations increasingly raise issues of the domestic realm and the politics of family as a mandatory part of public policy. Therefore an epistemological schism forms, which restricts the dynamic incorporation of *taqwa* from its comprehensive contribution to the building of public policies and for its private establishment within men as fundamental to a truly just social order.

Taqwa is one of those few principal theoretical ideals or concepts outlined here as part of the foundation of a paradigm shift in the movement to attain social justice in the context of today's Muslim communities. As I mentioned above, my first inspiration to consider these ideas from the Qur'anic worldview was Rahman's insistence that the purpose of the Qur'an was to establish a just social order.[52] As a conceptual ideal the word *taqwa* continuously surfaces in confessional discourse. Here I draw directly from female inclusive readings of their fundamental Qur'anic origin in order to mainstream women's voices into political reforms.

Therefore these articulations are premised upon some of the inter-relations between previously existing themes and principles such as *tawhid*, the unicity of God, *khalifah* (moral agent), and *taqwa* intentionally reconstructed to build more gender-inclusive understanding of human nature and to effect changes in laws and governance on behalf of Muslim women's mainstreaming in "Islam." *Taqwa* is essential to the moral attitude of the agent as an individual as well as a member of society since it assists in activating the *tawhidic* principle, both as a matter of personal practice and as the basis for extensive Islamic legal reform. Injustice is a sign of neglecting these concepts. Muslim women have been victims of such injustice in their homes, in Islamic cultural practices, and in public policies, in various ways in modernity as the idea of empire is transformed into nation state.

Despite the utility of these social justice aspects of *tawhid* and *khalifah*, I reiterate that theory alone will not suffice to bring an end to patriarchy and gender asymmetry. There is a crucial interplay between belief in certain ideas and the practical implementation of gender justice in the context of the present global circumstances. This book will address this further in various ways since the relationships between theory and practice, and between Islamic ideas, ideals, goals, and the historical development of *shari'ah*, all bear some effect on efforts to construct gender-equal Islamic reforms.

Justice and Human Dignity

I further developed my ideas about the importance of considering the implications and significance of underlying ideas about human nature as related to the politics of gender theory and reform when I read Alison Jaggar's groundbreaking book, *Feminist Politics and Human Nature*.[53] One objective of her book was to highlight the underlying philosophical ideas about human nature elemental to four major types of feminisms. From there I compared various ideas about the meaning of human nature in Islamic discourse, as described above, the term *khalifah* providing the irrefutable genesis to Muslim historical thought and practices – especially as eventually canonized in legal codes for over a thousand years. The idea of *khalifah* regarding gender issues was related to the formation of public policies. Islamic ideas of humanity are integrally connected to the mutuality of the Allah–*khalifah* relationship and are meant to determine people's actions, public and private. Although we accept that Allah is the ultimate judge of human actions, because only Allah knows the full cosmic, existential, and practical implications of all our actions, our intentions must continuously correspond to the call of our *din* as active agents fulfilling those intentions. Every principle underlying the context of building a living community committed to certain actions is articulated fundamentally in the Qur'an. The Qur'anic articulations are often specific to the time and circumstances of its revelation. Particularities are even more evident in the *sunnah* of the Prophet. He was the exemplar par excellence *under the specific circumstances of his community*. The fundamental principles, however, must be continuously re-evaluated from the perspective of the time of their specific embodiment throughout the challenges, changes, and limitations of history. Understanding and implementing the fundamental values were fine-tuned relative to their coherence to the circumstances and actual dictates of human life.[54] One aspect of evaluating values and principles is based upon their purpose or intended results.

Most importantly, justice is one value that is both universal in principle and relative to its manifestation in time and space. Drawing a coherent line between the universal and the relative is the place where living communities must be in continual dialogue. Legal codes are major considerations to human polity, governance, and social order. But no single set of legal codes could ever be expected to sustain or support the universal purpose of justice given the complex developments and constant change in human life. The past few centuries have stimulated human knowledge, with concern for both the inner human constitution and well-being and the many external areas of industry, technology, medicine, psychology, economics, militarism, biology, and globalism, which have developed at a mind-boggling and still increasing rate. For sustainable justice, these external areas of change require sincere and sensitive consideration of their moral impact on the totality of what it means to be human. Measuring current results by poverty and consumption alone indicates staggering disparities[55] that are actually within our global means to help eradicate. The problem seems to be the absence of the internal human will to introduce the means for eradicating this disparity. At one time it seemed we could simply refer to the world's religious leadership for inspiration along these lines. But religion has largely become victim to mere formal dogmas and creeds with little continued connection to the grand human spirit beyond solely personal terms, unintegrated and inactive in genuine terms of saving the whole of humanity and the whole human person, as it is of saving itself. Simultaneously, organizations formed to articulate and activate these religions into playing a more ecumenical role in issues of poverty, disarmament, family, and global conflict are constrained by their determinations of what is necessary to respect the integrity of each particular religion's dogmas and creeds, however diverse, while challenging issues of moral disintegration. Ecumenical discourse tends to accept the established status quo within the other traditions. In this way, it achieves the goal of mutual discussion, but fails miserably on how mutually to enhance the overall ethical grounding of living religious traditions and the catastrophe this world has become.

Joan C. Tronto[56] raises valuable and inspirational ideas about politically incorporating the voluntary moral contributions of nurturance and care – historically and currently performed primarily by women in the private sector. In the Muslim world, these contributions, especially their voluntary nature, are used to define and confine women's identities relative only in terms of the families. They are never looked at as detailed aspects of moral agency indispensable to human well-being and equally available for men and women to practice or implement. Tronto considers them transformative aspects of policy and governance even so far as to define the citizen as a care-worker. This removes the private and often privileged access that mostly male wage earners have to support networks integral to developing human well-being. As so deftly explained by Terri Apter, "Men often do get, when they marry, a partner who looks after their domestic needs, cares for their children, accommodates their changing occupational needs, and puts family responsibilities first and foremost. The 'woman behind the man' is the wife who takes care of everything else, so the man can concentrate on his career."[57] In most families the cost of maintaining care and the contributions of care-givers and care-workers are not realistically calculated in terms of the developments of public policies and economic theory. The ones who fulfill those contributions perform while invisible. Tronto challenges the inequity of defining the citizen in terms of production, wage-earning, and consumption when she politicizes an ethics of care as essential to comprehensive social justice.[58]

Sharon Welch agrees with this ethics of care in her work.[59] She thinks outside the box of each human being as a discrete entity responsible only for obtaining their piece of an ever-shrinking pie of global resources. Welch describes the patriarchal ethic as outdated with its "equation of responsible action and control – the assumption that it is possible to guarantee the efficacy of one's actions." She analyzes "the political correlates of this assumption addressing particularly the monopoly of power that one must have if one defines action as the ability to attain, without substantial modification, desired results."[60] Other than apathy and despair leading to non-action "when faced with a problem too big to be solved alone or within the foreseeable future,"[61] she suggests a feminist ethic of risk in response to such grand global predicaments. The best we can hope for is collective participation as a continual process contributing toward more holistic engagement in ethical practices that cease the "uneven rhythm of social change," so disheartening that they lead to "cynicism and despair" since "in some situations we cannot prevail."[62] She found inspiration to challenge the "presumptions of Western moral theories" while working with African-American women and men toward "alternative constructions of the aim of moral reasoning, the morality of rights or the morality of care and responsibility."[63] This ethics of risk is correlated to "a theology of divine imminence, that reinforces" it "and the passion for justice,"[64] challenging us "to relinquish 'power over' others" and inviting us "to participate in 'power with'." Like Welch suggests here, I have experienced the joy of working with women's collectives in a process-oriented challenge to gender oppression among Muslims. Nevertheless, I do not expect to see gender oppression eradicated in my lifetime. My work is part of the process; the results are truly in the hands of Allah in concert with human agents of free moral choice.

Muslims accept Allah's sovereignty over all things. Although we must struggle to establish the good, we never have control over the results of our struggle in the process. They belong solely to Allah even as they reflect the whole of human collective agency. Furthermore, the results are not restricted to a select few. Therefore, all people have the choice of agency as responsible care-takers or care-workers, learning and relearning what it means to achieve peaceful coexistence with each other on the planet. "Do not be concerned with the fruit of your action – just give attention to the action itself. Fruit will come of it own accord. This is a powerful spiritual practice."[65]

Diana Eck[66] describes her amazement, during a week-long interreligious dialogue between women from different parts of the world, when Japanese women confessed the absence of a Japanese word for "justice." She and others had "presupposed the importance of justice [w]as a basic criteria of value." Further discussion would disclose "[t]hat the word in Japanese would be something like what you mean by harmony." For the complex and yet simple implications of such distinctions in language, Eck confessed, "A sense of ethics must be won through the difficult process of dialogue, built from ongoing relationships." In describing the *tawhidic* paradigm above, I also used the words "harmony" and "equilibrium" as critical to the underlying objective toward justice.

> In Islamic cosmological thinking, the universe is perceived as equilibrium built on harmonious polar relationships between the pairs that make up all things. All outward phenomena are reflections of inward noumena and ultimately of God. All multiplicity is reducible, in some way to the one. All creatures of the universe are nothing but God's signs.

Furthermore, in our current time, justice for women is simply not like justice a thousand or two thousand years ago. It is more evident that despite women's continued child-bearing capacity, central to the biological function of human survival, the role of nurturance and care-taking could be integrated into dynamic economical and political public policies that contribute integrally to restructuring the care-work in family and society. Ideally, care is important enough to guarantee structural support in the public sector. It would also operate on more egalitarian terms of mutually shared rights and responsibilities.[67] Women and men are not merely their biology. The greatest teachers available to provide men with opportunities to learn about care-taking and its resulting egalitarianism are those who have most often been confined to this experience: women. Once men have learned more about this, women would still have exclusive privilege in the experience of childbirth but childcare and the construction of domestic tranquility must be incorporated as central to the larger framework of public duties. This requires policy reforms sensitive to women's domestic experiences, now enshrouded by taboo and misplaced discourse on honor.

Today we witness worldwide chaos and community-building simultaneously. It is crucial for continued self-reflection in Islamic discourse on harmony and justice to include both the inside and the outside as essential for building the moral agent (*khalifah*) in the context of the family. Muslim men and women speak a different language or fail in the process of an equitable "ongoing relationship" to bridge the language disparities with the result of different conceptualizations of justice and harmony and, not insignificantly, the disequilibria of male historical, political, and familial privileges. Thomas Sowell suggests, "What social justice seeks to do is to eliminate undeserved disadvantages for selected groups."[68] He also agrees with the notion of social justice as a process, and as an important part of the larger category of cosmic justice, which is up against conditions, circumstances, and consequences that can in no way be completely controlled by humans in order to be achieved at no cost. At least social justice can be measured relative to the advantages and disadvantages of its projected results. Cosmic justice cannot be so easily measured on the basis of results since the consequences can be endless. That is why my Islamic framework points out that results belong to Allah, as the collective effort of human agency to achieve those results belongs to all humankind. My concern here is that consciousness of cosmic justice must continually come into deliberation when working on other issues of social justice. I especially conceive of gender justice as a harmonious process in which women and men work together to remove barriers to women's full mainstreaming in all aspects of society, while simultaneously acknowledging and compensating them for the indispensable contributions they have played throughout history by way of reproduction, nurturance, and care-taking of family and community, by increasingly mainstreaming women in the process of public policy. Care-taking contributions have become so invisible but must now enter into full-scale public discourse in terms that reflect the immense voluntary donation of women as moral agents. No parallel contribution so essential to all human well-being has ever been voluntarily contributed by men just by virtue of being male and human.

The development of Islamic moral theory insufficiently incorporated explicit reflections on the dynamics of family as they bear upon gender. Women themselves were not considered full agents with a perspective of total choice in their contributions. Their identity has been relative to their role in the family as care-takers. Since domestic harmony is so important, it must be fulfilled. But to restrict the identity of women to only this role, even as they increasingly fulfill other community, political, and economic roles, unfairly violates the importance of care and restricts or doubly burdens women in the fulfillment of other aspects of their divine purpose as *khilafah*. Despite these historical developments about the moral agent, the *ahadith* and *sunnah* reinforce the thesis that *taqwa* is more than an outward attitude or performance. The statement by the Prophet, "God will not look at your bodies or forms, but at your hearts," moves the focus away from external gender disparity. Likewise, the famous *hadith*, "All actions are judged in accordance to their intentions,"[69] seems to emphasize situating the locus of judgment on the heart and mind in the actions, not on the accident of biology. Actions that qualify as either good or evil are then truly viewed generically, not in gender-stratified terms.[70]

Although the *hadith* "does not give us a definition of what the good and the evil referred to really are, we can clearly infer from it the express identification of goodness with conformity to the dictates of Islam or the [Qur'an]."[71] In the Qur'an, "whoever does good, whether male or female and is a believer" shall be rewarded (40:40). Such explicit emphasis prevents gender, class, or ethnic disparity as features of expanding and maintaining the development of a truly progressive Islamic ethical theory of care and compassion as a communal responsibility.

Ethics and Islamic Law: Shari'ah and Fiqh

Law is used in society and government to establish the necessary terms of basic rights and wrongs in collective living as well as to assemble the checks and balances for maintaining those rights. Before I look at definitions of law or *shari'ah* in the context of Muslim history and societies, it is iportant to devote some consideration of Islamic ethics in its own right as well as in terms of its extension to the legal tradition. The existing gender bias requires appropriate deliberation with regard to the needs and complexities of living Islam today. Little if any work has been done explicitly on the relationship between gender and Islamic ethical theory especially emphasizing the particular place where women experience oppression most: as daughters, wives, and mothers in the private domain. Too much of Islamic reform and the works of Muslim reformists extensively occupied with women's human rights addresses the issue of family through the law without considering the direct and detailed relation between Islamic ethics and the law. Discussions of the historical juridical formula of law and women's rights get all the attention while the ethical foundation of that law and the underlying ethical theories remain underexamined. However, from the perspective of this book, gender disparity was an underlying characteristic of *shari'ah* in its historical development[72] and as such still remains one of the most hotly debated topics in reform movements today.

The ethical foundation of the gender *jihad*, so far, has been subsumed under the extensive debates over *shari'ah* and *fiqh*. Despite the absence of direct or explicit corollaries between ethics, whether explained explicitly on the basis of ethical theory or operating as an underlying ethical presumption, the meanings of *shari'ah* have often been inferred by reducing it to one word: justice. As discussed above, it is clear that justice means different things to different people. It is also clear that patriarchal thinking asserts full justice to men who then limit it to women.

The fourteenth-century jurist Ibn Qayyim al Jawziyya said,

The foundation of the *shari'ah* is wisdom and the safeguarding of people's interest, in this world and the next. In its entirety it is justice, mercy and wisdom. Every rule, which transcends justice to tyranny, mercy to its opposite, the good to evil and wisdom to triviality does not belong to the *shari'ah* although it *might have been introduced in it by implication*. The *shari'ah* is God's just and mercy amongst His people.[73] (emphasis mine)

This quote helps us to begin an examination of that foundation. The words *"shari'ah"* and *"fiqh"* were not used as they became central to the Islamic intellectual movement after the death of the Prophet Muhammad. Ziba Mir Hosseini reminds us how crucial it is to "distinguish between *shari'ah* and the science of *fiqh*." She first points out that *fiqh* "is *not revelation*; it is that part of religious science whose aim is to discern and extract *shari'ah* legal rules from the Qur'an and Sunnah. Strictly speaking, *fiqh* is a legal science with its own distinct body of legal theories and methodology as developed."[74] Likewise, Feisel Abdur-Rauf reminds us to take care in making the "distinction between *shari'ah* as the idea of an immutable divine order, and *fiqh*, the human interaction between that belief and the sources of divine *shari'ah* from actual applications and implementations *that require human endeavors*"[75] (emphasis mine). These are but two examples of how most modern scholars emphasize this distinction.

This persistence of those who ignore this tremendous gap between the divine order and human juridical efforts to implement what they perceive as that order provides deceptive authority to conservative thinking. To object to rulings and selective implementation of *fiqh* by equating it with a divine mandate of *shari'ah,* especially when generally translated as Islamic law, is just another method of abusing the semantics of discourse in shaping its power and validity.

The next question, relative to the gender *jihad,* is whether or not Islamic law can be changed. "In theory, whatever means were used in the past to protect human dignity can undergo change, provided the new measures give effect to justice and fairness, since the essence of *shari'ah* is justice."[76]

In his groundbreaking work on reform,[77] An-Na'im made an important comprehensive effort in recent times to recommend the significance of this divine human nuance. It does seem, however, that his tendency to presume that readers would keep their relationship with *fiqh,* discussed as "historical *shari'ah,*" made it more difficult to follow the detailed arguments he intended in his reform theory. I was grateful after reviewing his work, because my lack of training in the law was then opened up to envision the importance of including women's perspectives in Qur'anic interpretation for more than mere theoretical reflections. As the Qur'an is one ultimate source of direct verbal access to Allah's self-disclosure and of the order of cosmic justice, then clarity about its multiple meanings, as developed over time and human mental and moral capacity, points to the explicit need for including women's experiences as essential to the work of human contribution and compulsory to the construction of how meanings effect ethical codes.

Occasions of inconsistent scholarly use of the word *shari'ah,* without distinguishing it as a human science, developed under certain times and in specific contexts, adds to the complexity of unraveling the correlation and distinction between the law of God, as the cosmic order of harmony, and the interpretations of God's law and the cosmic order as implemented through codes and rules of law for human society. Women and men seeking changes in human codes for implementing social justice, and re-evaluating the methods used to construct those codes and the expansion of ethical understanding, must especially acknowledge the traditional gender inconsistencies underlying the presumptions about what it means to be human. Many Muslim women continue to be passive recipients of social change. Meanwhile they live in countries forced by the changing global economy to enter the wage-earning public sector still defined along the lines of the privileged male. Women do not have equivalent participation in the policy-making of governance in the new nation-state, starting with the need for coherent, complete, and consistent analysis of how gender should figure prominently in the construction and standardization of new policies.

The major question in modern discourse is: can the law be changed? Rauf also points here to al-Jawaziyah, since "legal interpretation should change in times, places, conditions, and customs," to emphasize his opinion that "the majority of the jurist have accepted the principle of change in legal rules." He still leaves the meaning of gender as a category of legal rules underestimated or ambiguous. He does point out, however, that some accepted the possibility of "change in the explanation or in the interpretation of the texts, because of a change in their causes or in the customs upon which they are based, or in answer to necessity and public interest." Most telling, as historical precedent, Rauf quotes Umar, the second ruler of the Muslim empire after the death of the Prophet, as having said the "aim was always public interest what was evidently *sensible*"[78] (his emphasis). More than platitudes are needed to completely embrace women's complicated lives and near-exclusive responsibility for the moral upbringing of children and for sustaining peace and harmony in the domestic sphere. It requires extensive rethinking and reforms in public policy.

Indispensable with this change, Rauf is adamant that the nature and category of the problem be identified not always in a purely jurisprudential domain. Rather, the circumstantial domains of economics, politics, medicine, and technology have to be taken into full consideration. Here I would add gender as a category of analysis. He suggests, quite simply, that one should not ask the *imam* (religious leader in the mosque) a question requiring medical expertise. Correspondence between the jurist in the juridical domain and experts in the other domains is essential. He insists: "contemporary opinions and technologies, are forcing us to think of the morality of the issues that were not posed to us before."[79]

As these bear on gender rights, the necessity for reform is all the more apparent. For one thing, according to Mir-Hosseini, "gender rights are neither fixed, given, nor absolute. They are on the contrary, cultural and legal constructs which are asserted, negotiated and subject to change." Although she confess that she herself does not "extract rules from sacred sources by adhering to . . . legal theories and methodology as developed," she examines the validity of these in order to "expose the inherent gender bias of *fiqh* rules and their inner contradictions."[80]

Today there is virtually no context of expert discussion between jurisprudence and certain new fields of thought, like psychology – the discipline of human mental and emotional well-being – or with the increasing number of institutions to shelter abused women and children. Women have been voicing their experiences through this development of medical mental health but are also seeking resolutions in the shelters despite the disjunctive practices between social-psychological solutions and Islamic legal reform. Likewise, the experiences of the majority of Muslim women, with regard to their most intimate needs and concerns, remain silent and invisible in the process of the leading discourse of progressive Islamic transformation. The most basic and increasingly problematic example is domestic violence and abuse. International Islamic legal councils are not calling in the abused women themselves or referring to experts in women's personal lives to help direct and guide their decisions toward the intent of the divine level of cosmic justice and the codes and rules that are persistently used to determine the outcome of domestic disputes in the courts. Here again the absence of women as fully human is accentuated, as is the persistent divide between the domestic and the public.

Despite a proliferation of agencies in all parts of the Muslim world, where women address these domestic issues, the agencies operate primarily outside of or without support from both religious authorities and representatives and the leaders of progressive Islamic discourse. A massive renovation would result from combining juridical abstractions with women's real-life experiences. Admittedly, there has been an increase in legal and sometimes religious women experts referred to as representatives of the agencies that directly encounter the source of women's domestic burdens. Having mastered the patriarchal methods of discursive and public debate privileges the majority of the women whose voices are heard, whether or not they have sufficient knowledge as experts on the basic realities for the majority poor and uneducated female experiences. Thus many grassroots concerns are still inadequately integrated into discussions over legal or public policy reform. Then when religious experts are invited to assist the women engaged in the formations and sustenance of such organizations, they simply repeat double-talk and take refuge in the irrelevant repeating of the word "Islam" or haphazard quotations from the Qur'an or *ahadith* used in a way that actually continues the disadvantage of what circumstance demands. There is grotesque contradiction reflected in women being stoned to death, falling victim to honor killers, and the increasing levels of domestic abuse even as more and more women are increasingly better educated and play larger roles in certain organizations focused on women's issues. The policies remain unfair in terms of protecting the rights of the overwhelmingly poor and institutionally unsupported grassroots Muslim woman. Still the Islamists' calling for implementing *shari'ah* in its traditional patriarchal form sounds like an innocent and pious cry for protecting and maintaining "Islam," even though its existing historical formulas are patriarchal and simultaneously justify violent abuses against women.

Conclusion: Power

Looking carefully at key terms is related to the relationship between theory and practice of Islamic gender justice, sustaining the full human dignity of all Muslim women and advocating for a social-political structure that encourages the fulfillment of their purpose as full agents. I have drawn ideas about theory from female-inclusive reflections upon Islamic theological discourses, past and present, and on the basis of a hermeneutics of care that nurtures both the inner and the outer human well-being yet requires a political structure to ensure that it is justly and comprehensively activated. These comments simply expose the ways that the gender *jihad* is integral to all other aspects in discussion about social justice, public policy in government, democracy, and economics in today's reformist discourse. I will conclude with the observation that women's full human dignity, in terms relative to the real-life experiences of the majority of women in the Muslim world, is still marginalized, not only in terms of actual practice, but also in the power imbalance of women's multiple circumstances which still privileges men in the new reformist discourse.

Richard Valantasis[81] alerted me to the conceptual nuances of the term "power." The power paradigm wedded with the moral bankruptcy of gross individualism in the form of greed and desire as results from the madness of consumerism is a term that is most often used to reflect "power over," the will and action to exert control over others as utilities to achieve one's aims. Valantasis juxtaposed that understanding to consideration of the "power to." When gender activists and theorists assert the need for women's empowerment, those most accustomed to the term "power" in its "power over" dimension do not wish to have women's power asserted over them, reducing them to a utility for the benefits of others and dismissing their moral agency. Oddly enough, this is exactly what has been done with women's agency, the utilization of them and their empowerment or agency only as a utility to fulfill human care without recognition and more than mere lip service to the virtues of such an application. These discussions do disempower men, although they, as a class, have exerted their power over and dominated and destroyed the ecological environment and global economics for their own selfish utility, under the name "civilization." To empower women, or rather to fully acknowledge women's empowerment, whether in care work, public service, political authority, spiritual leadership, as well as any number of acts of agency, is to acknowledge not only their "power to," but also how it is integral to a third level of power discourse emphasized in feminist ethics, that of "power *with*." There is a reciprocal relationship between acknowledging women's power and the enhancement of the social-cultural roles they have contributed to benefit humanity. A lesson that can be learned by any who seek to fully apply the Qur'anic mandate of agency would result from accepting that women's power has made an essential contribution to human well-being which is not limited to biology. As such, power *with* others is a universal goal certainly commensurate with the dominion Allah has given to humans over the creation (22:65) and to fulfilling the ontology of agency Allah has assigned as intrinsic to all humankind.

2 The Challenges of Teaching and Learning in the Creation of Muslim Women's Studies

> Answers to the questions that naturally arise about gender relationships cannot be found by posing them to those who are unfamiliar with the principles and roots of Islamic thought.[1]

Islam is a tradition with an intellectual legacy that has developed sometimes coherently and systematically over the past fourteen hundred years, and sometimes in contradictory directions not only from previous generations, but also within a single generation. I have been engaged in research into and teaching about that legacy for more than three decades now. This engagement is especially difficult in the current generation, which happens to be characterized by great contradictions in development, articulation, and practical implementation. This generation is also faced with a particular politicization of Islam in general, exacerbated by diversity, and under heavy pressure from Western ideas of globalization, militarism, and the global economy. The major result is the demonization of Islam to such an extent as to defer deep learning and understanding to sensationalist verification. Although plurality and diversity is accepted and expected at this point in modern history, and the contradictions within the Muslim world are no surprise, the rise in extremism, exclusivism, intolerance, and violence in the name of Islam has helped to create a challenge in critical learning of gigantic proportion.

In the context of Islamic history and Muslims today, the rise in exclusivism frustrates total Muslim consensus over plurality. Indeed the exclusivism is internally reflected, with some Muslims aiming to remove other Muslims who believe in diversity. It seeks to deter them from even engaging in Islamic practices, whether ritual or cultural, and to convince them and others less informed that there is some simple measure to determine whether one is within the faith of Islam or outside it. Even as I was preparing the chapters for this book, one Muslim woman was involved in the procedures her mosque had instituted to excommunicate a member from its congregation. They have adopted these procedures of excommunication with no reference to *shari'ah* or its primary sources, the Qur'an and *sunnah*. Thus, the consequences of articulating alternatives to the status quo emphasize the problems of displacement experienced by Muslims, both those intent on practicing Islam within various community settings and those who feel personal devotion to the Islamic faith while experiencing or accepting relative isolation from the collectives. Those identified as Islamic authorities randomly exclude others from the faith even by using Islamically selective or illegitimate methods themselves. Discourses about the multifaceted aspects of gender in Islam are not merely a form of intellectualism. They are fraught with personal consequences for Muslim scholars, activists, and the real lives of all Muslim women.

I will nevertheless consider the juxtaposition of the Islamic intellectual legacy, historically and currently, to the recent concerns over gender reforms in Islamic thought and practice. My focus in this chapter will shift between my experiences as teacher and researcher – primarily in the context of U.S. academia – as a Muslim woman, and address Muslim women's studies within that context, and the larger areas of existing women and gender studies programs in North America, including the studies of women and religion. I will revisit challenges made within the academy to make a space for both protecting academic freedom and promoting intellectual exchange. In order to create a legitimate and dynamic discipline of Muslim women's studies, especially in the U.S.A., distinctive aspects of this area of study must not only be recognized but ultimately given assistance to develop. Throughout this book I address gender, as one of the most important issues in Islam today, both as an area in need of research and analysis and as a dynamic aspect of Muslim identity, practice, and contentions. What exists within the proliferation of Muslim women's studies in the last two decades has remained haphazard. In my brief and admittedly random review of this proliferation, I do eventually conclude with a consolidation of its multiple contributions at the crossroads of several different disciplines, while emphasizing that Islamic studies are essential prerequisites of the sub-discipline. My perspective grew both out of experiences as a Muslim woman scholar and out of full awareness of the potential contribution that theoretical work on gender has in actual practices and reform in the lives of Muslim women worldwide.[2]

Islamic Studies in Western Academia

The study of Islam entered Western academia as part of a larger agenda of Orientalism. According to Edward Said, "Orientalism is more particularly a sign of European-Atlantic power over the Orient than it is a veridic discourse about the Orient (which is what in its academic or scholarly form, it claims to be)." The two-pronged geopolitical domination and hegemonic discourse continues to shape every discipline related to the East (Far, Middle, and Near, as such descriptive terms indicate). Therefore, a power relationship is always at the core of the study. It seems that few other academic disciplines are plagued by such a persistent hegemony – not even women's studies, which actually has had some modicum of success in entering mainstream Western academia after several decades of struggle and, as will be shown here, also participates in the hegemony over many aspects of the potential development of Muslim women's studies.

Within the field of religious studies, some aspects of intersecting power politics can be distinguished to sustain the sacredness of the faith systems, but not so for Islam. In the political quagmire encompassing modern Judaism, for example, the convenient term "Zionism" distinguishes itself and disentangles the political realm from the sacred. No equivalent epistemological operation occurs for the separation of political Islam from the sacred, so one is never certain what is meant by the word "Islam" when it is used.[3]

Transition from Learner to Instructor

I have studied abroad, including at the American University in Cairo, Cairo University, and al-Azhar University, and taught at Qar Younis University in Libya, at the International Islamic University in Malaysia, and at other smaller institutes. However, most of my Islamic studies – learning, teaching, and research – were in the U.S.A., where popular media tends to cluster around a set of simple factors commonly used to characterize "Islam." While these characteristics might be meant to help non-Muslims understand the role of Islam in modern international politics, their reductionism leads to negative stereotypes that impede the learning process of Islamic studies in the academy, especially at the level of undergraduate education.[4] This forms an important condition to my experiences in the academic study of Islam and to the analysis I make about developing Islamic studies programs – especially the developing a critical area of Muslim women's studies.

Before I began teaching Islam, the academy was the more significant of two primary locations for formulating ideas on Islamic studies in the U.S.A. My initial encounter was inspired between Islam as an ideological framework or its worldview as a living faith system. I made my transition into Islam in 1972, while an undergraduate in the University of Pennsylvania, an Ivy League institution. At that time a tiny Muslim Students Association operated rather loosely on campus. I lived off campus and the greater Philadelphia area was steaming with local Muslim growth, especially among African-Americans. As a transitioning Muslim woman, I had no organized study programs to introduce me to Islam as a theoretical arena of academic research. I simply withdrew as many books as I could out of the university library and read them, with no ability to argue for their benefits or merits relative to the macro-context of Orientalist agendas with its incoherent sub-categories still used now to ascribe self-determining merits vis-à-vis the diversities of opinion. This independent reading was simultaneously available to me with the confessional literature from local mosques. My naivety resulted in heightened optimism. I knew little about Muslim women's experiences globally. A student life is often insulated from the world at large and constricted by a tunnel vision. Where my insulation led to optimism, this is neither less nor greater than my current students' pessimism, a tunnel vision due mostly to increasingly negative media associations with "Islam."

In the 1970s, media focus was still on the Cold War and U.S. military intrusion in Vietnam. Coincidently, my undergraduate years also overlapped both the Black Power movement and the full second-wave feminist movement[5] in the U.S.A. The resulting scramble in academic institutions to reflect these two movements, however randomly, lent itself to the development of new courses and programs. Critical studies of modern Islam and gender were nowhere in sight. In a Sociology of Women course I tooted the horn of neo-traditionalist form of Islam's moral advantages for the woman. A required twelve-page paper turned into a twenty-five-page exposition on the virtues of Islam and women. I got an A for the course. I knew nothing about the existence of women's struggles under Islamic law and customary practices and the instructor knew nothing about Islam. So how could she grade me except on the extent of my research and the coherence of my articulation?

I admit I focused on some romantic notions of the place of women in "Islam." That same focus would later became one of critical scrutiny and analysis after local and global inquiry into the developments of the Muslim world. In 1972, Islam offered me an escape from the overwhelming phenomenon of double oppression as an African-American woman. Part of Islam's mystique for females in larger groups of oppressed people, struggling for collective survival, is the appeal that they have been unable to experience: masculine honor and protection of the raised pedestal. No doubt some women amongst the empowered and privileged have reasonably articulated the struggle to be free from that very pedestal and the ways it acts to cage and limit autonomy, creativity, and empowerment, especially in terms of politics and economics. The experiences of this privileged minority bear little reality for the majority of women in the world, who struggle with poverty, national, cultural, or ethnic displacement, and whose collective identity with these forms of oppression give them no opportunity to experience relief from daily drudgery that such a pedestal offers, or the extent of its particularized male hegemony. As a young, poor, black female entering Islam, such a suggestion and other romantic images and notions of Muslim women's honor were accepted without critical examination. Local discourse assured females in transition that instead of being oppressed by the necessity to struggle in the white male, sexist, racist, and capitalistic world of paid employment and the cutting double standards politically, Islam offered care, protection, financial support, and adoration for women,[6] which would provide escape from that struggle and a rise onto that pedestal.

After more than three decades as an African-American Muslim woman, I have never experienced that honor, but I have faced the (external and sometimes internalized) humiliation of its absence. Now I am adamantly opposed not only to that superficial discourse, but to how it is advocated as a reality along with other dialectical games played to convince women to submit to the limitations of this façade of honor in the domestic realm and to accept second-class status vis-à-vis other women worldwide, as well as Muslim men in their own families and communities. When my experiences with Islam and Muslims eventually took me to live in Muslim communities across the world, diverse by class, ethnicity, and nationality, I began to encounter certain parties whose vested interests were in defending to the death such an ideal as a complete and actual reality lived by the "true" Muslim woman, or as the goal of Islam for the "good" women. I also observed the way they ignored certain limitations on women's full and free agency. One of the most effective ways to defend this is to keep women silent about their actual experiences. The main method of silence is to authorize neo-traditional concepts about women's roles – no matter how abusive – as integral to "Islam." That is why national and international public exposure of the atrocities experienced by Muslim women is such an affront to the image of perfect "Islam" that they wish to express. They pretend such practices do not exist, because "Islam gave women their rights fourteen hundred years before the West."

Paradoxically, many Muslim women still acquiesce to these images of honor in Islam, irrespective of actual experiences, which they shrug off as merely the consequences of men not practicing real Islam. They are unwilling and sometimes ill equipped to challenge whatever articulations of "Islam" allow double and triple standards. Many are burdened by the need to, at the very least, see to it that they and their children have a chance at male presence by remaining in a nuclear or quasi-extended family – whatever the degree of its reality or illusion – because it offers the advantage of looking like a working marriage.[7] Despite the length of time I have continued to struggle in the white, male, sexist, racist, and capitalistic world of paid employment against increasingly more oppressive opposition as an African-American, a Muslim, and a woman, I have become aware that the victimology of my experiences is not proof that I was not a good Muslim woman. I may experience many exceptions to some idealized norm in "Islam," but that only proves that the "norm" has a great deal more variance than romantically fantasized by both Muslim patriarchal thinking and Western Orientalist and neo-Orientalist studies with their media support.[8]

By the time I began serious work in the academy as a graduate student on issues of Islam and gender, I had already lived abroad and worked on these issues with other Muslim women. I had also already requested my first divorce and was managing the care of my eldest two children first with welfare as our sole income, then from a job as substitute teacher in the Philadelphia public schools and later in an Islamic Private School. While the Muslim community in Philadelphia made specific judgments about the virtue of my womanhood in the context of many mainstream Muslim communities, I continued my contributions and eventually rejoined academia for graduate studies. Between academic grants or scholarships, Medicaid, and some personal charities, I began my specific research on Islam and gender.

There were many obstacles to overcome in efforts to help provide more critical representations of the diversities of thought and reality within an Islamic framework. Oppositions are both intra- and extra-Islamic. One obstacle is being directly attacked by aggressive patriarchal interpretive restrictions in Islamic thought. Critical representations of such obstacles and encounters are one of the core inspirations for writing this book.[9] Here I start by recalling experiences and addressing limitations of the teaching of Islam studies in U.S. academia, let alone gender and race dynamics that obscure and exacerbate progress. I will then offer some ideas about developing a critical arena of Muslim women's studies within academia.

Personal Narratives from the Trenches of Academia

As an instructor of religion at Virginia Commonwealth University, a southern, state-run academic institution in Richmond, the capital of the confederacy, I share the pedagogy of all members in my department. We use the academic approach to religious studies, which conforms to the phenomenological method of examining religions in the classroom and relies upon the benefits of that approach in exposing students to a diversity of worldwide faiths, practices, and beliefs, historically and currently. In fact, that approach, and its distinction from a purely confessional theological approach that aims at indoctrination, is the subject of my first lecture in each class. This is indispensable as the starting point in order to set the stage for maintaining diversity and objectivity for both Muslim and non-Muslim students in these classes. It emphasizes that students are subject to a single standard of evaluation based on the research focus presented in each particular course. The uniform measurements of evaluation are also outlined in the course syllabus.

Although I use the academic approach along with my colleagues, other department members sometimes enjoy the opportunity to *veil* their religious identity as a valuable asset to this approach in religious study. While I also relish that opportunity to use the academic approach, I am unable to hide my identification with the particular faith system I teach, because of my overt style of dress. For more than thirty years I chose to wear the traditional Islamic *hijab*, or head covering, and long clothes.[10] The percentage of tenured Muslim women in Islamic studies is already extremely low. The percentage of tenured Muslim women in U.S. academia in *hijab* is also very low, with some increase only in the last decade. It is nearly impossible to find tenured Muslim women in *hijab* in the area of Islamic study in U.S. academia. Perhaps the constitutional conclusion in France in 2004 about the consequences of all external symbolisms of religions is supported in U.S. academia regarding Islamic instruction. Despite First Amendment protections it seems that in order for someone to teach the academic approach to Islam, one must either be non-Muslim or remove all symbolic associations with the faith.

Furthermore, the styles I wear were influenced by the Asian and African cultures where I have traveled the most. Recently, I have noticed how much I have conformed to wearing more solid or muted colors. Otherwise, this flamboyant advertisement greeted students even before class discussion opened and had its impact on students, as I will detail from my teaching in general courses such as Introduction to Religious Studies, Religion in America, and Comparative Religion. The truly effective learning experience takes the learner from her starting place to a place where she can begin to grasp the breadth of a new or unfamiliar subject matter independently. A curriculum cannot stand without proper acknowledgement of the learner. Short of undressing, I did begin to make accommodations with regard to other student sensitivities in my teaching.

I have been teaching Islamic courses primarily to undergraduate students for over a decade and a half, mostly at this southern university. This was an interesting experiment in many general lessons about teaching Islam in the context of U.S. academia. My thoughts on the subject have gone through several metamorphoses in all this time, and I have continued to adjust my teaching goals and pedagogy to achieve greater relevance and efficacy. Nevertheless, it is dismaying continually to face the same problems anew each semester on my own campus or during occasional visits to other campuses across America.

In summary, the characteristics of my identity in relation to the academy has the following three main features: (1) I am not only Muslim; I see all of creation through an Islamic perspective. The worldview of Islam helped me to understand more about the workings of the whole creation when added to my having grown up Christian and to a year living as a Buddhist. My experiences in learning and teaching Islam freed me from the constraints that ultimate Truth resides exclusively in one religion rather than accepting the sacred as permeating the whole world. (2) I grew up Christian, but also poor, black, and female in America. As a Muslim, I have traveled extensively for work, research, and human rights issues. I often feel *more* comfortable abroad than I feel in the U.S.A., the country of my four-hundred-year ancestry. (3) Although I obtained my Ph.D. from studying Islam in a U.S. university, my first professional teaching experience was in Malaysia, with little more than half its population non-Muslims. In that multi-cultural context the relatively peaceful coexistence of religious diversity encourages mutual respect for religion as an essential character-istic of human well-being. This helped me develop the spiritual confidence to evaluate my teaching on proficiency in the discipline. This confidence has been undermined in the context of teaching against a mainstream of mis-information, antagonism, and exoticism. When I returned to the U.S.A. and began teaching in a university climate hostile toward Islam – exacerbated by the popular negative media sensationalism that forms the basis of general public information – teaching became rather bleak. Unfortunately, Muslims themselves further exacerbated the negative by participating in some recent violent and extremist global events like September 11. Con-sequently, I mostly teach students who have been raised with intensely negative viewpoints on Islam. "Indeed, a University of Massachusetts study (Morgan, Lewis & Jhally, 1993) found that the more people watched television, the less they knew about the issues at state and the more supported the [Gulf] war."[11]

Instead of simply sharing information about a particular faith system, I struggle to create a space for appreciating its uniqueness. It differs from Christianity, a reality for one-third of the world's population but with a larger percentage in the Bible belt context of the southern U.S.A. Indeed, my teaching is up against this and the presumption of white supremacy. A kind of insulation is created whenever a culture has no need to be openly exposed to other cultural realities. Teaching Islam here often goes up against certain comfort zones, creating hostility.

Before tenure, I was required to teach two "Introduction to Religious Studies" courses each semester. In teaching this course I learned how to remove generic references using Islamic examples. For example, in discus-sions about the hero, one of my colleagues (not religiously obvious – but coincidently a white female Baptist and ordained minister) shows her class the Malcolm X movie. If I showed this, discussions would center on race and Islam, interfering with the main goal of the lesson: the universal charac-teristics of the hero in human civilization. I eventually discontinued any critical analysis of representations of religious ideas, metaphors, or symbols if they came from the Christian tradition. For example, since the cross is just two pieces of wood, two-thirds of the world's population would not know that it is the key to their protection against Count Dracula who would otherwise suck the blood out of their necks! Even this was not seen as the joke I intended, to demonstrate how religious symbols are ordinary objects empowered in context by the investment of sacred meaning.

As a religious studies academic advisor I assist potential and declared majors and minors. Before one semester, an African-American student was adamant that she would only take classes about Christianity taught by Christian instructors. I informed her that all instructors teach our courses using the academic approach to the studies of religion, not the confessional approach. Furthermore, other instructors usually do not include information about their personal religious affiliations. Although they span from Marxist atheists to ordained ministers, because there is nothing recognizable that distinguishes their religious or ideological preferences, it is easier for the students to focus attention on the subject of the lesson and away from the agent of that subject.

After my third year review, the dean of the Faculty of Humanities and Sciences referred to the evidence that student evaluations consistently ranked African-American female University instructors lower than their white and male colleagues. I already fell into a disadvantaged category for academic evaluation. Although I share some handicaps with other Islamic studies instructors in U.S. academia, as indicated above by Said, as a female Muslim of African descent, my instruction of Islam in a religious studies program in the patriarchal, racist, and xenophobic southern U.S.A. faces challenges not yet documented, but surely of particular disadvantage. After I attained tenure, I would discontinue teaching the Introduction to Religious Studies course for at least six years.

These are some of the ways in which what Ada Maria Isasi-Diaz calls "invisible invisibility" occurs: when people do not even know that they do not know you, and "when those values, traditions and customs intrinsic to being non-Christian are not valued, not remembered, not celebrated."[12] "This is part of the broader experience of every oppressed group: they must know about the oppressor's culture, but the oppressor need know nothing about them."[13] Meanwhile, "oppressed people need to know as much as possible about their oppressor in order to survive,"[14] and they are forced to give up certain aspects of being essential to their own cultural experience and identity development because those aspects are disadvantageous for the assimilation into the dominant culture or for participation in the dominant discourse. Western postmodern mastery over religious and theological discourse is just another form of cultural imperialism.[15] As I stepped into that box of privilege, most of what I said had the effect of shards of glass ripping against that solid cushion of insulation. The more insistent I became with attempts to articulate this divergent reality, the more deadly the shards became.

The American Academy of Religion

I have tried to share theses experience in a number of public forums focused on the teaching of religion, such as the American Academy of Religion (A.A.R.). The first presentation I ever gave about teaching Islam in U.S. academia was entitled "Teaching Afro-Centric Islamic Studies in the White Male Christian South," for the historic "Black Women in the Academy" conference, held at the Massachusetts Institute of Technology in 1994. I had only been at V.C.U. for two years at that time. That presentation was eventually edited for publication.[16] In reviewing the still vibrant optimism I had while writing that article, I shamefully confirm that some academic environments challenge instructors to lift up to greater heights, while others suck the life and spirit out of one's intellectual endeavors and thwart the potential of their creative contribution.

The A.A.R. sets the standards for the study of religion in the U.S.A. As with other national level professional groups focused around a particular discipline in the academy, it is a religious studies institution that intentionally endeavors to offer the best formats for exchanging ideas. I have appreciated being in the company of both Muslim and non-Muslim, male and female Islamicists,[17] and academics from broader interdisciplinary fields of Islamic studies, not just religious studies, and have especially enjoyed the company of those in other fields that intersect with Islam in their studies or addresses related to theological and practical issues. I have benefited from the Islamic studies sections of the A.A.R. in finding a collegial environment for mulling over ideas about Islamic studies in the academic setting of the U.S.A. Simultaneously, in attempting to contribute ideas about the *study* of Islam, including research and critical contributions to the study of Islamic reform, as well as helping to contribute in the intellectual formulation of those reform theories, experiences with the A.A.R. are widely varied. So far, the A.A.R. has not been the ideal place for developing scholarly ideas about gender and religion in the context of Islam.

The overwhelming majority of Muslim Islamic studies scholars in America are male and either white or transnational. The overwhelming majority of scholars of women and religion in America are non-Muslim. The unique but beneficial idea of creating space for the academic approach to a budding potential to form Muslim women's studies originated within the A.A.R. over the past decade and fell within negotiating the context of those two existing sub-groups of Islamic and women's studies.[18] To date, the roads between Islamic studies, Islamic reforms, and gender have met and found greater support outside the A.A.R. in forums set up by individual universities or institutions across the U.S.A. or in international human rights forums. Two A.A.R. experiences set the context for my comments on personal location and Muslim women's studies. One of these experiences occurred before the tragic "terrorist attack" on September 11 2001, and the other occurred after.

There is glaring evidence that 9/11 affected Muslims in general as well as Islamic studies in particular in the context of America. On the one hand, it has generated more interest in learning about Islam. This has led to an increase in academic positions for Islamicists at U.S. universities, and for researchers in a plethora of pro- and anti-Islamic institutions, nationally and internationally. Yet on the other hand, the simultaneous expediential increase in negative media stereotyping of Islam and Muslims outstrips these efforts at the level of the general public learning about Islam, as they face continually distorted ideas about Islam in modernity. Students in my undergraduate classes have helped to substantiate the claim that teaching and learning about Islam is a contested area occurring against the surroundings of negative public images and media reporting.

The A.A.R. experience I share first is the most recent one, which coincidently followed 9/11 by a mere two months. Perhaps the intensity of my comments about teaching Islam in America and the time when I was making those comments did little to open dialogue. None followed during the question and answer section. That presentation was for the "Identity, Scholarship and Teaching: Studying Cross-Culturally and Ethnically" Panel, in the Committee on Racial and Ethnic Minorities in the Profession at the American Academy of Religion meeting held in Denver CO.

My contribution to the goal of the panel could be seen as very narrow, very specific, and very personal. Yet I had hoped it would become a helpful contribution to the analysis of what this means to academia in general and to the study of religion and diversity in particular. I would especially like to posit some critical consideration to the study of Islam in Western academia, even more so to Muslim women's studies, despite my frustrations. Islam as an academic subject cannot be taught with equal effectiveness in every academic setting. Several factors adversely affect the quality of the learning experience. Furthermore, to use a Malcolm X metaphor, a Muslim woman academic is not an equal diner at the great dinner table of academic life. I reflect on matters of teaching and learning in light of a series of overlapping factors that adversely affect both teaching Islam and teaching as a Muslim female. I offer data collected from the experience of teaching Islam in hopes of contributing to valuable analysis and strategies for improvement in all aspects of teaching diversity. I have not established a standard to definitively measure or evaluate the information I have collected. This has been my personal experience, so the relative degree of how one or another factor might adversely deconstruct an environment conducive to effective Islamic studies could also benefit from a more objective examination.

Over my first few years, I collected information informally from two divergent sources. I read with detail the negative comments made on standard student evaluation forms – the final weapon for recalcitrant students to use their anonymity for particularly harsh commentary. I also took references from those students with whom I became very close, the ones who would often take every course I taught, and who clustered around me both inside and outside of the classroom. They would not only tell me what some other students were saying when I was not present, but they would also take their classmates to task for exaggerations during class discussions. They were the ones who informed me that my style of dress led others to confess they "thought you were going to throw that Islam thing at us, so they dropped the course."

Later, I developed two specific evaluative sources for collecting information directly from students about their perspectives, which could be constructively incorporated into my teaching and pedagogy. As stated previously, pragmatically speaking, a curriculum cannot stand alone without acknowledgment of and response to the learner. It was my genuine desire to improve my teaching to meet the standard of learner I am assigned to teach. I had also enhanced the use of technology in teaching Islam. A proposal I submitted specifically aimed at increasing images about the softer sides of Islam into the lessons was accepted for a teaching and technology grant.[19] Ironically, that was the same semester some Muslims decided to blow up the World Trade Center. Although the long-term profit from this grant has proven beneficial and I have created basic Islamic studies, with each topic increasingly better comprehended and appreciated, my best efforts that semester were no competition to the amplification of mass media sensational coverage considering their advantages in manipulating modern technology.

One of the strategies I used for constructive evaluation was an extra credit project for students to connect course materials with the use of technology. This became reduced to random lists of U.R.L. addresses with no substantive expressions of how the particular websites would be integrated into the course development to enhance student experience. Other students did submit ideas that helped to assess students' critical thinking about the course and its development – especially with regard to current events. My basic introductory course on Islam, now totally technologically enhanced, primarily covers the fundamental developments of Islamic theological ideas, dogma, creeds, rituals, and practices starting from its beginnings. Only a short amount of time would be available for applying that background information to current events. So I developed several courses explicitly on modern global trends and on Islam and women, but fewer than 10% of the students who had previously learned the basics ever signed up.

The other important source for collecting student feedback was offered for free credit in the form of two questions on the last of several non-cumulative assessment examinations. One question asks: "If there was one thing you would change about the course what would it be and how would you incorporate it?" With no reason for their choice they more constructively phrased suggestions for future incorporation. While student responses included specific additional topics, logistical information, or comments on things like attendance policy, there have been some helpful directions for meeting student needs more concretely.

However, one frequent suggestion is to teach Islam relative to Christianity. While, on the one hand, familiarity with Christianity is understandable, on the other hand, using Christianity as the standard for understanding all other religions has serious and potentially damaging results in continued misunderstandings. This is not a comparative course, like one available on Western traditions. That which distinguishes the three Abrahamic religions is too easily dismissed as insignificant or re-interpreted through a lens incongruent with the integrity of the non-Christian traditions by obscuring certain points crucial to their distinctions. When such points of distinction arise for critical reflection, this method has led students to reduce these matters by constructing such an amalgamation that important distinctions are meaningless.

For example, revelation and monotheism are essential to Judaism, Christianity, and Islam. The habit of overgeneralizing the meanings of these two terms actually violates the importance of their distinctions. Although all three revelatory monotheist traditions describe themselves as evolving from a unified origin – God and prophets – they do not form one religion. The significant distinctions of these two concepts help define the unique worldview of each faith system. Whitewashing the differences between Islam and Christianity may make teaching them more palatable to the average undergraduate student of Christian background in the south, but this method can also violate the integrity of Islam. At a most fundamental level, for example, Islam's idea of monotheism, or *tawhid*, completely rejects the idea of the Trinity. It is more important to engage in the distinction of Islam's view without using it to disagree with the idea of the Trinity in order to feign commonality.

Nevertheless, I have made many adjustments to adapt the curriculum to the particular learners, while remaining committed to teaching Islam within the integrity of its own worldview, and on the basis of its own principles. It is not the counterpart to other religious traditions, a sub-category to some standard established externally, nor a reaction to sensationalist media coverage. Meanwhile, I must still create courses that will draw in and keep a certain number of students each semester as part of the university's expectation of all instructors. Coincidently, millions of Americans tuned in to an Oprah Winfrey program, *Islam 101*. Despite the tremendous public interest in understanding Islam, it is still difficult to entice students into genuinely preparing themselves for an in-depth study of the complex issues of Islamic thought, development, reform, and, in particular, matters of Muslim women. I cannot realistically teach about the integrity and complexity of Islam at the level of undergraduate education if the goal is to reduce it to oversimplification to fit its most immediate circumstances or to resemble popular entertainment.

The other A.A.R. experience was also with a "special topics panel" focused on the study of Islam and gender. I was one of several women invited to participate on a "Women, Religious Studies and Backlash" panel for the section on the Status of Women in the Academy at the national meeting in San Francisco, Fall 1998. I availed myself of the opportunity to make a plea for greater inclusiveness and support while intentionally invoking the very places of tension between the powerless and the more powerful in the academy with regard to this special section. So I highlighted aspects of intra-Islamic backlash but also intra-academia backlash, in order to make it clear that U.S. academic settings – including the A.A.R. – can be part of the problem or part of the solution.

I was not viciously attacked, as I have experienced when facing Muslim confessional audiences about the problems of theoretically addressing gender justice, but neither were there comments on the points I raised, to ease the tension of the dilemma of double academic marginalization. At that time I had been involved with the A.A.R. for over a decade. This was my first direct dealing with either the Women and Religions sections or the sub-committee on the Status of Women in the Profession (S.W.P.). I felt hopeful that it could yield a place and time for coordinating bilateral discourse. The following spring I proposed a topic on Islamic Public Ritual Leadership and Gender,[20] which was accepted by both the Islam section and the Women and Religion section. However, the Women and Religion section orchestrated a special panel in conjunction with the topic. Since the A.A.R. does not permit a proposal to be delivered in more than one session, I opted for the Islam section. In my letter of apology to the Women and Religion section, I explained that I thought this particular topic would benefit most from the input of Islamic scholars more familiar with the field.

Having made the tough decision to reject the Women and Religion section, the following spring I proposed exclusively to that section the topic "Making Space for Critical Studies of Islam and Gender in U.S. Academia." The rejection letter stated the usual: no reflection on the quality of the proposal since many other factors may contribute to the possibility of a particular proposal being rejected, including whether or not a topic *might fit in with the other proposals for that section.* I sent a reply to point out the irony of trying to "create a space" while being rejected because there was no space. I indicated that the Women and Religion section continued to be unbalanced by the dominance of Euro-American, Judeo-Christian perspectives on the larger phenomenon of Women and Religion. Women of diverse faith perspectives will not fit unless they succumb to the standard already created without consideration of their religious peculiarities[21] or until a separate space is created. While preferably this space would be created within that section, some Women and Religion scholars have opted to split off from the larger group, for example the Womanist Religion section. While I applaud the proliferation of women's studies of religion sections, I worry about networking and cross-fertilization in the case of so many divisions.

Perhaps as a follow-up, or perhaps as a coincidence, the next spring three specially selected female Muslim scholars and I were sent an informal email invitation to discuss the status of Muslim women in the academy for yet another special panel of the Women and Religion section. I noted we were still not part of the larger body. I was uncomfortable with the informality of the joint email address that seemed to condescend our status as intellectuals or scholarly equals. Although these four women were from four distinct circumstances, someone unknown to me was hailing all of us on a first-name basis. I also had no insights into who had participated in the actual formation of an event that was ostensibly *for* us. I declined the offer with the simple: *Thank you for the offer; I'm afraid I will have to decline.* In response I was sent a message: *Sorry you won't be with us – as I recall, it was your idea that got this going originally.*

After conversing with one of the other four colleagues on the email invitation, I sent another message including: *I must conclude that this program was orchestrated in a way that continues to marginalize Muslim women and our concerns. The best I could come up with involves taking more time to plan it with some meaningful input from Muslim women academics themselves. If that can happen, I would be more than happy to consider it for a future date. This invitation will not address whatever "idea" I might have had originally.*

The final response on the matter read: *Forgive me. I did think that having an open meeting at the last A.A.R., getting input from 7 or 8 women who came up with this idea, asking another Muslim academic to work on it and co-write the invitation would have been sufficient.* She agreed to *discuss the matter further with S.W.P. committee at their February meeting, and share my thoughts with them.*

These narratives direct attention to several points. Just as the study of Islam under the larger heading of Orientalism was critically analyzed by the late, great scholar Edward Said in his book of the same title, as a matter of intellectual discourse that supports other political agendas of oppression and imperialism, so does the attempt to construct Muslim women's studies face formidable pre-existing obstacles and complications in academia. It is also subject to a new set of impediments that are obscure, unnamed, and even unknown. Yet "academic" contributions are increasing expedientially with little evidence of proper preparation for logical, critical, and constructive discussion on a topic which coincidently is not only one of the most sensitive in modern Islam, it is also a matter addressing genuine and oppressing problems for many women in the Muslim world, at every minute. One tedious component in my proposal is to begin with Islam studies itself. The remainder of this chapter will focus on the growth of contributions to Muslim women's studies despite the absence of any foundational theory for establishing clear parameters.

Over Two Decades of Research and Proliferation of Islam and Women Books

Upon quick observation it is clear that any non-Muslim woman who visits a large Muslim population and writes a book can have it published, thereby contributing to an as-yet undefined area of Muslim women's studies. That not only says something about the girth of random material on this subject, but also says that publishers, aware of a great vacuum and interest in this area, are willing to accept almost any articulation about real Muslim women under direct observation. They do not seem aware of any boundaries to determine what falls appropriately within this category of study. There are no consistent criteria of evaluation from the perspective of "Islam" as a component bearing on the lives of Muslim women or men. In creating such criteria, I build a rationale for locating Muslim women's studies as a sub-discipline of Islamic studies first, even when it crosses other areas of study or disciplines within the social sciences and humanities. Simply speaking, adequate knowledge of Islam is a prerequisite to formulating adequate analysis in Muslim women's studies. The Islamic intellectual discourse is as essential to understanding Islam and Muslims (women and men) as it is to understanding any number of topics related to them.

Furthermore, despite a proliferation of literature on Islam and women, by Muslim and neo-Orientalist or Western Feminist scholars in the past decade, precious little has been proposed to create an Islamic gender theory – whether from without or within. As such, this boom in literature remains rather haphazard. This has complicated and will continue to complicate what remains one of the most sensitive issues among Muslims. Rather than being helpful, this proliferation is viewed with great suspicion by both scholars of Islam and by Muslim laity. It is part of the problem of resolving real issues of concern to the Islamic gender *jihad*. Yet rigorous and intellectually solid academic publications could become vital in leading toward greater understanding and comprehension for the general public worldwide, as well as for better-informed participation by Muslim women and men activists in the matters addressed.

Although we may learn something even from the existing works, it depends on the goal of our learning. Within all this literature, certain presumptions prevail about the way in which specific variables affect the outcome of particular cases. Islam is always measured as one, if not the major, variable. It does not matter how inconsistently Islam is defined or how haphazardly it is referred to. Based on the stress already discussed about the use and abuse of the term "Islam," I reiterate that the extent to which those who claim to discuss topics related to Islam need sufficient background and a standard basis for defining Islam before their works achieve scholarly adequacy.

In addition, with regard to Muslim women's studies, it is too easy to listen empathetically when one encounters familiar language supporting preconceived notions about Islam as oppressive to women. It is also easy to accept perspectives with which one is already in agreement. A predilection toward the familiar emphasizes why some particular prerequisites are necessary for a comprehensive or reasonable understanding in the complex study of Islam and women. Instead the greatest lesson learned from most of this literature is the biases of the ones engaged in the study. Nevertheless, eventually this material can add to a growing wealth of material from which a genuine and critically beneficial discipline of Muslim women's studies might be wrestled.

Muslim women scholars, no matter what their discipline, have also contributed to the growth of literature on this topic. The mere fact that they are Muslim does not make them all experts in every area of Islam and Islamic studies. For many years I was invited to deliver a presentation on "Islam and Women." At first I accepted these invitations because, after all, I did have something to contribute within this vast and borderless area of research. I then just got tired of the same title and offered to work out an appropriate title using details about the larger framework of the forum, the audience, and the topics of interest. I was still limited to gearing my presentation specifically toward my expertise: gender-inclusive theological analysis. Few general audiences were ready for all the technicalities required for an adequate presentation, but at least I could narrow down that broad umbrella topic to address particular aspects more relative to my academic training and interests as specifically beneficial to different audiences anxious to learn about Islam and women.

On the other hand, it was amusing how invitations were extended to me from the flip-side of this pattern of overgeneralization. As a female Muslim presenter I was sought for very specific aspects regarding Islam and women, including areas about which I had insufficient training or time to become familiar, and I began to decline these invitations. Sometimes, if I knew of other specialists, better prepared for the topic, I would direct organizers to these experts. Often I was still pushed very heavily to accept the invitation despite my limited knowledge of the topic. The rationalization was that, since I know something about Islam and women, I should use whatever knowledge I had and the specified topic would make no difference. Several occasions of complete burnout eventually led me to reject all invitations that did not address narrow specifics of my expertise or experience.

Eventually extensive travel working on human rights issues increased my knowledge base of Muslim women's networks, human rights programs, and issues of family and sexuality regarding women within the framework of Islam. I now work better as a consultant to experts in these areas from my particular discipline: gender-inclusive interpretation for more gender mainstreaming. I could help create spaces for making meaningful, authoritative, and appropriate knowledgeable assistance across geographical borders in these forums as the challenge of Islamic legitimacy is continually used to disclaim women's contributions. However, other scholars continue to publish and accept invitations to discuss topics in which they have little or no expertise because of the lack of structure under this vast umbrella called Islam and women. This is so with both Muslim and non-Muslim scholars. Audiences must leave such forums no better informed than when they came, or unfortunately misinformed. This public role of scholarly work, sometimes referred to as scholarship-activism, can be problematic. While it emphasizes the need for properly establishing the area of Muslim women's studies, it also contributes to the chaotic state of a yet to be clearly defined academic discipline.

In critically developing this area of study one might also note how the overwhelming majority of the literature published falls under the case study category of anthropology, personal narrative, or historical reconstruction. These materials provide adequate evidence for the needs of Muslim women to find methods in attaining political, cultural, economic, and educational gender parity. However, recapping each and every particular cultural or historical context as *the* epitome of a non-existent monolithic Muslim woman obscures the very complexity of Muslim histories and societies.[22] As the literature increases without a theoretical foundation exposing a clear intra-Islamic basis for gender analysis, such literature often further obscures the root causes and distorts potential solutions or methods needed by a broad base movement to eradicate the persistence of unequal practices, gender violence, misrepresentations, and legal manipulations.

As such, the flood of books caricaturing veiled women, presenting them behind bars or posing a seemingly contradictory image – like a veiled woman casting a vote – must be viewed with greater scrutiny, attending suspiciously to the objectives of these texts. Each book needs to be examined on the basis of the goals and objectives provided by the author, the definitions and resources used to locate the work within Islamic studies and the detailed specification of the examples projected or analyzed. Authors should clarify their subject matter; locate it within some overarching aspect of the Islamic intellectual or legal worldview while providing justifications for not utilizing other subject areas in which they have expertise or at least to relate their methods and discipline to Islam. These are some of the most persistent problems that reduce the proliferation of works created to a scarcity, which provides the means for properly integrating specific studies within an Islamic gender framework.

* * *

The time it would take to correctly prepare to work from the perspective of gender and Islam might increase the time it takes to study and produce works from within the major field of the author, but it is worth the time if Muslim women's studies are to become a rigorous area of academic studies. It would require experts from their various disciplines to shuffle through a larger framework of Islamic studies, and then designate what gender possibilities might be made within Islam as central to their particular analysis. Another mechanism would be to coordinate more meaningful collaborations between specialists in various fields of study with Islamic specialists, especially reformist thinkers.

Meanwhile, such case studies, in addition to including the country of national origin, and the history and developments of Islam within the contexts of these women's experiences, must also equally locate the sample group on the basis of class, education, and methods of exposure to Islam's intellectual traditional and contextual developments. Information about the subjects' exposure to Western ideas would also assist this prerequisite contextualization. An intra-Islamic framework is a crucial part of the necessary background for entering the discussion. Sufficient research into the relationship between that framework, the specifics of the sample group, and the academic specialty of the author would be clear enough to notify readers of the exact nature addressed in the publications and presentation in order to define the extent of their benefits to issues faced by Muslim women and rights networks and to the learning process of students interested in this area.

I can eventually see that Muslim women's studies could be placed within several intersecting lines in academia – women's studies, religious studies, Islamic studies, certain social sciences and humanities – when case studies on real Muslim women's literature, histories, and divergent lives are clearly located in the ways discussed here. One prerequisite is developing definitions of Muslim women's studies wide enough to encompass all the variables mentioned here, while still narrow enough to be distinct from other areas of study. Muslim women's studies cannot presuppose a neutral background for engaging in one of the most vexing issues of popular interest today. Each of these intersecting parts form prerequisite building blocks in the scaffolding of modern Islamic studies for a truly academically viable area of Muslim women's studies. I have especially found that the sociological method of study often distorts the integrity of the Islamic worldview, the guideline toward which Muslims strive, albeit with varying degrees of sincerity, piety, consistency, or success. Instead, sociology simply traces existing atrocities, mostly decontextualized from ethnicity, class, local customs, national origins, religious understandings, and the relationship of those understandings to the sources of Islamic thought and development. In other words, it matters little what Islam is, only what some Muslims do. This is one area of academic discourse that is particularly charged, and the contributions accepted for publication in the past decade have been part of the problem. To pretend otherwise is both hypocritical and academically deficient. For while Muslim women's studies might be able to accommodate all of these intersecting lines, to adequately provide for an understanding of the diversity and complexity of Muslim women's lives, it is necessary for those who study or learn in this field to be appropriately familiar with the history, culture, and developments that precede from their particular discipline when approaching this sub-topic.

Nevertheless, even this material adds to a slowly growing wealth of material from which genuine and critically beneficial literature about Islam and women might eventually be constructed. Depending on the learning goal, a reader may learn from and apply critical analysis even to these works. If they distinctively point to the multiple variants that exist and which all deserve adequate analysis, they help to create a well-rounded discipline which is informative on a variety of levels within academia while simultaneously helping to remove the veil of mystique and exoticism of Muslim women beyond the simple reflection of preconceptions, prejudices, and biases of the ones engaged in the study. It is disingenuous to ignore the self-definitions of Islam as a way of life in which Muslims have variously lived for over fourteen centuries. Analysis of the "place" or "role" of women within the many contexts that claim allegiance to the Islamic way of life is one of many tools needed to evaluate how particular social groups reflect or reject those standards through interpretation and practice. These parts, as well as those "issues" deemed significant by anyone who encounters "Islam" and Muslim women – whether in their own lives or through some kind of relationship to others – help to prevent the intellectual hegemony and elitism that Said warned against in his classical work. Although his critique did not adequately address the specific issue of studying Oriental women, it was an important catalyst to achieve such advancement under this Muslim women's studies umbrella. Instead, it has been disappointing to draw attention to the way that it has become even more deeply embedded in the hegemony of discourse he addressed.

Returning to the importance I have given to work in Muslim women's studies to include a detailed discussion of the meanings for the term "Islam," at an abstract level I first agreed with Fazlur Rahman,[23] that the criteria referent for the study of Islam cannot be the plethora or varieties of the "little tradition" that have evolved among Muslims throughout the history of living Islam.[24] The assortment of understandings both reflect the Islamic worldview as based upon the referents and the diverse cultural and historical conditions which each collective of Muslims bring as influenced by the circumstances of their cultures, and the consequences of their historical circumstances, whether peaceful or under conflict. Negotiating between the influences of these interactions helps to better understand that Islam is one factor among many that we must study about individual cultures and the spread of the religion. The expectations established, limitations, and strengths of a specific cultural and historical milieu contribute to the variant implementations that take root or are totally ignored. For example, it would seem contradictory that some places which enforce greater general limitations on women, like Saudi Arabia or Afghanistan under the Taliban, do not practice any form of genital mutilation, whether the lesser "symbolic" removal of the clitoris or the full-fledged infibulations.

Knowing what factors cause which restrictions on women in concert with their interpretation and implementation of textual sources indicates that patriarchal practices among Muslims reflect some things other than the religious sources themselves. Yet, the consistent justifications given to these restrictions in too much of the literature generated to justify them to women and non-Muslim international groups have been that these practices are essential to "Islam." So they conclude: Islam oppresses women. Ultimately, those of us working not just as academics, but also as activists creating reform, must strategically negotiate these multiple factors at the level of policy and legal re-articulations with due research attention given to evidence of their existence and the consequences of their violation. Consistently across the Muslim world, the academic inclusion of alternative, female-inclusive interpretations have helped to advocate more liberative and egalitarian implementations in actual policy.

All these variants need to be incorporated into critical analysis of the specific case studies done on Muslim women in these societies. The absence of clarity about these variants has led too many readers to conclude that *each example reflects the goals, principles, ideologies, or worldview of Islam.* The patriarchal authority and control over what becomes accepted as "Islam" developed specific to cultural and historical contexts bears heavily upon the experiences of Muslim women and men in each of those contexts as analyzed in the case by case methods of study. How authority and control are determined and implemented, coercively or through acquiescence, is essential to the appropriate location of case studies work in contribution to this field of academic study.[25]

In addition, it is clear that the academic expertise of the one doing the analysis contributes in other specific ways to understanding the particulars of the study itself. The expertise primary to the author cannot be used as the sole basis for explaining the nature of Muslim women's experiences. Since "Islam is a faith tradition with an intellectual legacy that has developed sometimes coherently and systematically over the past 14 hundred years, and sometimes in contradictory directions from previous generations," it is important that intelligent consideration of Muslim women make clear correlations between this legacy and the areas of gender studies as developed in the West, especially as it has spread to become a global phenomenon in modernity.[26]

Finally, I hope eventually that Muslim and non-Muslim women and men academics who are working on these crossroads continue to orchestrate forums, conferences, and networks with a variety of motivating causes. I am especially interested in finding an opportunity for Muslim women teaching any subjects related to "Islam" to form a national collective that meets to discuss experiences in the academy, strategies of survival, and methods employed to excel.

All of my discussions about Muslim women's studies started at a meeting held at M.I.T. on African-American Women in the Academy. I cannot imagine what was needed to bring such a forum together, and despite many who claimed in 1993 that it was their desire to recreate such a forum annually, if not on a regular basis, it has yet to occur again. Muslim women academics are even more fragmented. Certainly, discussing the creation of Muslim women's studies should not take longer than it took to create women's studies in U.S. academia or should not be plagued by many more obstacles. This vision of the matter, however, does indicate how formidable a task it will be to create the sub-discipline or the collective.

Gender Issues

Whether with regard to identity, self-awareness, spirituality, sensitivity, inclusivity, mainstreaming, or political reform, gender is one of the major issues to be addressed by the world community in the past century. It is also one of the most crucial issues facing Islam and Muslims in modernity. Where the key Islamic issues might be seen as democracy, sustainable development, human rights, and globalization of the economy, all of these issues intersect in some strategic way with gender issues. In fact it was at the mismanagement of the element of gender and the vital significance of women's varied yet often unacknowledged skills and contributions that the earlier efforts at constructing sustained development met some of their greatest failings. "The failure to include women in the macro-economic policies as major and potential actors leads to the exclusion of *half the human resources and their potential* from the national development process. Therefore, mainstreaming women in the whole policy process is not only a matter of social justice but, it is an economic imperative"[27] (emphasis in the original). The leading models for gender analysis are still primarily from the place given or taking assertive advantages of individualism and consumerism to reconfigure the family – not as an extended unit of multiple networks of mutual self-support – especially for women, but in adapting the nuclear family, the structure most easily exploited for individualism and consumerism.

It is no longer possible to construct Third World and all other specified articulations and philosophical develops of feminism without due reference to the Western origins of feminism. That is why I still describe my position as pro-faith, pro-feminist. Despite how others may categorize me, my work is certainly feminist, but I still refuse to self-designate as feminist, even with "Muslim" put in front of it, because my emphasis on faith and the sacred prioritize my motivations in feminist methodologies. Besides, as an African-American, the original feminist paradigms were not intended to include me, as all the works on Womanism have soundly elucidated. In addition, socialist feminism has focused clearly on the significance of class as it further problematizes the origins of feminism in the West. Finally, Third World feminisms have worked tediously to sensitize women and men to the complexities of relative global realities to resolving universally existing but specifically manifested problems in the areas like gender.

Starting with Simone de Beauvoir's basic idea that feminism is the "radical notion that women are human beings,"[28] we move to examinations of what is meant by human being. Women are human beings in ways particularly distinct from men as well as in ways very similar to men. They are also similar to and distinct from each other as women, so likewise between Muslim women. The unifying principle of Islam, according to the Qur'an, is the notion of the human being based on a relationship with the divine; more specifically, the concept of *khilafah*, moral agency,[29] the ontological purpose for all human creation. This purpose, of direct responsibility to the divine, must be fulfilled here on earth and will only be fulfilled in a multiplicity of ways determined by and integrally intertwined with human circumstances and reasoning.

Islamic Thought, Feminism(s), and Postmodernity

In Western academic circles, the main focus of feminist thought seems incongruent with the establishment and sustainability of sacred systems, rendering them incorrigibly patriarchal and hence beyond redemption.[30]

> Post-Christian and post-Jewish feminist theologians contend that the biblical traditions are simply too broken to be fixed, that patriarchal values and symbolism are too essential and too central to their world views ever to be overcome. They do not see patriarchy, in its many levels of manifestation and meaning, as accidental or secondary to the biblical outlook, or as merely an unfortunate outgrowth or outmoded cultural habits. *Therefore, they contend, no woman will ever experience wholeness, healing, integrity, and autonomy while committed to a biblical religion.* (emphasis mine)

Shulamit Reinharz emphasizes the pluralist approach to her book *Feminist Methods in Social Research* [31] to demonstrate "the fact feminists have used all existing methods and have invented some new ones as well." Instead of orthodoxy, feminist research practices must be recognized as a plurality. Rather then being a "woman's way of knowing" or a "feminist way of doing research," there are women's ways of knowing, she reminds us, and we must remember "collective voices." Yet much can be said of the often-quoted remark of the black lesbian feminist literary and political genius Audre Lorde: "The master's tools will not dismantle the master's house." I do not propose to create or to engage in the creation of a new female-centered goddess tradition post-Islam.

While I acknowledge the potential contributions of both secularist and pro-faith perspectives in feminist work, I can only participate in gender reforms in (and outside of) Islam from a pro-faith perspective. I chose the literary tradition of Qur'anic exegesis as the specific discipline that would sustain my faith by equipping me with the tools to determine exactly how the masters' houses have been constructed, without limiting the sacred potential to human tools. I wrestle the hegemony of male privilege in Islamic interpretation ("master's tools") as patriarchal interpretation, which continually leaves a mark on Islamic praxis and thought. Too many of the world's Muslims cannot perceive a distinction between this interpretation and the divine will, leading to the truncated notion of divine intent as well as of the divine nature and essence limited to the maelstrom perspective, hence violating the actual transcendent nature of Allah. Western scholars are stuck between the variegated articulations and applications of these mutually existing and yet sometimes utterly contradictory paradigms, motivated by the need to find the simplest means to eradicate the significance of this trickster that takes the name "Islam" to suit its whims and to legitimate its reactive desire to build its own power agendas in place of its post-colonialist disintegration.

I see a link between these two – interpretation of praxis and ideas about Allah – because we cannot know how to "surrender to the divine will" – what might be considered as the fundamental "definition of being Muslim or Muslimah" – if we have a truncated notion of the divine. The notion of the divine is overwhelmingly as a male being, parallel to the cosmological notion rejected in Islamic orthodox theology of a male person literally made in the image of God. The idea of Allah as the sacred essence transcending all thing-systems (*laysa ka mithlihi shay'*) is too illusive for constructing and sustaining systems that exert power over others.

This brings to mind an important theoretical question: can there be such a thing as a post-Muslim? If a fully mature and responsible member of society selected of their own volition to embrace Islam as their worldview and complete way of life, and then with the same volition and full maturity rejected Islam, such a one – according to *shari'ah* – is punishable by death, for apostasy. Although I prefer the simple Qur'anic imperative articulated as "(*la ikraha bi-l-din*), there is NO COMPULSION in religion" (3:256), the persistence of the "death-threat" tactic does interfere with non-compulsory religious freedom of choice for Muslims. Given the complication of this, to actually openly declare oneself "post-Muslim" might be suicidal.

On the other hand, most of the world's Muslim population consists of persons raised in religious or non-religious households of parents known as Muslim. Upon reaching maturity almost none were given the opportunity to decide whether Islam was the right choice for them. If someone raised in such a household was not only allowed but expected to choose for them-selves, then those who wanted to leave could do so freely, openly, and with acceptance and respect for their choice. Instead, the legal ruling is generally understood to apply without distinction to those who never had the right to choose, so any expressions of dissatisfaction with being Muslim legitimates the punishment for apostasy and many would fear for their lives and safety, so might find it better to remain closeted about their real feelings on the matter.

Many of those first considered "Muslim feminists," as known in the West, had never been given the opportunity to choose Islam. One wonders, if the threat of death did not loom over them, how many would just as soon *not be* Muslim. Since they have had no choice in the matter, perhaps they are simply trying to make something good come out of being stuck with Islam. How will those who "analyze" the literature know which Muslim women writing in Muslim women's studies are pro-Islam, what definition of "Islam" they adhere to, or whether they are merely coincidentally Muslim? Surely what is being proposed as the problem, let alone what is being recommended as the solution, will bear a considerable mark of differ-ence. This is obscured behind a popular notion that any *one* who is Muslim, commenting on gender, is qualified to do so as if competency in one area of Islamic studies is the same or equal to proficiency in the any other area of studies. People like Oprah Winfrey, unfortunately, use a liberal male trans-national Muslim scholar to set the standards for all of Islam and women in her highly publicized television programs.

A person's qualification to comment on Islam is not prefaced upon one's "upbringing" by Muslim parents in a Muslim cultural context. Emphases need to include the aspects of volition regarding methods of study, defini-tions of Islam, cultural affiliations or identity, religious ritual observation, and spiritual motivations. Professor Leila Ahmad once commented that being "in the West," with its sizable community of new Muslims at various stages of transition (converts, reverts, born-againers) along with transnationals (immigrants, their descendents from non-U.S. cultural and ethnic traditions and neo-traditions), conservatives, and newly forming clusters of reformists still not clearly identified against liberals, she was asked, "Are you a practicing Muslim?" Now she must face new criteria in determining her status as "Muslim." In her memoirs she described how she was allowed exemptions from such concerns within the female space of her cultural upbringing, which also created its own female Muslim self-identity in distinction to practices and perspectives given in the dictates of the mosque discourse. This is an interesting new imposition. She remains *within* the boundaries of Islam in ways most meaningful to both her personal identity as Muslim and the methods and motivations behind her work. Her contributions *as a Muslim woman* are extremely valuable to the development of Muslim women's studies. Those contributions are, however, distinctively self-determined on the basis of both academic/professional affiliations as well as personal or public insider aspects of identification.

This "in and out of the closet" status is only more problematic when attempting to determine "what is Muslim women's studies," and then to further determine who is capable of rendering definitions and to engage in such a study. So this brings me again to the question:

[I]s Muslim women's studies merely a study of that vast complexity of real women living within Muslim cultures and history? Or is it the arena where a gender analysis is made not only of its sacred texts and primary resources but also of its self-definitions, self-implementations and deviances? How do these two interact in the completion of the discipline? It is a particular academic arrogance to assume any discussion of feminist theory without examining our many difference.[32]

There is no essential Muslim woman who applies her energies and love to the tasks of improving the status of women in the global context, as demonstrated by Azza Karam in her book *Islamism and the State: Contemporary Feminisms in Egypt*. She provides a thorough case study of women's collective activities in Egypt with detailed corollaries and contradistinctions between secular feminists and Islamist activists, a distinction previously unclarified in Western and some Muslim academic arenas.[33] Margot Badran, known for her primary contribution to the history of secular, nationalist, or cultural feminist methods and leading Muslim women's activism and re-examination of Islamic and cultural traditions from the early twentieth century, also based on a detailed case study in Egypt, recently wrote another noteworthy article with Nikki Keddie: "Islamic Feminism: What's in a Name?"[34] They contribute to the issue of plurality of Muslim women's activities and scholarship, while finally bringing clarification to the strata between secular and Islamist strategies and ideologies. While each bears the mark of the contributor, they have made a valuable contribution to remind readers how all methods have contributed to the larger issue and need for Muslim women's mainstreaming. Fortunately this is now more readily acknowledged by Muslim women's networks, creating less hostility and giving greater coherence to the significance and benefit of mutual collective work. A more recent need has developed and remains unclarified – the similarities and distinctions between liberal and reformist Muslim women's activism and thought.

Sometimes, with the Western secular or Judeo-Christian hegemony in the academy, distinguishing all of the nuances between Muslim women contributors to this field of Muslim women's studies seems just too much trouble to unravel. Sweeping generalizations are made on the basis of very selective information, further exacerbating an already complex and extremely sensitive issue. How does any one scholar propose to have *the* Islamic, feminist perspective on any notion which in itself is not monolithic? Yet those are the titles given to their works. I return to the notion that the only way properly to locate the proliferation of literature flooding the market is by clearly establishing a more comprehensive evaluative measure or criteria referent based on some framework of Islamic feminist theory.

Conclusion: Toward an Islamic Feminist Theory in Muslim Women's Studies

Constructing an organized and organic sub-discipline in academia with Muslim women's studies as the focus is a reasonably tenable idea. The establishment of Islamic studies and women's studies already sets two precedents. A careful examination of the development of these two disciplines by corroborating or cross-referencing the process and procedures used for both these larger fields of studies would expose that their beginnings were not as clear about the long-term developments as they would unfold in academia. The nuances, complexities, and cross-disciplinary components as each claimed a place within the academy indicate the space for the distinct discipline of Muslim women's studies as one continuum in those developments. Removing patriarchal biases from Islamic studies as a whole by integrating gender as a category of thought is one of the most significant means for expanding the interdisciplinary component. At the same time as this awareness is emphasized within the multiple sub-disciplines under the larger area, the space for gender-inclusive research developments would also further clarify the gender-specific aspects of study that might be best supported in a Muslim women's studies sub-discipline. Islamic studies is ripe for this radical reformation in research, learning, and thought.

Meanwhile women's studies owes its current location in the academy to over thirty years of coordination between the second wave feminist movement and the basic philosophical and epistemological theories that were developed within other disciplines until the specific demarcations of women's or gender studies were integrated. Careful examination of this academic development would also expose its nuances, complexities, and cross-disciplinary components as each claimed a place within the academy. Paramount to the disciplinary integrity of Muslim women's studies is the critical analysis of need for further diversification as was mandated within women's studies by womanists, lesbians, majuristas, and Third World women's particularities and complex specificities without forfeiting the general consensus that "women suffer discrimination because of their sex, that they have specific needs which remain negated and unsatisfied, and that the satisfaction of these needs would require a radical change."[35]

It is not too much to expect Muslim women to advocate the particulars of their circumstances being identified as Muslim, while simultaneously crossing numerous contextual planes of diversity in other aspects of their identity. This has been demonstrated by the multi-leveled discussions I have had to negotiate even in this chapter. The neo-Orientalist propensity toward academic hegemony has allowed non-Muslim male and female scholars to give the determinations of what qualifies as academically acceptable within the Muslim women's studies context while bold-facedly constraining the diverse intra-Muslim academic contributions. Overwhelmingly, Muslim male academics participate in or agree with this hegemony, because it justifies their own limited efforts to radically interrogate gender as a category of thought in the Islamic studies areas of the academy, which still privileges them over Muslim women scholars. Lesbian Muslim women will share some commonalities and some distinctions with both non-Muslim lesbians and heterosexual Muslim women. Already the discourse on non-heterosexual Muslims is being forefronted by gay men, with the attendant privileging of masculine heterosexual and homosexual underpinnings.[36] In other words, there is a plethora of roadblocks already being laid to limit the necessary and dynamic component of diversity that Muslim women's studies *will* eventually manifest within Western academic circles and institutes. How soon or how late each particular institute gets on the bandwagon will determine the quality of the scholarship available in their colleges and universities. The longer they wait, the more inferior and haphazard their own programs will be. Muslim women's studies is already in process earnestly, critically, and with the requisite scholarly discipline. Now comes the opportunity to facilitate this movement within the context of North American academia. The quantitative growth in Islamic studies in the academy is qualitatively redundant on Muslim women's studies. We are already trailing behind the establishment of clear institutional affiliations in other parts of the global realm of institutionalized education.

3 Muslim Women's Collectives, Organizations, and Islamic Reform

> Whoever does an atom's weight of good shall see it, whoever does an atom's weight of evil shall see it.
>
> – Qur'an 99:7–8

Introduction: Theory and Practice

I began my work on Islamic gender reform as a graduate student of Islamic studies, exploring theological ideas about gender in the Qur'an. I had no intention of, and no understanding of the significance of, translating ideas into practice because I was unaware of the full breadth of the experiences and politics of gender in Muslim history and societies. After I completed my research and earned my Ph.D., I was employed at the International Islamic University in Malaysia. I then began my relationship with a fledgling women's association that eventually became known as Sisters in Islam. Our interactions reflected the crossroads between theory and practice. Before working with this group I understood justice as a concept. While working with this group, I understood that "justice" could only have meaning when implemented in real human contexts. It is far easier to articulate the abstract idea than it is to bring it into practice.

To look at Muslim women's activism, this rudimentary discussion on the relationship between theory and practice shows how that relationship is integral to the Islamic worldview. In giving an overview of some theories affecting Islamic praxis throughout Islam's intellectual history, I intend to show how these ideas and theories significantly affect modern movements of Islamic reform. All of this stems from the idea that alternative interpretation of the Qur'an from a female-inclusive perspective is instrumental in reform movements for women and men in modern Muslim societies, but only to the extent that that perspective is not continually reduced to being secondary or subsidiary to the normative male social and epistemological privilege.

A theory flows from an idea[1] or a belief that something is possible or could come into reality. The projection of an idea does not necessarily include the process, procedure, or method that will bring it into being. Procedures and methods are actions that confirm the theory. On one hand, a theory can be disproved when actions fail to yield the desired results. Failure can also indicate errors in the process used to fulfill a particular idea or theory. On the other hand, a set of actions can prove a theory correct. In any case, a theory is nothing of substance unless it can be proven in action.

Actions can produce positive and negative results or consequences even with no direct link to an underlying theory. This signifies one reason why the theory behind actions is not always self-evident. It is also possible for the relationship between action and theory to get lost in the process of acting. We can act, even if we have no idea what we are acting on or what we wish to achieve. Although a theory may not be directly linked or articulated as foundational to a set of actions, this does not mean that there is no underlying idea. Underlying ideas are disproved and proven by successful actions even if these ideas are unknown, unconscious, or underdeveloped. However, since the results of the actions can be haphazard and unpredictable, it is more difficult to assess the causes of these results. They are as likely to fail, as they are to succeed, when no clear ideas lie beneath them in the first place. Indeed, it is impossible to say why they worked *unless* a theory is attached to them. For this reason, the theory or idea underlying a set of actions, whether failed or successful, needs to be ferreted out, articulated, explained, understood, and brought into service in order to determine or clarify a process, method, or course of actions that can lead to future success.

In particular, if a situation of gender reform regarding Islam and modernity demands some actions, those interested may act – either proactively (with planning and forethought, that is, by using a preceding idea or theory) or reactively (in response to a cause and its effect). The efficacy of reaction is fickle. It maintains the prominence and privilege of the cause of the action in the first place. The initiator of the events, the one that caused the reformists to respond or react, still *holds all the power.* Reaction is an action in response to a situation premised upon someone else's underlying theories or ideas. This is perhaps one way to understand the well-known Audre Lorde quotation, "the master's tools will never dismantle the master's house."[2]

Although some active response may be called for in many situations, to react maintains the advantage of those empowered to oppress or to create the problem in the first place. Actions, in the form of reaction, do not reconstruct the worldview of the situation. The original perspective or underlying cause of the predicament goes unchallenged by reactions alone. If we want to make a change then we cannot merely run around like ants and just be active. We must have ideas about where we want to go and why we want to go there, and from there determine how to proceed effectively. Theory is significant in providing direction and perspective.

Theory also supplies articulations about goals and agenda. What is our goal? What do we hope, plan, or need to achieve? How do we achieve it? What steps do we take to reach it? What are the obstacles in the way of our success? How can these be avoided, reconstructed, or removed? Theory helps us to conceive of a plan by mapping out the terrain that we are to cover relative to an overview of the existing situation. Although the theory itself is not a step-by-step plan, it maps out the big picture or worldview underlying potential approaches and lends understanding to how things operate. In the case of gender reform in Islam one underlying idea is women's full agency, or *khilafah*, before Allah. This is spoken of in terms of another underlying idea: justice and women's full human rights. What must be done to bring about a change in the status of women until they become full agents of Allah endowed with full human rights? Ultimately this is a proposal resting upon certain theories of justice.

To propose ideas about women and justice one must first determine the basic sources of that idea. Furthermore, how does that idea compare to existing views? What makes one worldview oppressive and another liberating? How are negative consequences of certain ideas avoided or effectively transformed? What makes a particular worldview appropriate to positive identity development without disrespecting others? After all, patriarchy did not start as an idea to oppress women. It started as a healthy idea to help establish and maintain social, religious, political, and economic systems within the framework of men's identity affirmation.

When justice is the underlying theory we are working toward in the establishment and transformation of asymmetrical gender practices, then we have to give some thought to our underlying premise and the basis for our work. If we wish to locate our arguments and activities for women's rights and access to justice within the religious framework, as within Islam, then we need to have some clear articulation of how we understand Islam. What is our theory of Islam and how did we arrive at it? How does our theory compare to other theories whether existing and historical? How can it be developed? Ultimately theory is a powerful state of mind. It is not a chapter, a verse, a *hadith*, or any one specific operation. This is a reductionist misunderstanding of the criteria of evaluation or reference point within the Qur'an and *sunnah*.

A theory is a perspective that helps determine certain goals. Clarity about a goal and its underlying perspectives helps to develop a process including actual steps needed to attain the goal. If the theory of Muslim women's inherent human equality could be reduced to a single verse, or a single set of verses, someone could easily come along and wager an argument completely deconstructing the validity of the perspective. Understanding the breath of an underlying theory is not so simple that it can be referred to in terms of a single reference, but rather requires a vision of the map or grounds upon which the theory rests.

In the Beginning Was the Word: A Theory of Gender Justice

In Qur'anic cosmology, the entire universe was created before the penultimate creation of humanity itself. Indeed, even the *jinn* were created before humankind. The significance of this has been the subject of much theory. By way of metaphor, I mention only one of these. It has been said[3] that Adam and *Hawa'*, Eve, the fore-parents of our continuing humanity, were not the first attempt at human creation. Others had been created before but having failed some essential divine test, were replaced by a new creation. One such test was whether or not they exercised their free will, even if the demonstration of this was disobedience to Allah's command to avoid the fruit of the tree, in the pre-earthly blissful paradise.

With regard to Adam as the archetype first created soul, according to the Qur'an, a test was given between humankind and the angels. While the angels confessed their ignorance, human beings were able to "give the names of things" (3:33). Thus, nomenclature is an important distinguishing aspect of what it means to be human above the rest of the creation. Nomenclature is the ability to give names. It is the particular metaphorical and literal use of language, or abstract reasoning. This "naming" is also the primordial stuff of theory.

The ability to name things implies a unique power over those things. Like all power, it can be used to privilege some over others. For example, the one who determines the name of a people also defines the classification of that people. When colonialists entered the lands of other indigenous peoples they chose classifications of "other" and "primitive" in order to privilege their own notions about human development and civilization.

In addition, the power of words operates in other situations as an illocutionary force. An illocutionary force brings a thing into being, or causes a status change through pronouncement alone. When the queen says, "I dub thee, Sir . . . " she invokes a radical change in the status for the one being knighted. When heterosexual marriage ceremonies conclude with the words, "I now pronounce you husband and wife," a major status change turns two individuals into a legal and social relationship as spouses. The divorce decree has the illocutionary force to reverse that status. Moreover, from the Qur'anic perspective, Allah's ultimate power of creation ex nihlio is the illocutionary "Be," "*kun*," and it is, "*fa yakun*" (36:82).

Another aspect of the power of words is measured in terms of their effect. "I love you," selectively uttered, has meaning. So does the accusation, "You are so wonderful." Such phrases of endearment can bring about a change in psychological status through a complicated process of response in the one spoken to. In the same way, negative statements like "You mean nothing to me" and "I never want to see you again" have a powerful effect and can bring about a change in status.

Our ability to perceive of and act in the world is powerfully influenced by language. Where Allah's creative power in the illocutionary pronouncement "Be" brings real change in the physical realm, human creativity brings about change in meaning. Imagination is a key component of this ability. I attended a lecture once where the presenter made reference to those who had experienced the status of slavery for generations. Some slaves had experienced no other reality. The very *idea* of freedom existed only relative to the experience of non-slaves and in the imagination. If a slave cannot imagine freedom, he stressed, then it is impossible to be free because freedom is not a practical reality; it is an idea, a theory.

I have an idea about Islam without patriarchy. Since patriarchy has always existed in the history of human development, then my idea stems from my ability to imagine an end to patriarchy. A theory can also grow from imagination and spurs us to find relevant sources of information and inspiration that help lead to transforming that image into its potential reality. However good or bad this post-patriarchy idea might be, it exists in my mind and is felt in my heart. Although I do not draw from my immediate experiences for what human civilization would be like without patriarchy, I have enough experience with the negative consequences under pervasive patriarchy that I utilize all my skills of mind, body, and will to work toward achieving an end to it. Like other underlying ideas forming theory, it is possible to share the idea with others who can contribute to ways of thinking and being without Islamic praxis enmeshed in patriarchy. However, to bring such an idea into reality requires more than imagination. Certain definitive actions are called for in order to bring a change in human relations so that women are integral actors to – and agents of – all actions, as well as beneficiaries – objects or subjects – of the results of those actions.

At the most fundamental level, this is what I mean about the relationship between theory and practice. Theory is the idea, and in this case the idea of particular changes in the status of women in Islam and the world, which is imagined in terms so eloquent that it can be passed on to others who can use their limited human empowerment or agency to transform the existing reality toward greater resemblance of that idea.

Islamic Law and Theory

The task of *shari'ah* has always been to make judgments about appropriate actions. The *fiqh* then constructs juridical codes and principles for codification. According to the well-known statement of the Prophet, "Actions are judged by their intention."[4] Since intent remains known only to the actor and Allah, the confirmation of that intent by action can never be known to another human for certain. Ultimately this *hadith* means that Allah is the only judge of the totality of anyone's actions, because humans can perform actions deceptively or hypocritically. However, despite not knowing the full extent of an action, the responsibility of *shari'ah* is to make a judgment on external action. This is an interesting paradox in the relationship between idea and action – although the idea behind a practice is not apparent, it is essential.

More notably, Islam is *din*, a complete way of life. The meaning of *din* points to a correlation between orthodoxy – right ideas, or faith – and orthopraxis – right actions. Faith or belief cannot be verified on an empirical level. It cannot be evaluated in concrete measurable terms.[5] For example, if a believer and an unbeliever are engaged in the ritual act of *salah*, it is impossible to tell the difference between them from the outward appearance of their performance. In this respect, let us take faith as a state of mind, a perspective, or a worldview which incorporates certain transcendent or unseen elements as essential and sacred. Therefore, for simplicity's sake, the relationship between faith and action in Islam will be taken as a parallel to the discussion about theory and activism. One is internal and the other is external. One is hidden and the other is manifest – and at best, a manifestation of the internal.

Orthodoxy in Islam covers ideas about Allah, humanity, and nature. Over the course of Islamic intellectual history, orthodoxy has not been monolithic. Indeed, certain notions of orthodoxy have evolved at one place or time that were in complete contradiction to ideas evolved at other periods of history. These contradictions have had fatal consequences for some and led to inquisitions that punished those who disagreed.

The foremost principle of Islamic orthodoxy is *tawhid*.[6] Allah is one, unique, and unites all of creations through His/Her/Its unity. Allah, the Creator, is uncreated. One question that proceeded from the idea of *tawhid* was how could words proceed from Allah in form of revelation, the Qur'an? Either the words are uncreated and eternal with Allah as reflected in the very nature of *tawhid*, or the words are created, as emanations from Allah. Debates over Islamic orthodoxy included right understandings of revelation and definitions of belief itself. The answers to these questions were used to determine if a person would be considered Muslim or apostate. Even today, the practice of identifying someone as not Muslim stems from the variant understandings of orthodoxy. Women who advocate the necessity for gender reform within an Islamic framework are even challenged by patriarchal and narrow conservative standards on what it means to be Muslim. To disagree with the idea that men are superior can be projected as anti-Islam! This is why theological theories behind gender reform also need elaboration and explanation.

Reformist thinkers in Islam and modernity are proposing alternative understandings of Islamic orthodoxy. They are challenging the meaning of Islam and offering expanded notions of *tawhid*, especially as each term operates in the context of historical reality of real social and political contexts, as well as as reflections of the underlying universal principles. How these two terms are understood affects how the social and political order is established and maintained. There are also reconsiderations about the nature of the Qur'an and the role of interpretation within the framework of Islam. Again, the underlying theory is important to Islamic reform.

The other prong of Islamic orthodoxy as *din* is orthopraxis, or right actions. At countless places in the Qur'an, faith or belief and actions, *iman* and *amal*, are linked. Indeed right ideas are not sufficient in and of themselves. Faith depends upon some demonstrated action or orthopraxis. Historically, orthopraxis was the arena of Islamic *shari'ah* with the task of articulating right actions into positive juridical terms.

Shari'ah divides actions into two categories: *'ibadah*, formal rituals, and *mu'amalah*, social or human relations. I limit this present discussion about *'ibadah* with the presumption that it is fundamental even to the most controversial amongst us.[7] Suffice it to say that *'ibadah* is equivalent to the five pillars: *shahadah* (witness to affirm faith), *salah* (formal worship), *zakah* (alms-giving), *hajj* (pilgrimage), and *sawm* (fasting)–*Ramadan*. These five rituals are formal, stylized, and not self-encoded actions. Like all such formalized liturgical practices they are determined to set parameters between the sacred and mundane.

From the perspective and goal of this chapter, however, *mu'amalah*, social intercourse, mutual relations, or just relations, is the most significant category of action. The following *hadith* helps to describe just relations: "Verily, your Lord has certain rights over you, your people have certain rights over you, and your soul (or self) has certain rights over you. So give each the rights that are due."[8] This notion has three arenas of application. One arena is relative to one's own soul or self. In this respect we might point to proper food, water, shelter, and exercise for physical, intellectual, and spiritual well-being. The significance of right relations to oneself is obvious in terms of overall well-being, but right relations with self also affects one's ability in terms of the arena of doing justice in relation to others and to Allah. The arena of right relations with Allah has significance that can never be truly fulfilled except within the context of just relations to self and others. Relations with Allah can be perceived as both the ultimate goal as well as the motivation for right actions.

My focus on just relation between self and others presumes a dynamic integration between the rights of self and Allah. Just relations are the individual and collective responsibility to fulfill one's own rights equally with the rights of others. In fact, the *hadith* cited above uses the word *ahl* for people or family. It has been variously used in the Qur'an to apply to a small clan of people or family, as well as to designate a larger kinship group or tribe, to ultimately the whole of the world's Muslim peoples. Given a radical understanding of the global village, I confer on this term a even greater meaning than any single or particular community and propose that the term *ahl* is associated with all "people," with the human family. All are descendents of Adam and Eve, the primordial parents. All are due equal rights. In my reading, relations with other people form the most significant subtext of this *hadith*. As such the *mu'amalah* category designates the social dimension of human activity and must been seen as the pentacle of Islamic praxis and the primary objective of *shari'ah*.

Theory and Practical Gender Reforms

Since the underlying ideas about nature, humankind, and Allah affect the ways people act, Muslims accept that ultimately only Allah can judge actions. Yet our *din* calls us into action. We also evaluate actions on the basis of their results. In the context of evaluating Islam and gender for the sake of reform, we can ask this simple question: how are women treated by individual men and by Muslim patriarchy as a whole? If answers to this question show grave inequalities between the humanity of women and men then reform is not only warranted, but justified.

The first theoretical concern is to determine the underlying ideas that cause this inequality. That is, are women in an inferior position in Muslim society because of Islam itself? Again, determining what is or is not Islam is the basis of answering this question and for the sake of this chapter I will stress the partnership between the primary sources: Qur'an and *sunnah* and the primary agent, *khalifah*, and servant, *'abd*, of all Allah's creatures with moral competency – humankind. Muslims continually claim to articulate an Islamic position with reference to the sources. Yet the variety of conclusions drawn from these sources leads to an important realization. Even though Muslim scholars and laity are analyzing the same resources, the resulting diverse conclusions indicate that there are key elements in the interpretive process that lends itself to particular results. Since a single source can and does lead to diverse conclusions then the hermeneutics of the very act of interpretation is emphasized.

In hermeneutics, the analytical focus shifts from the source materials to the interpreters of that material. More precisely, how does anyone come to render an understanding of anything, especially something communicated through human language? Language or abstract reasoning through a symbol system has the distinct characteristic of variant meanings and multiple understandings. What causes these variant meanings is both the language itself and the reader or the listener. Thus we must consider in some detail what the process of comprehension within human beings is.

That process cannot be taken for granted. The most basic aspect of that process is that people understand and use language on the basis of their contextual experiences and the potential of their imagination beyond those experiences.

Primary to theories on gender is the proposition that men and women experience the world differently, whether for reasons of biology and nature, or through experience and culture. As one subgroup of the human species, women may have experiences that are unique from men, the other subgroup, and vice-versa. Yet, the record of Islam's historical intellectual development reveals one thing very clearly. With the exception of *hadith* transmission and Qur'anic *hifz* (memorization), women did not participate in the formation of Islam's paradigmatic foundations. Put another way, not only did men, men's experiences of the world – including their experiences with women – and men's ideas and imagination determine how Islam is defined for themselves, they also defined Islam for women. Men have proposed what it means to be Muslim on the presumption that the male experience is normative, essential, and universal to all humankind.

When we examine these presumptions, the tendency of patriarchy abounds. I take patriarchy as a term discussed by Elisabeth Schussler-Fiorenza in *Bread Not Stones*,

> I use *patriarchy* as a heuristic category. I do not use the concept in the loose sense of "all men dominating all women equally," but in the classical Aristotelian sense. *Patriarchy* as a male pyramid of graded subordinations and exploitations specifies women's oppressions in terms of the class, race, country, or religion of the men to whom we "belong."[9]

For I do not limit patriarchy to merely an affirmation of men and men's experiences but also extend it toward a hegemonic presumption of dominance and superiority. That includes both the presumption of male as normative human and the tendency to extend humanity to women only in functional juxtaposition to that norm. For example, the patriarchal formulations of Islamic law through out history hold condescending utilitarian perspectives on women. Not only is the female looked down upon, she is treated as an object in *shari'ah* discussions, not as a discussant. The woman is a recipient of its decisions, not a decision maker. Decisions made concerning her role in the family and society were made from the perspective of those who did not and could not share her experience and therefore judged on the basis of second-hand perceptions. What is more, women are subject to double standards and exclusions in matters of state policy, education, employment, and economics. This is the one constant in all of the history of Islamic thought that seems the most difficult to extract in order for genuine female inclusive reforms.

The results of the double standards between women and men are apparent when levels of human development are measured. From matters such as educational level, public health, mortality rates, representation in the political process, and others, the United Nations development statistics indicate that women's status in Muslim countries remains far below the status of Muslim men. Is this the natural order? Is this a reflection of the divine decree? In short, are there any indications in the primary sources of Islam, the Qur'an and the *sunnah*, that women's humanity should be so oppressed? The basic theory underlying Islamic gender reform movements is justice founded upon the ideal that *Islam does not oppress women*. The next goal of theoretical development is to look into both the primary sources of Islamic thought and the vast intellectual discourse throughout history for verification or proof of that theory. If the theory is incorrect, then definitive evidence must be provided. No one – not even the staunchest conservative patriarch – proposes that Islam oppresses women. The overwhelming consensus of Muslim scholars and believers is that the primary sources of Islam extol the virtues of humankind on the basis of *taqwa*, the moral capacity toward orthodoxy and orthopraxis (49:13). *Taqwa* has never been discussed relative to gender stratification.

Although the revelation to the Prophet Muhammad and his normative behavior are accepted as the divinely inspired sources foundational to all of Islam, actual contexts, human perspectives, and experiences affect both the formulas of the sources as well as their interpretations. Furthermore, even when interpretations are rendered, there still remains the important issue of application and implementation. How are ideas and theories concluded from the Qur'an and the *sunnah* best implemented in specific social contexts? Implementation reflects time, place, gender, level of knowledge, resources, and circumstances of history and culture. The process of establishing gender justice in Muslim society is neither simple nor straight-forward. There is not one strategy, one method, or one process. What works today may be unsuccessful tomorrow. What might work in one cultural circumstance may vary from what works in another culture. The necessity for continued efforts to achieve gender justice, however, is premised upon the fundamental theory that Islam is just for women, and that Allah intends full human dignity for women.

Although there are no detailed goals in theory, it has ultimate principles, like justice for Muslim women. On the other hand, activism must have clearly defined goals and expectations that are attainable in the course of some process. Discussions about basic understandings of Islam as a matter of theory are often hidden from the arena of praxis or actions in the context of Islamic reform. Perhaps this is because of their complexity and irreconcilability. However, in other ways, these underlying or hidden ideas are exactly what shapes or determines what actions need to be taken, as well as why they are effective or ineffective in particular circumstances. For this reason, I am once again inclined to stress that knowledge of the underlying ideas is important to the actions themselves and to the efficacy of the actions. Haphazard actions can only produce haphazard results. Although reform movements benefit from all kinds of efforts – no matter how poorly articulated or unarticulated – the goal of recognizing and operating in various social systems that woman are full human beings cannot be reached and maintained without knowledge of the perspectives that underlie and thereby affect actual practices.

Ultimately, women and men who are interested in the future development of Islam as a system of social justice must act in accordance with that interest and remove authority from those who seek to prevent the manifestation of Islam as a system intended for the fullest realization of human potential. While not predetermining a selected set of actions, this perspective provides the underlying theory to verify the need to act. Actions are seen as a necessary extension of faith. This perspective is clearly borne out in Muslim women's collectives and organizations.

Muslim Women's Activist Networks and Organization

Non-government and non-profit organizations are run as special-interest groups of civil society. In the past few decades, Western agencies under the umbrella of global development have discovered the benefit of these organizations in the context of the Third World and have supplied them with impressive philanthropic funding and other material support. This support mainly benefits global development agendas and helps to create more democratic governments. Another benefit of Muslim women's collectives or N.G.O.'s is their contribution toward more gender mainstreaming, especially in their processes likely to directly help the poor and those at the grassroots. International funders have preferred to support these organizations rather than disperse funds to the bureaucrats and administrators in some context of the nation-state because the totalitarian bureaucrats and their cronies may maneuver actions that limit certain civil liberties.

This financial support is without a doubt indispensable to establishing and sustaining the institutions or organizations created or run by the special interest groups in the context of Third World women and other disempowered groups. They focus their research, activities, and strategies of reform on issues of concern to women and the community as a local or regional collective. At one level, N.G.O.'s, although working within the legal context of a particular nation-state, are free from partisan obligations. That can bring greater autonomy to their involvement in local concerns over the force of political agendas, which might forfeit the basic moral motivation and qualities of their efforts to become accepted, acknowledged, and ultimately referred to with authority. Still there are often subtle restrictions placed on their agenda and focus areas when the results must fulfill the expectations, support, or agendas of the funders.

There are also beneficial women's N.G.O.'s or auxiliaries funded or supported by the government. They retain some semblance to a non-government status but because of contributions and liaisons with governmental funds, their agendas are often applied under the umbrella of other government programs with realistic knowledge that women are productive members of the society and cannot be excluded from the development process if the nation-state hopes to compete in the global market.

Some Western feminists have posed several questions worth consideration with regard to women's organizations. First, the status of women as citizens of the nation-state is historically and currently unequal to the status of men. Attention drawn to transforming the definitions of citizen help to discern more conducive ways for women's mainstreaming.[10] Second, the consequences of separate public and private spheres have dominated the way public policies are formulated, invested in, or negated. Are such policies gender-inclusive or not, and if so, to what extent? Is the private sphere the primary arena of women and a major factor excluding them from due recognition as agents in community life? By totally ignoring women's work done in the private domain because it seems voluntary, such work is considered by-products of women's nature and not identified as reflecting the agency of the women contributing them. Consequently the significant values of these contributions are often ignored by the public sphere. With the devaluation of the private sphere comes the greatest determinant of women's rights and status in society. Likewise, women are underpaid in public work, since they are not considered to be fulfilling their primary role.

How can we utilize the relationships between public policy and women's experiences in the private or domestic domain to help rearticulate the mutual value and limitations in different types of work? My particular concern with women's work and the separation of public and private spheres in the context of "Islam" is both the conceptual framework of the tradition, primarily developed by men using the sources to conclude that male experiences and perspectives deserve the privileges given to them, and the resulting devaluation of women's status, no matter what contributions they make. Whatever kind of work the men do, it is deemed the most valuable. If women do the agriculture and men take care of the animals, taking care of animals is more important. If women take care of the animals and men do the agriculture, then agriculture is more important. Furthermore, these general evaluations have interacted with major ideological, economic, and political themes exported from the West, especially since the Enlightenment and the movements of colonialism over the past two hundred years.

Another motivation and point of origin in focusing on women's organizations is to draw attention to efforts made almost exclusively by women to address the needs of a silent and invisible female half of the population as well as the whole of the community, and the networks of inter-relations that assist in supporting women's development of their human identity with faith in Islam demonstrated through agency and activism. First I will focus on those women collectives and organizations that do not receive funding from governments or national, international, and humanitarian funding agencies. It is women as moral agents of care who have given not only to their immediate families, but also to neighbors, communities, men, and children on a voluntary basis. Their experiences may prove to lead to the much-needed bridges between women's issues and other agencies with social welfare agendas. However many contributions their ad hoc or quasi "organizations" generate, or however much they alleviate immediate family or local welfare matters or address crises, they may never receive public recognition, and remain silent or invisible at the government level. So much of Muslim women's grassroots work remains behind this veil of silence and invisibility.

Simultaneously there has been an explosion of communal, national, regional, and international Muslim women's organizations in the last two decades. In some cases these organizations merely reflect vagrant flaunting of selective tokens to help provide images for continuous justification and support of the organizations as actors or legitimate representatives of disadvantaged women, or at least as discussants on the realities of women's inferior status vis-à-vis men in various communal contexts.

Muslim Women's Grassroots Initiatives

Muslim women's grassroots collective care-taking is overwhelmingly affected by both gender and class issues. Women living in poor communities are not always accessible to state or international funders who must justify their contributions along the lines of larger development and social welfare issues. The maximum good of these contributions is measured best by the production of those organizations and collectives that can articulate their relationship to the development needs. Simply working to help move women from a second-class status to a status of access or to achievement of symbolic or real equality is not enough. Otherwise funders become charity organizations giving handouts just as invisibly devoured as the unmet and still mostly unacknowledged needs of the silent majority of Muslim women. This does not help improve systems or structures of victimization. Class issues and the construction of local, national, or internationally recognized Muslim women's organizations deserve greater investigation in order for Muslim women's efforts to be evaluated comprehensively. Yet the distinctions are obvious when we see the women whose works are acknowledged and those whose works go unacknowledged. Meanwhile, certain Muslim women's organizations and networks are provided with large grants and support while they do little to actually provide direct benefits to the women whom they claim to represent.

This chapter looks at two distinct levels of indigenous Muslim women's organizations. I start with local or grassroots organizations and further restrict them to the context of the African-American Muslim communities. Within this restriction I can still describe some features of networking in the context of Muslim communities. I have a particular interest in exposing some of the history, benefits, and developments of Muslim women's organizations as they characterize agency in the complexities of modern Islam. I will not make a comparison between the grassroots organizations and the highly visible and internationally recognized organizations, but the distinctions will be glaring. The importance of incremental steps from obscurity to authority will also be demonstrated. I will not comment on women's auxiliaries to existing government and non-government male organizations.

In predominantly Muslim countries, status quo authorities and the institutions created or run by them have used the moral force of Islam to manipulate women's organized participation – even at its purely voluntary level. The women are supported to the extent to which they in turn support the status quo. Theoretically, N.G.O's sustain the right and privilege to contradict the status quo and challenge government policies, if the status quo seems detrimental to their constituency or the citizens they represent. In short, they put a lid on unbrandished governmental control over private lives. Until the end of the twentieth century, women participating in oppositional non-government organizations in countries with Muslim laws were either non-Muslims, or were engaged without reference to Islam except as part of the problem. It was argued that facilitating and maintaining alternatives against oppressive Islamic regimes outweighed the loss of identification with the women they claimed to represent.

However, such denial or rejection of Islam causes most Muslim women clients to feel skeptical of these groups' intent. This skepticism reduces the effectiveness of such groups because their women clients are reluctant to participate in or support the group. They are even unwilling to speak to them about the nature of the problems they face for fear it will be exploited to demonize "Islam." The overwhelming majority of Muslim women worldwide feel that their Islamic identity is integral to who they are and to whom they wish to be. They are also increasingly aware of the tactics used by the West in exploiting the poor status of women as a weapon to stir up discontent, within Muslim communities as well as without, at the general level of Western citizens' animosity toward Islam. Although abuses experienced by Muslim women are real, they are decontextualized from the multiplicity of factors that helped to create them and instead "Islam" is pointed to as the single cause.

Sister to Sister: African-American Muslim Women's Networks of Support and Empowerment
I have never been a Muslim except as an African-American. Despite this fact, I have done very little academic work on the complex realities of African-Americans as Muslims. Most of my work has been focused on theological premises that are equally beneficial to gender issues at both my location in the African-American Muslim community as well as outside that location on the international level. Yet African-American Islam is unique especially because of the history of African-Americans. I am part of the awesome legacy of the soul and survival of African slaves brutalized by the dehumanization of the institution of slavery in its peculiarly cruel American racist form. The testament to the skill, morality, and excellence of our people is not only that we are still alive today, despite pervasive racism in America, but also in the ways we continue to struggle and prosper within the context of white superiority. Whatever systems of institutionalized, social, and cultural racism that followed the legal eradication of slavery also form a part of the collective Black experience. In the early part of the

twentieth century, around 1930, the first alternative religious movements for the unification and esteem-building of disenfranchised African-Americans came in the name of "Islam." Again, its definitions and practices were varied. However, it was the first time that faith, spirit, and religion were considered integral to the total transformation in the oppression of Black people. Later, African-American Christians would draw from their religiosity to resist racial injustices also.[11]

With Islam the fastest growing religion in America, it remains a viable alternative providing religio-moral identity to a considerable number of previously Black Christians. Islam in America was formed around what is now the largest single ethnic group – more than 40 percent of the total American Muslim population descend from African slave ancestry.[12] Despite the huge disparity in ethnic representation among Muslim American leadership against the actual percentage of African-American Muslims, one feature that was initiated by African-American women in all types of communities has continued and expanded on the American Muslim landscape – indigenous, grassroots women's collectives. The origins of the grassroots organization are not exclusively Islamic, however. The lessons gleaned from the literal break up of traditional families by slavery itself, and the coercive power of economic discrimination afterwards, taught African-American women an ethics of care indispensable to survival and empowerment. It was but a small step to initiate these same practices in our communities as Muslims. It comprises two dynamics: the need of one member, one family, or the communities; and the development of collective help and support. The insight required to coordinate between needs and means for providing support started long before the transatlantic slave trade as implied through the well-known African idiom, "It takes a village to raise a child."

African-American Muslim women have been gathering collectively to directly address the everyday issues and needs of their communities. They have done so despite burdens in their own lives, under the moral imperative of mutual care as the cornerstone of human well-being. They operate primarily on a volunteer basis, whether with other collectives of women only or in concert with men's collectives as well as the existing authorities and establishments. They endeavor to provide food, clothing, shelter, rehabilitation, upliftment, and education to other members of the community. They are rarely discussed at the level of local, national, and – least of all – international forums, which claim to represent Muslim women, because they work within the community with the goals promoted by an ethics of care but without a goal of recognition or of seeking funds, although their services would be greatly enhanced by both. If what they give could be bottled and handed out on the open market of humanity, it would contain the primal living example of whatever is most fundamental to a theory, a theology, or an ethics of care.

Care is a fundamental aspect of human life. Care consists of "everything we do to continue, repair, and maintain ourselves so that we can live in the world as well as possible." . . . Most of us think about care in the intimate relationships of our lives: care for ourselves and our families and friends. In its broadest meanings, care is complex and multidimensional: it refers both to the dispositional qualities we need to care for ourselves and others, such as being attentive to human needs and taking responsibility to meet such needs, as well as to the concrete work of caring. To care well requires that both of these elements be present: a disposition to care and care work. Care thus always involves thinking about who is responsible for what caring, and about what that responsibility means. . . . As a perspective from which to think about social and political life, a care perspective demands that, as we try to make moral and political judg-ments, we use the concrete and contextual to support our more general political, social, and moral judgments. An ethic of care is in this way a subset of what Margaret Walker has called "an ethics of responsibility." . . . There are critical moral and political questions for us to ask in deter-mining who is responsible for the ways that care work is done, and what caring work is done and what caring work is left undone.[13]

The intrinsic empowerment of grassroots African-American Muslim women's caring networks is in its direct relationship to their responsibilities "for the ways that care work is done" and in meeting the needs of other community members, with the faith perspective that builds personal dedication in care work. It is not motivated by what grants them the greatest global recognition, money, status, or legitimacy. Being women who struggle through untold hardships to sustain a genuine place in whatever they themselves think is "Islam" motivates and sustains their communal contributions. At the same time they seek to grow and flourish while creating a mirror of hope and mutual self-support for those whose hard-ships highlight not only the personal struggles they bear, but also the complete and utter failure of whatever discourse predominantly calls itself "Islam" despite the extent to which it ignores such basic needs among the women. While they may suffer in the name of fulfilling "Islam," they pray only to be better Muslims.

Over time, women's collectives may form into, or from, study groups, make efforts to form nurseries and schools, build activity centers for children, develop scholarship programs, oversee teen organizations and form gatherings to engage all Muslims. The most popular form of collective activity that has formed uniquely in North American communities is the women's retreat. These retreats are usually held in places away from women's daily responsibilities in the domestic sphere. They may include a conference, workshops, entertainment, banquets, fashion shows, and shopping for Islamic wares from other female Muslim entrepreneurs. The multipurpose retreat brings Muslim women together where they inevitably share experiences and vicariously support each other in their mutual struggles to be Muslim even when what stands as status quo "Islam" in their local communities might totally neglect them or is the cause of their oppression. They are strengthened by the company of each other in their efforts to learn the truth about "Islam" as the core basis of their spiritual identity. I will briefly profile two Muslim women who have formed and remained central to such Muslim women's collectives in the Richmond area, Muslim Women United and T.R.U.T.H. The women who have founded or presided over these collectives have been especially important to my faith experience and the nature of the work I do when little has inspired me in the Richmond area.

I came to live and work in the Richmond, Virginia, area after teaching at the International Islamic University in Malaysia. I spent all three years of my contract there working within the larger community of Muslims, especially women and as a core member of Sisters in Islam. A similar organization does not exist in Richmond, but Muslim women have demonstrated their exemplary roles as care-workers and leaders characteristic of the African-American women's survival and advancement. Latifah Abdusubur and Jennah Amina Qadir[14] are two of the most courageous and generous women demonstrating this kind of leadership as care-worker that I have known as a Muslim. Despite personal struggles, they have both contributed more to the Muslim community – through which they claim their identity – than many other community members, who have often been recipients of their noble deeds. Latifah is the chairperson and chief organizer of Muslim Women United. Jennah Aminah had a vision to start an organization called T.R.U.T.H. Neither one of these women has sought recognition for her contributions. Yet they have continued to serve out of personal spiritual motivations drawn from what Islam means to them. They are care-workers, but not for money.

Muslim Women United, Richmond, Virginia
According to their mission statement, "Muslim Women United (MWU) . . . was established in 1989 by a group of muslim women . . . who recognized the need to uplift and enlighten muslim women in the practical application of Islam through education, networking, programming and philanthropy." Latifah was a principal player in organizing this group and has been the primary chairperson of this organization. In the late 1980s she moved to Richmond from another state where the Muslim women had already formulated activities for women. Muslim by choice for nearly thirty years now, she did not find such activities here and so met with other African-American women to start M.W.U.

Latifah is one courageous Muslim woman activist who had struggled for years as a single parent to her children while her husband, their father, was in prison. Upon release from prison he began to take responsibility for his family and to continue his efforts to develop himself as an upstanding member of the Muslim community. She notes: "A proven prison statistic is that the majority of men, including Muslim men who have been incarcerated for a number of years, are trying to 'catch up.' They desperately try to regain the past and in so doing, they reach for that which has passed them by. Trying to recapture the missed years, and regain their youthfulness, or the past they thought they had lost." So his manner of responsibility did not last a year. He was soon chasing after young, single, and non-Muslim women until one of them became pregnant. When Latifah finally asked for a divorce, the man married the young pregnant woman who then converted to Islam.

My attention was drawn to the strength and stamina of the Muslim woman activist with visible signs of the burdens of betrayal overshadowed by her continued generosity providing services for other Muslim women through contributions with M.W.U. My response to her was, "I could not do what your do." She replied, "That's what everyone says." What is it that she does that causes others to recognize her as unique and to aspire to her role modeling? Whatever it is, it is the crux of my own aspiration in writing to acknowledge Muslim women's networks worldwide.

Since its inception in 1989, M.W.U. has had its ups and downs. Core membership has fluctuated between five and nineteen. These members come from various local community collectives, not always able to work together for the sake of a Richmond-wide experience of practicing Islam.

They experienced one major rift between core members from one local collective that led to a complete break. New members followed their decision to remove themselves from M.W.U. Later they returned as members. A maximum of ten women have bonded with and beyond the projects in which the organization has been engaged.

Such varied projects have included conferences, workshops, luncheons, festival celebrations, special event issues, "problems and solutions for Muslim women," and invited speakers, and these projects have been inclusive of all Muslim women in Richmond, irrespective of their particular allegiances to sometimes contesting mosque organizations. Some side activities, like an occasional sleepover, and all their planning sessions, are not open to the general public. They have engaged Muslim men and children – including a "Father–Son" function – with non-Muslim specialists, as well as with Muslim women. They now belong to a regional network of Muslim women with organizers from similar groups along the U.S. east coast. Different women are responsible for various committees with specific areas of focus required to bring about their many activities. Their primary annual function is a regional retreat with workshops, speakers, banquets, a bazaar, and entertainment. The annual retreats bring together two to three hundred women, primarily from Virginia, New York, New Jersey, Maryland, and North Carolina, with scattering numbers from other major east coast areas.

Latifah is a woman who can do what others cannot. What does she do that encouraged me to single her out among the collective that has worked together with various numbers and toward a variety of goals all beneficial to creating and sustaining the sense of faith and spiritual well-being among their sister Muslims? She lives what she speaks and speaks what she believes in an exemplary manner that gives her the quiet fortitude of Islamic leadership in concert *with* other Muslims, not in imposing her authority over them. She has been known for her skills and presented several workshops on this topic from Richmond to Pennsylvania. This kind of leadership is more exemplary of Muslim women's grassroots organizations. It creates an arena of productivity, *din*, and hope with no need for exerting the false self-appointed authority essential to local, national, and international male Muslim collectives.

What I admire about her is her extensive ability to sustain the careworker role, even when the care promised to her for being Muslim, woman, wife, and mother has not been provided to assist or relieve her from the burdens of husband, children, divorce, and other outspoken Muslim women, ready first to complain but never to orchestrate and participate in extending the best available as Latifah does through her belief in Islam toward a community of friends and strangers. She is the epitome of the fundamental understanding that faith alone does not make Islam, but only with her faith does she bring forth meaningful actions and the fulfillment of good deeds. She tells this story, on her own behalf.

"Call Latifah" is the word in the community. Her organization has been instrumental in aiding the needs of the community. On one occasion, she was approached after a *jumu'ah* service and told that a family needed assistance. Latifah was able to organize M.W.U. members and off to the grocery store they went. She and the other M.W.U. members cried, as they witnessed one of the family members pick up a bag of sugar and kiss it.

T.R.U.T.H.
Jennah Aminah Qadir began her Islam in the Nation of Islam temple in the Bronx, New York, with Louis Farrakhan at it head. It was 1969. When W.D. Muhammad inherited the organization he recommended that the followers accept what was good from his father's legacy. Jennah took that lesson to heart and has continued from that moment until the present, focusing on her own understanding and implementation of Islam as both growth and development. Her life has been characterized by many such transitions. Mother to four children, all adults now with an array of under-standings about Islam, she had left Richmond only to return in 1999 to bury one of her daughters, who had placed her life in the hands of drug addictions and paid the ultimate price. In Ramadan that year she was awoken to the word "truth." Although she tried to return to sleep she spent several hours wrestling with what that word could mean. Eventually, she came to this conclusion: Together Righteousness Unites The Hearts: T.R.U.T.H. She has devoted herself as a care-worker to demonstrate just that point.

Sometimes she has done so single-handedly; now there are 11 members working, at different levels, to support her vision. Again her contributions are not for money or personal recognition. Initially she charged a subscription of one dollar a month to any sister who was interested in receiving a monthly newsletter that advertises local and regional events benefiting the growth and union of Muslim women's hearts. She single handedly collected, alphabetized and distributed an information list with over 300 Muslim women, mostly in the Richmond area. T.R.U.T.H. organizes sister functions for women to take care and be taken care of. One such function,

"Pamper-Me-Plus," provides opportunities for women specialists to perform their services at reduced rates to other women who may never take the time to give themselves a facial, foot massage, or certain foods for body and mind.

When one Muslim woman needed a heart transplant, T.R.U.T.H. organized a walk-a-thon to raise money from those willing to pledge per mile. Hundreds of dollars were presented to help the heart patient through her ordeal. Nothing was put in Jennah's pocket although she works as a vendor of Muslim wares and on occasion does odd jobs for wages. During the last few years she provided daily care for an ailing mother with diabetes, high blood pressure, bone cancer, and foot disorders, wheelchair-bound and requiring dialysis three times a week in addition to other continued visits and admissions to the hospital. Jennah Aminah has an especially intimate level of personal spirituality. She is the only person I have ever known who makes occasional calls after *salat-al-fajr*, the dawn prayer, just to check on how I am doing. She reads the Qur'an every day and enjoys the *tarawih*, a special twenty-unit prayer during the month of Ramadan, as well as collective and individual *dhikr*, prescribed acts of remembrance.

As Tronto reminds us, "care is needed" and care-workers provide that care. Latifah and Jennah are care-workers for love through their faith in Islam. They are the living embodiments of one of the better notions of Islam to which any Muslim can aspire, agency through service. Both women demonstrate the priority of unity – as the words "united" and "together" imply from their respective group names. However, unity is never used for uniformity, as demonstrated by the inclusive nature of the forums they conduct. Muslim women and men, adults and children, from all mosque affiliations and all from convenient geographical locations and with diverse perspectives on Islam are invited and attend. One visible indication of this is seen in the variety of dress for the women's retreat – with women who wear no head covering to women who cover their face – all present are equally welcome to participate in the forums organized. The indigenous African-American *hijab* is not monolithic. It reflects styles worn by non-Muslim women, elaborate and colorful wraps like their African sisters, and various styles worn by Asian and Arab women. Through their examples, inclusive Islam moves from potential to reality. In that reality, the woman care-worker is the community exemplary for compassion and care.

Pro-Faith, Pro-Feminist Movements

In the 1990s a pro-faith agenda was proposed among some Islamic groups and used as a force of strategic, yet radical, operational force for women's organizations, research, and individual activism. The acquisition of this agenda is a recent move for Muslim women's groups. Its distinctions are most simply articulated when juxtaposed to Islamist movements that advocate a return to pristine Islam, as if that would solve very complex modern problems, and to those Muslim women and collectives working from a feminist or pro-feminist perspective with standards set by the prevailing Western and secular feminist movement. I give some analysis of the historical development, methodological approaches, and perspectives of one such pro-faith group in Malaysia, in which I became a core member in 1989, Sisters in Islam. Not allowed to use the word "Islam" for registration purposes, they registered in 1992 as an N.G.O., under the name "S.I.S. Forum (Malaysia) *Berhad.*" They retain "Sisters in Islam" for authorship purposes and all other forms of public recognition. I will contribute only a few comments about their tremendous record after registration, when my status as core member would change after I returned to the U.S.A.

The Pro-Faith Agenda

Without restriction to a particular religious affiliation, the pro-faith agenda for human rights has two main components:

1. Humanity is interconnected and the destiny of the planet depends on cooperation across ethnic, national, religious, or other boundaries. Such a connection necessarily operates by full validation of diverse religious, spiritual, and cultural backgrounds.
2. Commitment to the sacred as a transcendent or ultimate reality contributes significantly to the understanding of an ethical world order.

It is understandable that spiritual or religious motivations effectively mobilize human participation in sustaining that order. Paradoxically, it can act as a means for upholding the rights of all global inhabitants, or as an impetus to violate the rights of other faith orientations and interpretations, contrary to the perceived integrity of their particular faith. In its more positive modes of operation, this commitment can be expressed in terms particular to one religion as well as in more general terms of moral virtues and ethical principles like equality, justice, and freedom with a transcendent or sacred focal point. I refer to it here from the positive end of the existing paradox, without ignoring the pretense of using the same pro-faith perspective leading some to narrow exclusivism. Gender is one common denominator that has led to cross-fertilization and diverse collectivity over shared concerns in concert with the specifics of various women's differences, including faith perspectives. "Interdependency between women is the way to a freedom which allows the *I* to *be*, not in order to be used, but in order to be creative. This is the difference between the passive *be* and the active *being*."[15]

The process of articulating justice in Islam was offered first by Muslim male elites throughout Islamic history. However, since gender as a category of thought is a recent intellectual criterion, their perspectives on full humanity gender were based on being a man. The woman was a utility to facilitate the development of a man's full Islamic humanity. The colonialist period introduced those outside the faith into the gender discourse. While many Muslims have ascribed to this extra-Islamic and often secular approach, the methods for attaining full implementation of the principles were not scrutinized for either the intra-Islamic problems via the secular, Orientalist, pro-West, or even anti-Islamic bias. The book *Tarir al-Mar'ah* (Woman's Freedom) by Qasim Amin[16] is still referred to by way of precedent, even as its perspective was aimed at "freeing" Muslim women from their own culture, including or especially from the components of those cultures that come from religion. Thus the impetus to remove religion from the human rights discourse has many arguments.

From the perspective of developing a pro-faith agenda in Islam and human rights, the Qur'an first articulated the notion of human being in binary terms between "believers" (often simplified through interpreting it as "Muslim") and "non-believers," those who denied the truth of faith and of the sacred. Second, the Qur'an discusses relationships between particular Abrahamic traditions living in the Arabian peninsula at the time of revelation, as well as the idol worshippers and polytheists in that context. Opposition launched against the fledgling Muslim community, after the first thirteen years of pacifism, was eventually countered by explicit calls to fight against their opponents, specifically on the grounds of "Islam." The Qur'an also begins to critically nuance even the notion of believer with extensive discussion about hypocrites: those who give the appearance of being Muslim in public but betray it in private. Finally, the Qur'an presents many aspects of the binary relationship between males and females in the seventh century context. Yet all are human beings, including women and those outside of the Islamic faith, although this was difficult to reconcile under the precedent of historical experience, and Islamic thinkers soon developed a particularized religious dogma.

That which makes one "inside" the community of believers, and consequently subject to all rights imaginable, also delineates those who are "outside," reducing their human rights relative to their cooperation with the insiders' goal to preserve Islam. This is the implication for the legal status of *dhimmi*, non-Muslim citizens in a Muslim polity. They have responsibilities, prohibitions, and protections in a second-class status. This binary has become a rigid perspective *inside* the Muslim community as well. To point out inconsistencies between the status of women and men "in Islam" is to point to women's outsider status from the privileged male Muslim, conceived as the penultimate human being and exemplar of "Islam." One is also called an outsider for pointing this incongruity out. To struggle to create a horizontal relationship of reciprocity – despite its *tawhidic*, intra-Islamic, and Qur'anic origins – threatens the status quo by implication of shared responsibilities and privileges. It is not surprising that the modern movement toward full human rights for women *in Islam* started outside an Islamic framework, or was influenced by Western colonialist or Western feminist discourses.

The step to move women's rights' discourse back *into* the core of the Islamic worldview was radical, for several reasons. The first reason was that it points to the means for "dismantling the master's house" by using the "master's tools." By invoking *'usul* methodology, rules formulated by earlier generations of exclusively male Muslim thinkers could be shown in their wide diversity and internal self-interrogation. Islamic thought is a consolidation of its historical epistemological transformations and social and political contexts. This precedent legitimates the continuation of historical inquiry at this current juncture. The aim is not to deconstruct Islam, but to radically *reconstruct* the tradition from within; in particular, to incorporate on-going human intellectual developments, with a specific integration of *gender* as a category of thought. In addition, at the epistemological level, the aim is to leave open the idea, mentioned elsewhere in this book, that the Ultimate is *unknowable*. What humans have come to know as the divine always evolves within the limitation of mundane human knowledge against the ultimately unknowable divine. Allah cannot be fixed by any one moment, any one text, and any of the multiple interactions with that text. But as human knowledge and epistemology continues to develop, so do human ideas about Allah. Most importantly, the pro-faith agenda created a mandate to include women, women's experiences, and

perspectives in reformulating the creeds and codes on the basis of underlying principles essential to being human within the Muslim intellectual
process.

Sisters in Islam, Malaysia

I first interacted with Sisters in Islam in October 1989, shortly after arriving
in Malaysia to join the faculty at the International Islamic University. At
that point, I was not joining an organization: it was primarily a study
group. As their research continued, I brought out the significance of moving
away from secondary sources back to the primary sources, particularly to
the Qur'an itself. My research on the Qur'an had been done with an eye for
gender justice, egalitarianism, and the capacity of agency for women. It
indicated that much of what plagues the lives of Muslim women results
from the authority given to implement and acculturate male interpretations.
Little wonder that such interpretations espouse theories of women's inferi-
ority and utility before men. Despite the difficulties of this intellectual field,
to respond to the status quo by using sources external to primal Islam, such
as the writings of modern Western and Muslim secular feminists, was less
effective. Status quo authorities would simply de-legitimize them publicly
by marking everything outside of "Islam" as un-Islamic. The well-intended
but critically uninformed general Muslim population did not question these
claims. Liberal theories of the West were categorically rejected as un-Islamic
and therefore could never be seriously considered viable options for
Muslims. In addition to problems of legitimacy, it is true that the application of such theories alienates Muslims from a significant aspect of
self-identity and points to one premise of reformist discourse. Islamic
reform is a product of an indigenous Muslim transformation through our
Islamic historical tradition to our current Islamic circumstances.

When Sisters in Islam changed the research strategy to focus primarily
on the Qur'an they felt an elevated self-confidence. We were no longer
dependent on centuries-old patriarchal interpretations of the sources as the
only viable ones for determining our roles today. This was proven to be one
of the most significant aspects of our effectiveness. When the core of our
strategizing for change gained ideological authority equal to that heretofore
exclusively belonging to males, women acted on the right to voice
opposition to mainstream discourse. This led naturally to a third unantici-
pated strategy, which proved pivotal in the position of Sisters in Islam
vis-à-vis public opinion.

Some disturbing events were making the local newspapers again, in particular a hotly debated polygamy case. Sisters in Islam drafted editorial responses to popular status quo public opinion. Our editorials in the local papers were our first published self-representation. Although signed by each of the members, only the group title was published: "Sisters in Islam," later given the acronym S.I.S. (from *Sisters in Islam*). It would soon become a catch phrase for female-inclusive alternative opinions on modern Islamic issues. Our responses to this first issue, polygyny, were focused on intra-Qur'anic considerations that deconstruct its practice as an unbridled right of Muslim males. We rescripted the issue through Qur'anic evidence showing it was a serious and conditional responsibility. Nowhere had there been such a well-articulated, Qur'anic-supported contradiction to the popular notion of polygamy as a privilege and irrefutable right of Muslim men. Our editorial not only discussed how the Qur'an considers it a responsibility, but also rendered it virtually impossible today to undertake properly such a responsibility while fulfilling the requirements needed.

As other issues pertaining to women hit the press, S.I.S. responded with similar editorials offering detailed source-based arguments as authoritative alternative viewpoints. As our responses to various issues became anticipated, since they had gained considerable public attention, so too would those not favoring these new opinions pay attention. This was a departure from the norm where modern liberal thinkers argued cogently against the "accepted" authority of narrow-minded clerics. Our responses were clear and rational articulations, substantiated through innovative female-inclusive experiences applied to interpretation of the primary sources. S.I.S. prepared for the next-level strategy: to launch the core group of eight in a public forum as we presented the publication of two pamphlets: "Are Women and Men Equal in Islam?" and "Are Muslim Men Allowed to Beat their Wives?"

At that time an underlying pro-faith premise for Sisters in Islam was that we would not abandon our cultural or spiritual heritage as Muslims, with the social harmony and personal spiritual strengths it grants us, in favor of an agenda exclusively defined and set by male elites whether from our own cultures, those relative to it, or those totally ignorant of our realities, just because they used the name of "Islam." It is clear that the male definitions of appropriate Islamic behavior and intellectual thought have influenced women to acquiesce to oppression if not to openly or secretly abandon Islam. We reclaimed Islam as our own by including our input to clarify its definitions and the interpretation of its primary sources. This offers a legitimate alternative to oppressed Muslim women and conscientious men in understanding a primary aspect of their identity. In addition, we dedicated ourselves to changing the course of development for religious institutions when detrimental to the spiritual, physical, emotional, intellectual, political, educational, and economic, i.e. the human liberation of Muslim women.

It is primarily male thinkers that have produced what passes as fundamental paradigms in our religious heritage. Many ordinary Muslims have come to consider these narrowly produced paradigms as universal – even divine. Yet the vision of past scholars was limited in two particular ways: (1) by their social-cultural and intellectual-spiritual circumstances; and (2) by the noticeable absence of women's ideas and reflections in considering what Islam means or what it means to be human in Islam. S.I.S. advocated a compulsory expansion in the vision of Islamic thought by explicit inclusion of the voice of women's experiences and epistemological perspectives. A comprehensive paradigm shift from within can effect a radical change for the future of Muslim women and men and can increase Islamic efficacy by shifting from coercive participation to voluntary dedication.

Evolution of Strategies

As Sisters in Islam worked toward this goal a variety of strategies evolved. What began as an ad hoc group of professional Muslim women, meeting to discuss highly publicized events that adversely affected the lives and perceptions of Muslim women, would also evolve. At this initial stage, S.I.S. was very similar to other Muslim women's collectives, distinguished by the level of expertise, class privilege, and professional status of its members. The concern over the lives of women adversely affected by conditions for Muslim women at large *united* us to give critical consideration of these conditions, to raise our own level of consciousness or understanding, and to determine immediate and long-term actions to give care in resolving these adverse conditions.

After launching the booklets in a public forum on gender issues as discovered by the research and consciousness-raising strategy, future activities were given consideration. This raised S.I.S. from an informal social group to a semi-formal and goal-oriented organization. The group proposed an explicit strategy toward that goal. It centered on answering fundamental questions in the context of women and Islam. Is our current situation a true and accurate reflection of the full potential for women implied and intended by our religion? Are things the way they are suppose to be, or is this a consequence of particular circumstances in Muslim societies where men have rendered the interpretations that sustain their privileged position?

Since Muslim women's personal lives and social roles came under the jurisdiction of the *shari'ah* courts in Malaysia, S.I.S. had reasoned, then any case could be questioned when it led to unfair treatment of women by breaking the spirit of the law. Court officials could be held liable. This had led to a previous forum before I met S.I.S. when they had met with Islamic court officials to point out inconsistencies between implementation of the letter without the spirit of the law due to patriarchal prejudices of individual court officials. The results of this meeting had not been very satisfactory, perhaps because each liberal argument they would raise against the court conclusion of results was countered by the haphazard exclusivism of court officials speaking in the name of "Islam," randomly quoting sources against which S.I.S. had no will or viable articulation. Obviously, this did not lead to any specific means for guaranteeing systemic progress toward positive and comprehensive change, or uniform results.

When S.I.S., a grassroots *women's* organization, came forth offering holistic Qur'anic hermeneutics to challenge current responses to the issue of women's rights, it was a novel strategy. It supported the idea of a broad-based reconsideration of what it means to be Muslim and of how "Islam" can be interpreted under various circumstances, including our current circumstance. With less dependence on a select class as the sole authorities of official interpretation, ordinary Muslims might focus their energies and intellect on a more meaningful direct connection with that aspect of their identity. This is attractive to intellectuals in general. More important than that, women began to see that the distance between their lives and the meanings of the Islam passed down to them was not the same as the distance between themselves as believers and the Creator – some patriarchal interpretations had interceded. S.I.S. initiatives were met with enthusiasm for providing a means for creative regeneration of thought and establishing dynamic and relevant Islamic paradigms. It meant no longer reacting to "Islam" as projected by media, traditional institutions, governments, or cultural relativity.

This perspective and goal distinguished S.I.S. them from the two most well-known types of Muslim women's organizations in Muslim majority contexts at that time. One type relied on viewpoints, arguments, and rationales from outside the Islamic heritage. Their effectiveness was reduced because their arguments failed to identify with broad-based concerns over identity and this diminished their support. The other type was status quo oriented, reflected by Muslim women's organizations as auxiliaries to larger Muslim male-led initiatives, like the youth movement known as A.B.I.M. The attractiveness of these groups for Muslim intellectuals and youth, male and female, has been in the fervent stand against Western hegemony, the anti-colonialist position, and the dialectic of offering a fundamental core of self-assertion for Third World Muslim peoples. This raised ethnic and Islamic identity in the post-colonial period and heightened the sentiments of autonomy and self-identification.

Coincidently, both these types were visible and outspoken at the 1995 International Conference for Women in Beijing. Sisters in Islam presented at Beijing in the N.G.O. forum and mediated between these two poles. They gave a "yes" to Islam, but "no" to the history of Islamic patriarchal articulations and implementations that had robbed women of their full humanity dignity and Islamic agency. The other two types of groups were irreconcilably at opposing strategic ends of the quest to affirm Muslim women's identity in the global complexities essential to attaining those ends. Some of the polarization between these two groups has abated and a part of that abatement was the tendency of more concerned Muslim women entering into the debates and seeing the contradictions but believing in their potential reconciliation. Sisters in Islam had set up a track record of reconciling the contradictions and that was important to its initial public image and its expression of potential developments for women's well-being. In my days actively involved with Sisters in Islam, we were also primarily a volunteer women's group – albeit at a class level above what might be considered "grassroots" for Muslim Women United and T.R.U.T.H. discussed above. At that voluntary level we operated without resorting to larger international funding organizations and with no particular government affiliations. It was also non-hierarchical, with no president, chairperson, or executive body. This operative collectivity was another one of the aspects that I loved in the time I spent with S.I.S. Meanwhile, my tendency toward theory was put to the test of actual practices and my participation in activism has its origins within this early group.

S.I.S. Forum Inc.

In 1992 I completed my contract at the university and lost my residency status in Malaysia. This was the same time that Sisters in Islam completed its formal registration as a Malaysian N.G.O. As a non-Malaysian and a long-distance core member my status would become more one of a consultant. As a registered group, essential changes to the intra-group dynamics were instituted and have continued to develop along the lines of the standard male corporate lines. From a group of equals to a structure with an Executive Director, with salary and salaried workers, the organization has substantially increased its membership. The motivation to work on defining and sustaining Muslim women's human dignity still stands, but the subtle difference between a voluntary reciprocal membership structure is now overridden by the formulas of other professional groups. The attraction of public attention has gone beyond mere local levels to explicit networks regionally and internationally, especially in coordination with extensive international funding organizations.

It is beyond the scope of this chapter to do justice to the long list of accomplishments of this organization once this professional status was formalized, international funders were multiplied, networking became extensive, and progress within Malaysian civil society and government agendas were more closely coordinated. Sisters in Islam has organized local, regional, and international activities like workshops, lectures, conferences, and publications, and through its central office provides resources for multiple levels of research and learning, and is actively engaged in looking at systemic reformations and policy changes. At the same time, issues and perspectives particular to the Malaysian context hold sway over other issues and determine the ways they are addressed. There have been considerable advancements in acknowledging the accomplishments of Sisters in Islam. There have also been suggestions for its future development, including comments from a special session in 2005 held with Khaled Abou el Fadl concerning greater autonomy for women-centered self-reliance within the larger arena of reformist discussions and developments. Interestingly enough the basis of his suggestion was the initial basis of the group's formation: to build a women-centered trajectory *through* the history of the Islamic intellectual heritage by engaging the tradition in a female-inclusive method within the context of modern circumstances and challenges.

Indeed, the discourses now appear even more open to various individual and collective contributions and challenges. Sisters in Islam played an important role in identifying the necessity and competency of women engaged in these discourses for reform. Their agenda was independent of funders' requirements or government approval.

Conclusion

Muslim women have always collected to address the care and concerns of their communities. The mechanisms for their valuable contributions to become transformed into government-level mechanisms for the concerns of all members of society warrants substantial analysis of the arbitrary divide between public and private spheres of operation as well as analysis of the relationship between theory and practice. With no need for dominion – whether useful or intrusive – women's civic contributions may have been overlooked as simply a reflection of the feminine nature, but have surely indicated the intense level of agency required to perform these various functions and are not restricted to women as natural extensions of their instincts, but rather as demonstrations of what is potentially accessible to all humankind for transforming communities and governments.

4   A New Hajar Paradigm: Motherhood and Family

"The Fire of Hajar"
For one short span, she was our Hajar,
my bright young bride, the helpmeet
of a lonely aging couple.
How she grew from round-cheeked girl,
capable, aproned, baby strapped to high hip,
into a woman beyond our ken, strange giant
straddling rockscape, midwifing a new earth!
Twice Sarah put Hajar's hand in mine,
as God willed, first to marry, then to desert her.
But it was I who let her hand drop.
Our last night we spent alone in God's wilderness,
one last time to circle, in the crook of my body, hers,
the baby nestled between her breast and belly,
my arm around them both.
Then I dropped her supple girlish hand and freely
I admit the tears that wet my dusty beard,
fell brackish into that dry ground
as I walked, willing, to the slaughter
of my own bared neck, my Hajar-love.
I walked away.
She called, "Ibrahim!" She knew
what I had to do, but still she called,
let me hear my name shaped by her lips

one last single time, "Ibrahim!"
At the pierce of that cry, I wanted
to bundle her up and carry her home again,
protect her from this howling barren land.
I turned around. But one look at her face –
she was already fiercer, older, a woman
I do not know. She chose too.
"To whom do you leave us?" she said quietly.
For a minute I could not answer. Fire
like the fire of the trials of my youth, this fire!
God who made the fire cool and safe for me
will make this scorched desert for Hagar
a garden surely.

When I said "God is here,"
she took my words and threw them back
at me, "Then I'll take God. I'll take the God
of this wilderness over your home and city."
She turned away. I know that turn.
I as a young man chose to accept from God
a hard vocation. But an old man knows
what it means to drop the supple hand.
I walked away bent nearly double,
picking my ragged path back home to Sarah.
I took one last look.

Hajar was walking into her own
soul-scorching days, head-on,
far from me now, her shadow thrown
by the lowered sun across a wild country,
turning into something stark and strange.
Be cool and safe for Hajar, fire!

– Mohja Kahf[1]

From Hagar to Hajar: Then and Now

In the 1990s a pragmatic academic trend began in women and religion studies to draw attention to shared aspects of history and ideology between women of Judaism, Christianity, and Islam.[2] This trend focused on women as daughters of Sarah and Hagar. It was a successful strategy helping to forge epistemological relationships between women, in place of patriarchal conceptualizations of the Abrahamic tradition. In a much-beleaguered area of religious studies, this gender-based dialogue was intended to concentrate on shared concerns, and create ecumenical publications, conferences, workshops, research projects, and reforms. However much benefit this new awareness brought to my own concerns about gender, religion, and justice, a few presumptions were already built into the particular Sarah–Hagar paradigm as configured. These presumptions privileged Judaism and Christianity by presuming that the stories of Hagar were taken from the Old Testament/Hebrew Bible. This privileged historical reading left unresolved issues of difference between Christianity, Judaism, and Islam. Although the focus is on gender, it reinforced certain other hegemonies, at the expense of more comprehensive intellectual and political alliances against oppressions. One simple distinction is in the Anglicized spelling of the name. There is neither a letter "g" in Arabic nor any words pronounced with the hard "g" sound. The soft "g" sound relates to an Arabic letter, which is "j" as used in the Library of Congress transliteration system. Therefore Hajar is the preferred spelling used in this chapter.

Additionally, the presumptions failed to acknowledge certain aspects of ethnicity crucial to the Abrahamic experience. Although Abraham's paternal bloodline is the same, the two maternal bloodlines bear on current historical and political circumstances. Gender discourse does not render ethnic, racial, class, and other situational contentions mute. To reduce the story only to a presumed relationship between Sarah and Hajar overlooks the fact that they are foremothers of Jews and Christians or Muslims and Arabs. The tension that looms over the subsequent and continuous annihilation of Palestinians means that significant players – real people and real families – will not be resolved by such an oversimplified reading. This reading carefully reads-in certain concerns, and silences others.

In the Bible and Qur'an, Sarah is the wife of Abraham by one form of customary marriage existent at that time. However, Sarah is beyond childbearing age and no longer hopes to produce an heir for Abraham. She avails herself of another existing customary practice to resolve this problem. Hajar, an Egyptian slave woman, is given to Abraham as a concubine-spouse. One significant discrepancy over the privileged status of Abraham's *only* son occurs between the Judeo-Christian story of Sarah and Hajar and the Islamic one, leading to different conclusions regarding the heirs of these two women. There is no competition implied in these customary practices with respect to household status. *Any offspring resulting from the liaison of the master with the slave woman Hajar becomes heir of a household ruled by Abraham and Sarah.* Several competing assumptions with regard to this cultural practice are no longer discussed in today's use of this paradigm. However, I will refer here to several such assumptions in order to reconstruct issues of gender and family in Islam and will do so specifically to focus on the experiences of female heads of households in the African-American Muslim community and beyond.

The Institution and Practices of Slavery

Some attention must also be given to the institution of slavery in its multiple historical formulas. All forms of slavery severely limit the freedom, dignity, and human potential of those enslaved. Noting first that the Qur'an acknowledged the existing practices of slavery in the seventh century, and that it was not a major source contributing to the eradication of the institution of slavery, interferes with the guidance I seek from the Qur'an with regard to my priority over underlying principles of human dignity irrespective of class, race, or gender. Slavery was not only alive and well throughout the entire course of Qur'anic revelation, the Prophet Muhammad's exemplary relationships of freeing slaves, adopting a slave, and cohabiting with slave women are remnants of his fixed location in history, not reflections of ultimate moral integrity which must adopt to changing circumstances in order to sustain the efficacy of their essential values, rather than mimic previous particular historical or cultural forms. Today, there is clearly universal consensus over the idea that slavery violates human dignity, so it is not only unacceptable as a form of labor exploitation, it is morally unjust.

Moreover, the particular race-based slavery practiced in the Americas proved even more heinous than other practices of slavery throughout human history, with centuries of residual racial discrimination following it even up until today. Again the dominant Western practices in terms of race obscure some nuances of other historical practices of slavery during the time of the Prophet and by earlier civilizations, including European, Muslim, and African. Although race became significant to slavery only with the transatlantic slave trade some four hundred years ago, Black Africans were enslaved before that. So also were other racial and ethnic groups. Black Africans even enslaved others from their own race. Fair-skinned people of Europe, Persia, Turkey, and other parts of Asia enslaved fair-skinned people as well as darker-skinned people. Likewise, darker- skinned people enslaved people with fairer skin.[3]

One major distinction in these historical practices of slavery of concern here is with reference to the offspring resulting from a sexual liaison between a male master and his female slave (whether by force, mutual consent, or customary acquiescence to the circumstances of a woman's enslavement). In Islam, for example, descendents of a slave were full and legitimate heirs to the inheritance and legacy of their father-master. Some who became enslaved might have formerly been masters of other slaves. Under Islam's historical practice of slavery it was possible for the sons of concubines to become masters, prominent political leaders, and rulers of the empire.[4] A Muslim leader sometimes married one to four permitted wives; these marriages were usually arranged with other prominent families and tribes and often helped solidify political alliances. After the ceremonial marriage consummation, his preferred sexual partners were the concubines selected for his *harim*. It was not uncommon for him to produce through these slave women the future heirs to power in the empire. Slave sons became rulers. This could never occur in the form of slavery practiced in the Americas.

Slave women's subhuman status was not viewed as a threat to the advantage for the ruler since there could be no regional contentions after his death from the people of any of his prominent wives who still held position, ties, and allegiance to their heritage. The dominion of the empire was less subject to conflict after his death. Islam, by Qur'anic edicts, elevated the position of all a man's offspring through inheritance, heritage, and legitimacy. As with the existing customs at the time of Abraham, primacy was given to paternal line. The value of the father's seed has been variously constructed and reconstructed historically, culturally, and biologically.

The Sarah and Hajar story partially indicates how women were perceived as vessels to carry male and female offspring with male progeny to continue the paternal heritage. Little or no functional significance was given to the wife's roles beyond this utility. Nothing seemed to matter in the household as much as continuation of the paternal family line. It was indispensable to other concerns that women may have had. Interestingly, Judaism eventually transferred the descendent line from that of the father to a matrilineal one, perhaps as a result of conflicts between Sarah and Hajar's offspring regarding their priority over legitimacy. Ishmael, Abraham's first son, was born of an Egyptian slave woman. So when the scriptures command Abraham to take *his only* son, the politics of transmutation that equates that to mean Isaac, Sarah's *only* son, are difficult to explain. This new construction of lineage only coincidently appears less patriarchal. Around the time of this transmutation, Hajar and her son are banished to the desert. Matrilineal lines continue in Judaism, but not in Christianity or Islam, even as other male privileges continue or are resumed for all three faiths.

Motherhood Constructs: Prisms of Paradigms, Not Biology or Divinity

I have a painful response and long experience with the oft-cited prophetic statement, "Paradise lies at the feet of the mother," an idiom pretending that unconditional honor belongs to the one whose biology was created with the capacity to hold life under her breast and then in due time release it. It has been my nemesis, I suppose, for I have struggled in the public space to argue for the dignity and honor of every Muslim woman while I have suffered at home to maintain the care and nurturance of those to whom I am mother without knowing the ways to bridge the great schism this has created in my own identity as Muslim woman and mother.

But it is just an idiom. It is not an actual goal to be achieved by policy, economic structures, and legal codes, especially in neo-conservative circles and other places of male privilege. It is not a statement of fact. It does encourage some women with this biological capacity to yield the whole of themselves into conformity with misogynist fantasies and ideals. Such a woman must conform to a "role" which is more easily manifest if the bearer of the child is not also the one who must make a way for that child to survive in a harsh world – like our beloved Hajar in the desert.

In my life, as a five-times-over mother, I have opened my body to receive the sperm of men as celebration of a love I thought we shared – and perhaps we did, for a moment or two, perhaps even at the moments of conception. After carrying the seed of that act for nine months until its fullest fruition – for not all such seed reach completion – I opened my body again in surrender to Allah's call. It yielded up the fruit that was planted between my legs, not in pain but in labor. I have been transformed in the act of delivery.

The moment of crowning is better than orgasm itself, well worth what might have proceeded – be it real or illusion – of the love I covet.

The fathers meanwhile were present at both moments of opening. They also cry out in both, but for each a different manner of abandonment: the one, abandonment of their ego self into my body; the other, an acknowledgment of my body-self as it opens to bring forth the fruit of the seed, a new life, in the act of delivery. But, no matter what, on both occasions, and in no time at all, they wipe away the sweat from their brow and walk away.

Sometimes they never come back. And I am alone, the mother.

No one celebrates the altar at my feet, for like Sojourner, I must plow the dusty fields and draw the carts upon my back. Even as my breasts harden and weep with the fullness of milk, the whip draws blood. Both flow freely in my awakening: there is nothing romantic about the one who works like a man to save her young from the mighty grips of death and despair. She grows hard in the task. Little thought is given to her: in opening to receive the seed, she also opened to be the one who was loved and cared for. But no one is there for her.

How does an idiom about "paradise at the feet of the mother" fit the struggles of poor and single mothers? "Only within a patriarchal structure is maternity the only social power open to women."[5] When I submit my resume for jobs, grants, or creating short bios in other public roles, the twenty-plus pages is impressive to some, but if a short biographical sketch is composed I always request they include that I am the mother of five children as the most important achievement. This chapter is partially inspired by the living hell for many single female parents, or women with disabled or un-able fathers, husbands, and brothers in a Muslim community that pretends such an idiom is a statement of fact and therefore ignores the agony of these women making them invisible. It is not intended to direct attention to their plight for the purpose of pity. Rather, I use the particulars of this experience as a major criterion for challenging all reformist dialogue that is held primarily by men whose "fight" for justice focuses so exclusively on the right to preserve or extend greater privilege to the ones already privileged – Muslim men. They offer little or no direct contribution to the discourse and practice of family,[6] nor to the eradication of poverty with its negative gender consequences. Neither have they participated in, recognized, or allowed entry into their discourses the words and experiences of the ones who demonstrate the critical failure of elitist reform discourse in the first place – poor mothers.

On the contrary, most Muslim male reformists wantonly secure their own families according to patriarchal traditions. The number of women in the Muslim world whose lives and suffering are allowed to remain invisible discredits the aspirations articulated by such men as progressive Islam. It is disappointing to note how frequently some who are considered the most progressive are at best liberal in their gender agendas as evidenced by the embodiment of their own domestic experiences. Their failure to listen to, understand, or incorporate the self-expressions of the diversity of Muslim women renders them deaf to the intense ways these women need assistance in the name of reformed Islam and the agency they could contribute in constructing reforms beyond the double jeopardy.

If the most oppressed amongst us – those with a life of suffering and despair that lies writhing under the floor of the fancy conference halls and behind the walls of elegant five-star hotel rooms inhabited by those considered champions of Islamic freedom and justice – are not equal participants in the discourse, then reform discourse remains a hypocritical façade. The inconsistencies of elites seeking to enhance their privileges, for example by taking full benefit of their wives' care work, in order to focus exclusively on power politics as philosophical and theological foundations for a reformed Islamic future, allow this discourse to ignore those whose lives represent the level of survival and struggle most reflective of the need for this movement.

Motherhood

"As a universal category equated with nature, 'motherhood' does not survive historical deconstruction."[7] As I will subsequently contend, motherhood, like family, is socially constructed. The "role" of mother has been variously conceived and variously fulfilled. "The history of motherhood also requires careful examination of the status and image of women in particular cultures. Although not all women are mothers, all mothers are women: gender arrangements play a crucial role in organizing the institution of motherhood and shaping its ideologies."[8] Many forces, including religion, influenced the conceptions of the ideal mother. "All religious systems develop norms for behavior and relationships, including family relationships, with explicit and implicit ideas and prescriptions concerning sexuality and parenthood, mothers and children."[9]

At different times and places in the history of family – particularly for wealthy elites – all that was required for one to be a "mother" was actual biological reproduction. No conception of caring for the child was associated with it, including the first aspect of infant survival, nursing. In Islamic history, this is borne out by Qur'anic references to wet-nursing, and by the *sirah* literature describing the Prophet's own wet-nurse, Halimah. No charge of un-motherliness was ever launched against Aminah, the biological mother of Muhammad, because nursing one's own infant was not part of the understanding of "motherhood." The mother was the one who gave birth. Even in Arabia by that time, the father's clan or tribe was responsible for the child's upbringing. We can only speculate what other aspects of child rearing were associated with the biological mother.

Today's new technologies further complicate even the basic physiology used for conception and motherhood. Who is the mother – the donor of the egg, or the one who carries that egg to full gestation? Islamic medical experts and legal thinkers have had to react to some of the new reproductive technologies, even if only to declare them un-Islamic. Paramount in their consideration is determining how circumstances of birth for such offspring potentially determine the subsequent eligibility in conjugal relations. Questions of legitimacy and inheritance must also be resolved.

Such changes also emphasize the complex concerns over family and the ways people conceive of the role of the mother. "However mothers are characterized, they are always female parents – that is, they are women." So "certain fundamental and long lived ideas about women,"[10] about the body and about sexuality, are likely to be reinscribed in our social constructions of the role of the mother. In many cases the good woman is equated with the good mother. This moral association allows for the conception that women's sexuality and reproductive potential are meant to serve the household or the husband. This naturally leads to particular kinds of domestic ideology.

Aliah Schleifer[11] built a case around the concept of motherhood as one of sacrifice and martyrdom. The evidence for the case is very skeletal,[12] even while it mimics ideas about motherhood promoted during the Middle Ages in Christianity when "the association of motherhood with suffering and of suffering with holiness" made it "possible for women who were mothers to be eligible also for sainthood."[13] When we extol selflessness as a particular virtue of the mother – but not as a general category of virtue for all humans – we are setting up a standard of motherhood that is exceptional to other human functions, even within the family. Inadvertently, we are requiring women to fulfill those virtues, while exempting men and children. We have an entire array of virtues and values of "mothering" that become a special prison for women who try to emulate them; while idioms alone are set up to facilitate or coerce those roles no structural systems of support are provided by public policy as behooves a full citizen in relationship to human and societal well-being.

The evolving structures and ideals should alert us to "the historicity of motherhood – an institution constructed over time and differently enforced and experienced in different times and places." Indeed, "(m)otherhood never was purely "natural"; it has always been shaped by religious systems, power relationships, and material structures. Its historicity and contingency have become increasingly apparent in our times."[14] "It is also a historical construction – embattled, vulnerable, requiring recreation in each generation. To recognize its historicity is to begin to assume responsibility for the character of its reconstruction."[15] To incorporate critically the paradigmatic implications in the life of Hajar as relived in various ways by Muslim mothers today lends much to reconstruction in Muslim Personal Law.

Special care and consideration prevents this reconstruction from falling into the trap of extolling the sanctity of motherhood as "natural," thereby ignoring the burdens of care work for all mothers, but especially the multiple levels of work expected of single mothers. Certain Islamic idioms like "paradise lies at the feet of the mother" should not be used to shield civil society from taking a hard and fast look at the ways women are treated in the family and the complexities of circumstances for women as mothers. "The 'sanctity' of motherhood . . . failed to protect those who gave birth and raised children in urban poverty or rural slavery." Such women were assaulted by their status and still expected to be paragons of the virtues of selflessness and sacrifice useless for their and their children's plight – survival in a contemptible margin of invisibility. In such a plight "the bankruptcy of the ideal (of motherhood) was exposed, along with its role in enforcing race and class as well as gender privilege."[16] Unless the larger social and legal structure is set up to lend meaningful support to the particular virtues it extols in its "ideal" of family and motherhood, then it is responsible for sustaining a double bind, victimizing women who parent children alone. They must uphold the virtues of the family while competing in a public sector that disregards their familial roles because they are not the standard used to measure the predominant male participant whose essential status is determined by their exclusion from maternal care-taking.

Family in Islam, or Gender Relations by Any Other Name[17]

As with the construct of "mother," the concept of "family" is a term frequently used in various contexts with little critical reflection upon its meanings and their implications. In fact, family is so often promoted as the cornerstone of society, that the constituent parts of what constitutes family are lost in the process. Many derived concepts are built upon despite adequate definitions and variously constructed notions that contribute to public acceptance and that come to eschew a set of values as "family values." Another impetus to my research on family began with the United Nation's declaration of 1994 as the "Year of the Family," one year before the Women's International Conference in Beijing. After this declaration, which promoted national discussions on "family" values, there immediately followed a public campaign in the U.S.A.

It is easy for international bodies like the U.N. to make such designations and expect universal consensus from international communities. My primary question, along with other women's organizations in South and Southeast Asia, was, who has the authority to define "family?" With these women I worried that the definition authorized would result in certain plans, whether exploitative or beneficial to all members in the real complexities of family circumstances and structures. How would certain limitations embedded in the underlying presumptions of family further exacerbate problems existing for so many families? From this concern over definitions and settings of basic "family" paradigms I began some deliberations over policies with regard to actual families. Although I have continually revisited ideas about Qur'anic flexibility in accommodating more than one model of family to propose intra-Islamic justifications for the social construction of more egalitarian notions, my own experiences and ideas about family were transforming continually. This chapter revisits some of the stages of that transformation. Moreover, my ideas about "family" have proven to be more significant in influencing my experiences as a Muslim woman than I had imagined at the time I began to research the topic, to say nothing of the time I surrendered to being Muslim.

Although my task here has been to dismantle some of the implications of various conceptions of the term "family" starting with Hajar, a few historical examples, and developments within both early Arabian cultures and other global developments, the major goal is demonstrating how and advocating why it is necessary to reconsider family in the context of Islamic reform in modernity. In particular, the future of the harmonious continuity of Islam in the face of global realities requires Muslims to be more conscientious about the underlying implications of "family" in the ways we establish, protect, and promote family in Muslim societies as they bear upon Family and Personal Status Law. Such unexamined definitions of family in legal practice allow certain kinds of abuses within the family to go unchecked.[18] These abuses are especially experienced by those members most dependent upon the family for survival, protection, support, well-being, identity, and legal status, like women, children, the elderly, and persons with handicaps or disabilities. It is my contention that the failure of civil society, including Muslim civil society, to look carefully at the underlying notions of the term "family" while simultaneously relying upon it as a "cornerstone" of social well-being, the source of a system of "values," and the place for the development of morality, implicates those societies in the commitment of the various crimes and abuses which occur within the family.

Kinship and Family in Pre-Islamic and Early Arabian Muslim Contexts

My goal in focusing attention toward the underlying implications of various forms of "family" is three-pronged: (1) to advocate for more egalitarian notions of family in the context of Islamic societies in modernity; (2) to demonstrate how such notion are more commensurate with the Qur'anic social and moral ideals; and finally (3) to indicate how the willful progression toward the implementation of such egalitarianism in the context of real families will be instrumental to the survival of the *ummah*.

In his early twentieth century work, Robertson Smith looks at the "family" before and during the lifetime of the Prophet.[19] Using the word "kinship" in his title alerts readers to the specificity of his references without deluding anyone into thinking there was some agreed-upon, static, or ideal form of "family." Attention is more easily directed toward two functional aspects underlying all families: (1) the formulas for establishing and maintaining conjugal relations or marriage; and (2) the more expansive construction of relationships, the bonds of kinship, formed around those eligible conjugal configurations for survival. Relationship is the key component characterizing "family." Family is a construction of relationships. Paramount in this construction is the procreation, protection, and care of offspring.

The principal basis underlying the construction of conjugal ties or procreative relations is the social understanding of the roles of males and females. Women as biological child-bearers must be joined with men or male sperm in order to fulfill the child-bearing capacity. Although I do not deal here with the significance of women as child-bearers to the determination of reproductive rights, such a matter also bears upon the social construction of family.

Some of the conjugal forms that existed in pre-Islamic Arabia were maintained under the new social-moral order of Islam. Others were condemned by actual practice during the Prophet's Islamic mission, or simply became obsolete as a result of adaptation and change. For example, at that time, the woman is the only progenitor whose relationship to the unborn child could be proven. There was no means available to determine with certainty the paternity of a child, when the father might have been any one of a number of men with whom a woman had had sexual intercourse. In turn, certain child-rearing patterns were adapted. Smith focuses on historical implications that lineage was maintained through the female line in pre-Islamic Arabia. "The word *ab*, commonly translated as 'father,'" referred to the "one who acted as guardian and provided nourishment."[20] Here, the emphasis "was not primarily a matter of blood," since adopted children and blood children were considered the same, and thus prohibited from marriage or forming certain conjugal relations.[21]

Elsewhere, the practice of *adat perpatih* in certain areas of Southeast Asia is a cultural tradition with a matrilineal and matrifocal emphasis. Thus, the mother line was given greater attention. These historical examples indicate the ways in which family constructs respond to ethical-spiritual, social-intellectual, and economic systems at hand.[22] This is not for the sake of judging or comparing these systems with our current knowledge and/or human civilizational context and development. I can use them here, to provide additional information important for understanding how "ideologies of motherhood (and family) are persistent and adaptable."[23]

Although emphasis was on maternal relations when there was no certainty in identifying the biological father of any particular progeny, still, caring for the offspring, the other aspect of human survival, was necessary. The mother's people took this up. The human species must procreate to survive, but short of that basic necessity, there is no single form or consistent model for the construction of "family" or kinship that allows for care and protection of the young. The sustenance of the children in early Arabia was formed around the female progenitor not like the patriarchal systems we have justified as natural or ideal.[24]

> But we now see that before this [paterfamilias] state of things, there must have been one in which there was indeed a family system in which the center of the family was a materfamilias. The house and the children were

hers, succession was through mothers and the husband came to the wife, not the wife to the husband.

Remember the two key features of "family" cited above: conjugal relations and the construction of extended relationships for child upbringing. Conjugal relations result in procreation – even when that is not deemed the only reason for such relations – as in the case of Islamic Law. Procreation can also result in uncaring situations like rape, as in camps of Bosnian Muslim women in Croatia, or after the transatlantic slave trade. It is women, however, who always fulfill procreation in the form of reproduction. In this respect, women's role in procreation is basic and fundamental. However, systems for the protection of and care for those procreated are always contextually or culturally motivated.

The historical focus on Arab women as progenitors and on the woman's tribe, clan, or group including genealogical and material inheritance was one means for securing the future of that people. How long this formula existed or whether it was the only solution is not as much of concern here as using this for evidence to the ways "family" and "motherhood" as constructs have evolved. An Islamic ideal evolved to grant equal protection to the fathers' paternal rights as biology had protected the mothers' rights to claim their children. Attaining mutual paternity rights could have been the basis for the construction of some aspects in Islamic law, like the prohibition of polyandry.

While the Qur'an restricted polygyny, it is self-evident that, before modern medical technology, it was impossible to mutually recognize and thus protect the father's paternal rights when a woman had more than one conjugal partner. "The modern patriarchal family was created so that each man would "own" a woman who would reproduce for him. He then had to control the sexuality of "his" woman, for how else could he be sure that *'his' child was really his?*"[25] (emphasis mine). However, the maternity of a woman is still evident even when a man has more than one wife. Hence, although the Qur'an limited the number of wives a man could marry, mere biology does not provide precedent, motivation, or moral-social rationale. The prohibition of polyandry was one of a few substantive changes between Islam and pre-Islamic Arabian kinship groups. Another change surrounded the understanding of foster children and is a significant indicator of the social and historical construction of "family."

According to Smith, at the time of Muhammad's birth, "group" law meant the force of custom. Variant group ties of extended sizes or subdivisions of blood relations existed. Wide kinship grouping was advantageous as it increased power and resources against the harsh desert lifestyle. "Kinship then among the Arabs means a share in the common blood which is taken to flow in the veins of every member of the tribe – in one word, it is the tribal bond which knits men of the same group together and gives them common duties and responsibilities from which no member of the group can withdraw."[26] Men cut off from their tribe would seek protection from a tribe they encountered. Such protected strangers, *jar*, "were freely admitted . . . and in the insecure life of the desert a strong tribe or a strong chief could not fail to gather a great number of dependents."[27] In a similar fashion freed male slaves "were often adopted by their patrons . . . In like manner refugees were frequently admitted to the tribe of their protector by adoption."[28] However, "to preserve the doctrine of tribal homogeneity it was feigned that the adopted son was veritably and for all effects of the blood of his new father."[29] As mentioned above, such foster children and blood children were considered the same, with marriage prohibited between them.

Pre-Islamic Arabian "familial" construction bears upon Islamic changes in the rules of inheritance. There was no inheritance to women. Only those who took part in battle, drove booty, and protected property were eligible to inherit. Three things were of common interest: blood feud, inheritance, and booty.[30] Thus merely attributing greater paternity rights to women was not the same as considering women greater than or even equal to men. Women were vulnerable, in part because they could bear children, and if they were kidnapped or fell victim to the constant wars and raids between tribes, the woman was absorbed into her kidnapper's tribe with whatever children she bore belonging to that tribe.

Inheritance in Islam reflects the old tribal system in so much as there are fixed shares for near relations and afterwards a gratuity for kinsmen present. However, the definition of kinsman changed from 'asaba: those "who battle together,"[31] where membership is utilitarian, based around the three common interests mentioned above, to a more literal blood relation when faith in Islam became the common interest. In this new system of Islam bloodline was alternatively emphasized for greater egalitarian, as was the share of inheritance allotted women.

Islam changed the emphasis to one of blood bond from one whose "purpose . . . [was] to unite men in offense and defense."[32] So, by the time of Muhammad, the son follows the father and the father's tribe. And the Qur'an exhorts, "Your adopted son is not like your son" (33:5). A distinction is given to biological blood ties as the exclusive basis for constructing "family" by determining which conjugal relations are permissible as well as who is eligible for inheritance. Although Muslims, united as believers in Allah and His Prophet, form a single *ummah* – a word which incidentally comes from the same root as the word for mother – it is clear in the Qur'an that blood relations – also sometimes discussed in terms of "relations to the 'womb'" (4:1), are more distinctively emphasized over particular manners of certain pre-Islamic bonds.

The absorption of the offspring in pre-Islamic Arabia into one tribe or another reminds us of the two principal components of "family" already mentioned: reproduction or procreation, and protection of offspring. Quite naturally, procreation or reproduction is indispensable for the survival of the species. In the animal kingdom some males fight for the opportunity to mate with available females. In some species, the males will kill the offspring of other males, either to establish their claim over the available female, who will no longer lactate and then go into heat ready to mate with the king to have his own offspring to protect his line of descendents, or simply to reflect territorial dominion and leave precious resources more readily available for his offspring.

As human beings, we are capable of both moral excellence and degradation or abomination unknown in the animal kingdom. Not mere subjects of biological determinism, we construct mores, norms, and laws as part of civil society to ensure the continuity of the race/species. The emphasis then is that we do participate in the willful conceptualization and construction of conjugal forms, procreative choices, and systems of care and protection that facilitate survival and continuity.[33] To pretend that we do not do this consciously, or to ignore the willful aspects of our family concepts, reduces us to an animal-like state of mere biological reproduction.

In short, "family" is no epiphenomenon that occurs naturally. To suppose this is to pretend that all that is needed is physical survival – that there is no need to honor the rules of civilization or to acknowledge the Islamic ethos with its goal of forming a just social system in order to facilitate the willful surrender of the human will to the will of Allah. Overlooking the conscious intent in social constructs means there is no need to obey the limits set by Allah. On the contrary, as human beings we are created vicegerent or trustee over nature, *not* mere subjects of "nature." Biological determinism is not the moral basis of Islamic society, so why should it be for family? This historical look demonstrates the willfulness of human kinship arrangements and family.

As elsewhere in this book, this discussion is premised upon certain ideas about history and development, Islamic and otherwise. Let us examine other significant global phenomena affecting the construction of family in modernity: the industrial revolution, colonialism, post-colonialism, and the advantages and disadvantages of extended and nuclear family constructs as affected by these phenomena.

Colonialism and Post-Colonialism

The term *ummah* (or community) was applied to a united Muslim empire until 1924 with the end the Ottoman Empire. Since that time, any mention of *ummah* is more symbolic and sentimental in focus. The *ummah* was once a genuine political realm or empire, but now it is a social and psychological realm up against the global establishment of the nation-state. At the same time as the *ummah* empire ended, Western colonialism rapidly expanded. Many of today's Muslim nation-states came under colonial rule. Those not under direct military or political rule are surely under the ideological and economic influence of the colonial West.

The colonial process within these newly formed Muslim nation-states included the wholesale borrowing from Western legal systems for matters of tort, criminal procedure, and family law, as well as the more important matters of political law, economics, and constitution. One trend in the post-colonial Islamization movements reflects the failure of various Muslim nation-states that had wholeheartedly adopted Western positive law. To offset the effects of feeling this failure, and to demonstrate the a priori prominence of Islamic tradition, many Muslims are seeking the re-establishment of Islamic law. This is especially true in the areas of family law, personal status law, and the *hudud* ordinances, or penal codes derived from the Qur'anic articulation of harsh punishments for certain crimes. Again, the means for implementing Islamic law have been variously constructed.[34] The effect of these new configurations on women and the family is another part of the backdrop for my considerations. The ideas of family underlying these new configurations are often severely detrimental to present complexity in real family circumstances up against the globalization of gross consumption and the emphasis given in enlightenment articulations that what it means to be human is primarily a notion of discrete individualism.

Furthermore, the phenomenon of the new global economy bears heavily upon considerations of family in local contexts under the umbrella of building pluralist nation-states. Despite the fact that Muslims have applied some of the most advanced modern research to debates over modern economic systems, the primacy of capitalism – with its bastard child, consumerism – has never been challenged. Select Muslim nation-states have benefited from the precious oil resources that the Creator just happened to put under their feet and have rushed to benefit in global economic terms. Economic reforms did not address economics as an ethical issue, resulting in greater consumerism. Muslims and other ethical thinkers need to debate the politics of economic power within the context of the gross disparities of consumption.

A critical look at the global economy shows the many ways in which large populations of the world continue to be victimized and sustained in poverty, especially affecting women and children within existing notions of family. According to statistics[35] from the United Nations Development Program (U.N.D.P.), 86% of the world's consumable goods are consumed by 20% of the world's population, while the remaining population – four times the number of the wealthy top 20% – must divide the remaining 14% of the world's consumable goods. The lowest 20% of the population consumes a paltry 1.3%. We live in a world where the massive existence of poverty is accepted simultaneously with gross consumption and waste by a small portion of the world's population. Meanwhile, what is viewed as normative is based solely on the consumer gluttons whose lifestyles and perspectives are advertised the world over as the goal toward which all people aspire. The moral implications of this are fundamental to the family in the future of an Islamic ethos that claims universal social justice and human dignity as a goal.

The Nuclear Family Moves into Domination over the Extended Family

"With the industrial revolution the men departed to the factories and the offices and women's sphere of power shrank, but her role of responsibility for domestic piety and family morality became almost complete."[36] There is evidence that the idea for the nuclear family, one man cohabiting with one woman and living with their offspring, had some history in medieval times in Europe. However, for our purposes, the most significant factor impacting on the construction of the nuclear family – fast becoming *the* basic family structure in modern society – was the industrial revolution.

In cottage industries long preceding the industrial revolution, production was centered around the home, and was part of the family structure. All family members had roles to play in production, and the absorption of other members was directly related to maintaining the family as the center of productivity. Whether a son brought his wife, or a daughter brought her husband into the family or married out of it, depended on the nature of the family business that needed to be maintained and the resources that perspective and actual conjugal relatives could provide.

The industrial revolution changed the face of modern society, promoting an exploitation of human resources in an unprecedented manner. Human labor was needed for the smooth running of systems of mass production in huge factories away from the home. Slavery was no longer an option. The nuclear family structure provided the most expendable arrangement for supplying the human resources needed in the factories and industries. The nuclear family is still the most popular familial construction in modern civil society today. In modern Muslim society much lip service is still given to the "extended family," but a cursory look at various consequences of globalization and shrinking village-life resources leading to mass urbanization shows a new culture of nuclear families with different configurations of connections to extended family members – even if only limited to visits on holidays. The effects of this lip service and of the spread of the nuclear family are part of my concern here.

In cottage industry (where productivity centered around the home), men, women, and children all had vital roles to play. How were these roles altered under the pressures of survival in the new labor force of modern industry? For example, cottage industry observed a natural clock, with most work starting at or just before dawn and ending after dusk. The invention of electricity both facilitated the running of factories and provided lights, allowing them to run all night long. In such cases, how is it decided when a worker has worked enough? What if that worker is a child, a single mother, or person with disabilities? New questions and concerns like this led to new labor laws, like child labor laws to help build better conditions against exploiting minors. That is, civil society constructed codes to maintain that which is deemed to be "civil" about society.

In the nuclear family construct, a number of tasks once fulfilled by an extended membership of the predominate family units would come to fall squarely on the shoulders of the more isolated conjugal pair – though of course, not equally. The domestic space became the irrefutable responsibility of the woman. This included all forms of childcare from skills development, moral upbringing, education, and nurturance, as well as all domestic services like cooking and cleaning for the physical and psychological well-being of all members. While not evaluating the value of these tasks intrinsically, their utility and necessity merits acknowledgment of their good. Successfully completing these tasks constitutes success of the family.

A cursory look at family arrangements today will demonstrate how the larger percentages of these tasks still fall upon the woman–wife–mother. She was considered the primary care-taker, a role presumably determined by the absence of out-of-home responsibilities. This was a convenient arrangement when men performed tasks outside the home to acquire the means for providing material support for the family. This arrangement still remains and is considered ideal or natural vis-à-vis various understandings of gender and gender relations in "family." This arrangement associates certain menial tasks with the female member of a nuclear pair, and relegates her to a role that is defined by services that are barely recognized and rarely warrant praise in the larger social and political system. Nevertheless, when these tasks fail to produce the kind of offspring deemed desirable, she – and in many cases she alone – can be castigated for this failure.

If these tasks – moral upbringing, child care, domestic services – are indeed intrinsically significant, then their significance should become an essential component integrated in public policy no matter who performs them. As a result of their significance, civil society should construct ways to assist in maintaining them when actual families evolve as a consequence of diverse forces affecting the function and understanding of family, as we have seen increase after colonialism.

Remember, family is a construction of gender relations. It is the socially determined structures of conjugal relations who constitute an eligible partner, especially – though not exclusively – for the continuity of the species, through procreation. It involves not only how children are procreated, but also what kind of environment is created for the basic care of all members and upbringing for the children. This explains why considerations of "family" are essential to discussions about procreation or reproduction. It is the society that determines reproductive rights and responsibilities. If the goal to continually recreate ourselves as the human species is to be understood fully, then it entails detailed consideration of how we construct family or what we consider as appropriate gender relations. In a variety of social settings this necessarily extends to include the "roles" of males and females, since children are potential adults who will contribute to forming new "families" and to patterns of procreation and productivity. Children within any one social setting are raised to become appropriate adults intended to fulfill appropriate roles for males and females. This bears heavily on the development patterns for children in their upbringing.

Thus the word family is also a word for gender relations. What constructions of gender roles will best serve particular social structures as conceived in various contexts? As Muslims, the ethos of the Qur'an and traditions of the Prophet lead toward a social order that facilitates the surrender of both individuals and the collective to the will of Allah. At one level this basically means following the rules of Islam, or obeying Allah's commandments. At a more fundamental or existential level, however, this is more than rules alone. It means individual and collective development of a mindset that places remembrance of Allah uppermost. For when a rule does not exist, only a mindset in surrender can formulate such a rule or make a moral conscientious decision that is commensurate with the ultimate goal of surrender. As Audre Lorde puts it, to provide "the power to seek new systems of being in the world . . . as well as the courage and sustenance to act where there are no charters."[37]

The New Global Economy, Or, Your Worth in Paper Money

The new global economy is singularly the most significant factor since the industrial revolution to impact upon family life and its meaning. This impact needs to be sufficiently examined in the Islamic context and in Islamic constructions of gender relations or family. Instead we are falling headlong into its effects and the unexamined conceptions of family are left to fend for themselves – just like the industrial revolution left the nuclear family couple to fend for themselves.

For example, salaried income – the bastard child of the industrial revolution – has become the single basis for determining individual and collective worth and dignity. The notion of an upstanding moral individual or institution no longer exists without an economic base. Those institutions that we support and develop, including non-government organizations, community-based organizations, Islamic associations, educational facilities, and other constructions for learning and research are all salaried or capital-dependent. Likewise, wage earning affects the construction of the family, which once operated around a non-wage-earning primary caretaker. This is one fact that Islamic resurgent romanticism consistently overlooks in the promotion of the ideal Islamic family. Either the family suffers economically from the absence of the female's necessary financial contributions, or the family is deluded into pretending that she is in all respects an at-home mom, since working in the salaried sector does not relieve her from any of the chores attributed to her when she was at home.

Increasingly, salaried income has come to be the evaluative measure for worth of the individual. At one time in history the goal of university education was the development of the learned person. Now, universities are increasingly becoming corporate bureaucracies with the goal of producing competitive wage earners. Professional positions and jobs are evaluated on the basis of the salary they offer. While both wage-earning and the evaluative measure of wage-earning are increasingly extended to the female, the consideration of the tasks heretofore exclusively performed by her as primary care-taker who was not obligated outside of the familial home environment has gone unchanged. Instead, she suffers from a double burden.

The "family" as the basic unit of care in society cannot survive with dignity in a world where one's sole measure of worth and the basis of one's dignity is a paper money system. Yet the well-being of the home is also dependent upon the nurturing and care-taking once considered in and of itself a "role" that was identified with the mother/wife. She is still expected to fulfill this role, but she must likewise go into the public sector and compete in terms sufficient to secure her increasingly necessary wage contributions to that family. The only way to resolve this dilemma is by more egalitarian family structures and ideals.

We are living in a time of unprecedented change and development in human civilization in light of new technologies and globalization, especially of the economy. These changes bear heavily upon the moral attitudes of humankind. Extensive discussion is warranted about the ethical implications of these technological and economic developments and the global economy. These discussions should include analysis of gender roles. This nuclear family is not only the family of the male–female couple as stewards only over their biological offspring; it is also decidedly male-dominated. Despite the disruption of the extended family networks of all traditional societies, including Muslim societies, this focus on male dominance appears to be a compensation for all the other negative consequences that result from the loss of the extended family network with immeasurable value to women, wives, and mothers who have become exclusively responsible for the care of all members. The care-taking role of the woman has suffered the most negative consequences in the demise of the extended family since her role within the family has been severely stretched.

In conjunction with a woman's primary care-taker role in the nuclear family, increasingly, wherever there is mass urbanization, the father's role as sole provider of *nafaqah*,[38] material support, is challenged. Material support, since the industrial revolution, means wages. Wages are mostly the results of work that no longer takes place in the home. The cultural acknowledgment of the role of wage-earning between the isolated nuclear couple was the male, leading to the assumption that the non-wage-earning female fulfills all other needs. This assumption idealizes the woman who only reproduces and cares for offspring. Many assume that this is natural, and hence a voluntary contribution with no bearing upon female agency. In reality, women's lives – including women in Muslim majority contexts – are adversely affected by global economics that presume the fulfillment of multiple extended tasks without the domain of an equally extended family or public policies that explicitly carve out resources designated to help with this care work.

While this transition to the nuclear family has become normalized globally, the new global economy has increased the need for two wage earners to provide decently for the family. The choice for a mother to attend only to the house and children is rare. Of course, poor families, the majority of the Muslim families worldwide, never presumed such a choice. One of my concerns about male dominant concepts of family is that women's work inside the home goes unnoticed. This is most evident when weighed upon the wage-earning scale. There are many tasks that women are expected to fulfill as primary care-taker and keeper of the domestic sphere. For simplicity's sake, if each of these tasks were compensated by at least the minimum wage in the West, at home mothers have an extensive balance overdue. After all, when she leaves the house to earn wages in the public sector, she must pay someone else to fulfill these task, or simply work double shift: one paid, one unpaid. For that matter, with Technology-Assisted Reproduction (T.A.R.), where surrogate mothers carry the child for some other couple, they are paid tens of thousands of dollars. Reproducing a child could also be weighed on the wage-earning scale. All these tasks are applied to mothers and wives as only "natural." Coincidently, childcare and housekeeping are not defined as extensions of motherhood in the time of the Prophet or in the formation of *shari'ah*.

In the context of modern industrial societies, these responsibilities must be reflected upon and integrated into all aspects of reformist discourse. Simply overlooking the realities of these complex but inherently essential tasks associated with mothers for the sake of healthy moral upbringing of future generations, simply because these women have the biological capability for child-bearing, is a serious overestimation on the part of too many cultures today. It stands in stark contrast to the Qur'anic statement, *"lil-rijaali nasiban min-maa-ktasabu wa lil-nisaa' nasibum min-maa-ktasabna*, for men shall have a share of what they earn and women shall have a share of what they earn . . . truly Allah has knowledge of all things" (4:32).

In light of the added reality of global economics, more and more women are also burdened with the responsibility of contributing to the family income. All this severely strains the notion of the self-sufficient nuclear family unit. When a woman faces the multiple roles of parenting in the nuclear family with the presumption of sufficient wage-earning from the male, but without the extended network of support, she is already overly burdened. Next to these, working wives and mothers are doubly burdened. Yet an even more illogical reality faces the many women today who are single heads of household with no financial support, except what they are able to provide, and no structural system to alleviate the plight of their families. This leads to my notion of the new Hajar paradigm.

Hajar

Once a year, millions of Muslims converge on Makkah to perform the pilgrimage rites or *hajj*. Included among these rites is running between two foothills, Safa and Marwa, seven times, symbolically re-enacting the plight of Hajar who was abandoned in the desert with her child as a homeless single parent. All needs of the child now fell upon her shoulders exclusively. Never mind the magical rhetoric of "with Allah's help." Faith is a spiritual and psychological posture that describes a partnership between one's practical efforts and one's understanding of a spiritual relationship with the divine. Allah provides as we provide. Faith alone does not. Yet the need for nurturing the child has not displaced the idealization of the mother as exclusive or primary care-taker.[39] Hajar was forced to make a way where there was none, for herself and her son.

I wonder how many Muslims who run seven times between Safa and Marwa actually reflect on the realities of a woman who entered into a customary practice of her cultural heritage and bore a child for a man soon to be recognized as the father of monotheist, scriptural religious traditions. Hajar was raised in a context with certain customary codes that promised she would never have to worry about her or her child's livelihood or protection. What did she feel when such an unprecedented responsibility fell upon her shoulders – to say nothing of life in the desert! Once isolated from a network that had carried the promise of provision, protection, and care, nowhere in the exegetical literature of Christianity, Judaism, or Islam is the reality that this woman faced juxtaposed to the understanding of normative family at that time or in the present. Her status as single head of household is never commented upon, no one was held accountable for its resolution, and later legal codifications in Islam would still overlook it. Such patriarchal practices and texts do not elaborate on her plight. At some point in Muslim historical records it is implied that some Bedouin Arab tribe took in her and her child. She saves the Arab lineage with no serious analysis of her parenting experience in their commentaries. The silence over this discrepancy is my consideration here.

Islamic personal law is built upon a notion of family that does not include a woman thrown into the desert, forced to construct a healthy, happy life for her child and to fend for herself. Islamic law for family, as constructed and still maintained, is not only premised upon an ideal of an extended family network, it presumes that a woman will never, for any reason, become responsible for providing for and protecting herself and her offspring. Yet this reality happens more and more frequently the world over. At the time of the Prophet, in the extended family network of the tribe, a woman was only seen as having no other responsibility beyond the safe delivery at the birth of the child who potentially contributes to the future. The newborn child Muhammad was considered an orphan because his father, 'Abd-Allah, had died during Aminah's pregnancy. Motherhood was solely based on her child-bearing capacity. The establishment of guardianship through the patriarchal line was the only means available for him to become a legitimate heir and a recognized member of the patriarchal society.

Furthermore, as Islamic law has developed, if a wife or a mother has material assets by inheritance or other means, now extended to her wage earnings, these assets are exclusively for her. She has no responsibility toward *nafaqah*, material maintenance of the family, the household, or even herself. If her husband dies, she is supposed to be taken in, provided for, and protected by the extended family. Likewise, the law presumes that if she divorces her husband or is divorced by him, she returns to an extended family network. All material needs of her children are the responsibility of the father and the father's extended family. Other aspects of protection are presumed to be available through an entire network. For a mother, the implications of this nurturing and supportive environment must make it easier to imagine that a woman has nothing to focus her attention upon except the moral and emotional welfare of her children. Ironically, even in that system, no actual tasks of nurturance or guardianship were presumed to fall upon the mother.

The reality that many women face today is nowhere near the ideals presumed within the concept of family sustained by Islamic law and underscoring Muslim cultures. Suad Joseph proposes an examination of the relations between the family and the gendering of citizenship in the Middle East by analyzing what she calls the "kin contract." Furthermore, "the binary between public and private . . . situate citizenship in the realm of the "public."[40] Women's citizenship is intricately linked to their roles in the family where family and state can be said to be mutually constitutive.[41] "For women, this means that their citizen rights are often mediated through the very patriarchal structures (kin, communities, religious sects) that control (and care for) them."[42] "(M)ost Middle Eastern states constitute men as citizens through their roles as heads of patriarchal families and treat women as dependent mothers, wives, children, and siblings."[43] The idea of a woman's agency apart from various notions of family, as they bear upon changes in family or diverse realities of women as mothers, must be restructured in policy terms of state and *fiqh*. The ways and means for achieving the fulfillment of family needs without patriarchy or without the ideal of extended family is not sufficiently studied under the area of Islamic studies. For this reason, women like Hajar can only be considered deviant, with no practical steps proposed, either for the individual or the community, to construct other models of family and motherhood to assist these women at addressing both their internal struggle of identity as Muslim agents and their external struggle to retain the honor of human dignity stolen in patriarchal presumptions of marriage as the subjugation of women. This "ideal family" is the bind of the unexplored Hajar paradigm.

The African-American Family, Islam, and Women

African-Americans began turning to Islam in the late 1920s. In addition to the establishment of the Moorish Science Temple and the Nation of Islam, which both borrowed many underlying ideas from the fourteen-centuries-old tradition, many African-Americans in major urban areas along the U.S. east coast also joined global Islam with reliance upon its orthodox dogma, creeds, and practices. These numbers slowly increased over the next few decades. At the beginning of the twentieth century, transnational movements, even amongst Muslims, were motivated by secular and financial interests in coming to assimilate with mainstream white America. They gathered in ghettos or moved far from urban centers, especially from African-Americans, whom they avoided at all cost and on all levels. They married white Americans, especially non-Muslim women, named their children according to the names prevalent in their new secular culture and did little to represent Islam or to promote its expansion in America.

By the mid-1960s, changes in U.S. immigration laws brought more immigrants or transnationals from Muslim countries, mostly students, but also their wealthy families. They were more dedicated to preserving and promoting their cultural identity as Muslims. They constructed cultural enclaves in the form of mosques and other organizations. This new transnational population was soon coordinated with public life in America and by extension with those members of the African-American community who had already gained interest in Islam. By the 1970s Islam was becoming a part of the American landscape both in transnational and indigenous-transitional elements.

African-Americans who were the first part of this growth of Islam in America were representatives of the totality of the social, cultural, moral, political, economic, and spiritual history of African-America. This is particularly important regarding my focus on African-American Muslim women. They are a part of the repository of many events that make up a complex history, affecting notions of identity, including motherhood, family, and community.

Extensive research on the African-American family has been contributed over more than three decades, particularly after the 1970s *Moynihan Report*. Without referring to the biases of the report itself, I have benefited from the subsequent research in order to make a coherent link between the development of the African-American family and the African-American Muslim female head of household.

Research on Black women's unpaid labor within extended families remains less fully developed in Black feminist thought than does that on Black women's paid work. By emphasizing Black women's contributions to Black family well-being, such as keeping families together and teaching survival, such scholarship suggests that Black women see their unpaid work as a form of resistance to oppression than as a form of exploitation by men. Less attention is given to ways that Black women's domestic labor is exploited within African-American families, an omission that obscures investigations of families as contradictory locations that simultaneously confine yet allow Black women to develop cultures of resistance.[44]

The African-American family is a reflection of the African family and of the tenacity and flexibility of African-Americans to survive the brutal history of slavery in this country. Slavery was followed by de juro and de facto oppressions that would further exacerbate the presumption that family has clear and narrow boundaries, necessarily established in patriarchal terms or like those delineated for the nuclear family construct. Unlike the nuclear family, premised upon the conjugal relation between two heterosexual adults, the African family was, and in many ways continues to be, based upon the consanguineal core of blood relations. The structural privacy of the nuclear family that focuses primarily on that married couple is not universal. Families survive with a complexity of adult relations based upon the significance of having and bringing up children. Within the context of comparative family studies, the African-American family shows itself to be an enduring institution with its own set of values and mechanisms for flexibility and adaptability, which manages to meet family needs.

In this flexible and adaptable model of family, the existence of female-headed households was less endangered due to complex networks of support and community relations. In addition, females without seemingly fixed male partners were not subjected to the negative stigma implied by some Islamic legal configurations of family still prevalent in most Muslim traditional cultures.

How is Islam, a more recent yet major addition in configuring the identity of African-American Muslim women, distinct from other configurations of African-American women? Islam is a major identity factor, with its history of meticulous ideas about community, family, and relationships. None of these ideas reflect the post-slavery survival mechanisms for African-American families despite many important corollaries between ideology and praxis. I have already discussed the sources of the Islamic ideology and related its development of *shari'ah*, a detailed system of laws and codes. What I am considering here are areas of reform in the law based upon the multiple actual experiences of all mothers. The Qur'an is emphatic that Muslims are characterized by both belief and action. Certain actions are prescribed, both regarding ritual practice, *'ibadah*, and social relations, *mu'amilah*. As the Qur'an was revealed in seventh-century Arabia then the law was developed, it established juridical principles to help construct what could be understood as morally acceptable behavior within the context of a just social order. It did so in a manner that reflected the time, place, and circumstances of the ones constructing the law. It is equally important to take into consideration the time, place, and circumstances of other Muslim communities, especially modern ones, in order to continually determine right praxis. In this regard, the special history of African-Americans, as a significant part of Islam in America, should impact upon ideas about attaining and sustaining social justice in the context of an African-American Islamic identity.

The experiences of African-American female heads of household must be looked at holistically, vis-à-vis reform notions of Islamic law. The argument for this stems not only from the basis of our particular experiences as African-American women who have chosen Islam, but also on the basis of the Hajar paradigm, which gives an historical precedent to an important parallel within the entire Abrahamic legacy, including the Islamic legacy: especially since the law was developed without considering her experience, while retaining it as liturgically indispensable to the fulfillment on one of the five pillars. With larger numbers of women facing a similar reality, there is even greater imperative for the law to accommodate this reality instead of continuing to turn a blind eye to it. The legal accommodations I refer to must include mechanisms to help ensure the safety and well-being of families with single women as head of household, to prevent the double burden of the negative stigma of fixed ideals of family, mother, and female as well as of the public sphere.

In this complexity, the American Muslim community has several competing paradigms of family and marriage: family from traditional Muslim cultures, as a reflection of the unique African-American historical experience, and families within the context of Western cultures and U.S. legal codes. African-American Muslim women have entered into marriages, only to exit them in percentages no one dares admit. In selecting this topic, I want to emphasize the tenacity and bravery of such women who not only engaged in single parenting, especially including sole responsibility for material support, but also often offer innumerable public services to the Muslim community.[45] We are in denial. We do not focus upon the realities of these women's experiences, because to do so would be to admit that their lives are far from the ideal perceived to be their right or due in "Islam." Of course, when attention is focused on them and this discrepancy between right and reality we implicate the woman herself, otherwise it reflects badly on Islam. Our failure to admit this will not make this reality go away. That's rather like little kids who say, "Cover your eyes and the monster won't see you."

Should any shortcoming befall such families, we do not address it as a matter of collective community responsibility, inadequacies of legal structures, or their implementation, nor as a matter of systemic forces playing at even our most intimate developments as individuals and members of kinship groupings. We simply hide behind the rhetoric, "Islam gave women all their rights fourteen centuries ago." The context in which those rights were given, the complexities of historical development, and the challenges of current circumstances with painful realities for women in families are totally ignored. Furthermore, if we can blame these shortcomings on the parent who spends the most time and resources toward providing for endangered children, then the community does not have to look at its role in failing such families. Instead, it projects a very impractical expectation – the best Islam has to offer will result, no matter what actual circumstances people live in. If individual families or women cannot live in the fulfilled promise of Islam, the implication has been that the fault lies with *their* own faith or personality. Women are left to face this burden alone and silent. "Over the years, female-headed families have been among the most maligned and misunderstood of all Black families, being forced to bear the responsibility, as it were, for all the ills of Black America."[46]

My concern is that the formation of Islamic family law was based upon certain notions of family that have ceased to exist in most parts of the modern world, and that have *never* existed in the context of many parts of the world that have transitioned and continue to transition into Islam, like the African-American Muslim community. Yet the legal ideals of family are presumed to remain unencumbered by global or regional realities. If Islam is for all places, for all times, and for all people, then how do we deal with *this* reality from an Islamic perspective? In the case of Islam in America, especially in the case of transitioning Muslim women, we expect they will represent the best while they are offered the least. We offer no substantive consideration of the realities that so many women face when left to raise children single-handedly in a predominantly non-Muslim and un-Islamic environment with fixed and exclusionary definitions controlling success in the public space for acquiring a means of survival.

Toward Egalitarian Concepts of Family for Holistic Legal Reforms

Although the story of Hajar is not detailed in the Qur'an, Muslims claim her and ritually re-enact her plight during the pilgrimage, *sa'iy* – running seven times between Safa and Marwah. Pilgrims have the opportunity to focus on her predicament and the reality of a single female head of household. In every situation where Muslims are ravaged by war, faced with refugee status – with estimates that Muslims make up as much as a half of the world's refugees – wherever poor Muslim countries supply male and female laborers for wealthy Muslim countries, including the brain drain, real families are split off from even their own ideal notions. When women assume greater responsibilities for protecting and financially managing the family, they achieve a larger social role. They are certainly more than mere vessels for safe delivery at childbirth.

The purpose of looking at the Hajar paradigm anew is to give precedent to the expectations of the "nurturing mother," who is also housekeeper, cook, laundry woman, educator, valet, driver, and ad-hoc medical assistant, and who must also contend competitively within the patriarchal public sector to provide protection and a means for living a life of dignity. Yet no elitist progressive discourse has focused strategically and pragmatically on the reforms needed in order to construct legal, political, and ethical systems that provide access to sources of financial, moral, and psychological support – especially in the U.S.A. where poverty has plethora of humiliating legal and moral consequences. What does this mean for a Muslim woman without a vast fortune? The Hajar paradigm is the reality for Muslim women heads of households whose legal category in *shari'ah* deviates from the patriarchal, man-centered norm. Yet it is through the law they expect their honor and dignity to be upheld.

In most traditional Islamic schools of law, custody, or *hadanah*, of the child goes to the father and his people (except the Maliki school). The reasons for this again reflect cultural, historical, material, and tribal trends. In all schools, maintenance of the children is supposed to be the responsibility of the father or his extended family. In the context of modern U.S.A., custody of the child as well as maintenance most often goes with the mother, with the focus on underlying notions of nurturance and care, and also cultural and historical reflections of specific presumption of family not presumed to bare on maintenance. Muslim families in America have bought into both these ideals without increasing the means for support.

If a women needs to divorce, earn an income, protect her family and community, she *simply* does so. It is within this realm of pragmatism that Islamic gender roles make sense. Many African-American transitioning Muslims want to be free from from having to "do it all." They want relief from having to bring in an income and manage all domestic affairs. Many women would like men to have a comparable desire for family stability, and if performing fixed gender roles is the method to achieve that goal, so be it.[47]

However, because there is no formal structure to sustain the paternal maintenance responsibility of traditional Islamic law, there is no guarantee of child support unless divorced women avail themselves of U.S. laws and policies surrounding child support. African-American women are often distrustful of these laws as un-Islamic, even when they are forced to provide financially for the children they presumed by an Islamic idealism would only require them to nurture and morally support. This leaves child maintenance to the whim of fathers, who often receive sanction from male authorities of the transitioning Muslim community that excuses them from the traditional *shari'ah* requirements to fulfill the child support responsibility while discouraging women from seeking support from the U.S. established legal means. All the while, the idealization of the full-time nurturing mother, according to one woman, is that "She is free from financial responsibility according to this religion."[48] The magical expectation that children are provided for and women are pampered and protected mothers, with paradise at their feet, is a negative fantasy afflicting the single mother's realities of survival.

Therefore, this massive recall by Islamists for the full implementation of historical *shari'ah* codes must include rethinking universal principles in the primary sources, rather than becoming a mere overlay of obsolete codes onto modern complexities. It behooves us to take into greater consideration the workings of the law and to become more responsible with regard to holistic and radical reforms. This is especially so in the U.S.A., where the Qur'an and Islam might be deemed our ethical guide, with no legal structures organized to enforce the full implementation of its universal guidance. This circumstance has permitted neglect and abuse of Muslim women in families in ways particularly relevant to modern global changes. Meanwhile, because of a presumed ideal of *shari'ah*, the realties of the single female head of household and her children experience additional yet undue damage.

Conclusion: More Egalitarian Concepts of Family

Although Islam is a coherent and integrated system that includes the legacy of complex legal formulas known as *shari'ah*, the underlying notion of family in *shari'ah* has a patriarchal bias. As Muslim cultures move into modernity with the extended family giving way to the nuclear family, both notions have reconfigured and yet retained a patriarchal bias. This results from family retaining the primacy of marriage. According to the Prophet, "Marriage is half of faith." When a "marriage" dissolves, however, *family* may still exist. Securing the survival of family as a primary unit of society is not the same as securing the patriarchal bias of *shari'ah* constructs. New configurations of family – with or without the heterosexual couple – must reconsider the ways that all members of the family may play various roles in care-taking, protection, and provision. As noted above, African families surviving slavery and the economic and political aftermath have been important sites for other configurations of family, including different dynamics of the extended family. As African-Americans have adopted Islam, they have sometimes forfeited the integrity and survival benefits of their own heritage. Women have been valued primarily with regard to their relations to husbands, and sometime fathers. The realities of single, female, heads of household do not include the sanction or support of this focus on male familial leadership and support. However, if an African-American articulation of Islamic identity is to be formed in a meaningful way, then our whole history must be taken into consideration. This history shows the virtue of women surviving and helping children to survive. In this task, women still need the benefit from networks of support. I recommend an extended concept of community to offer that support, through public policy change, Islamic legal reform, and the moral imperative of family well-being. We should neither depend upon nor carelessly disregard the reality of Hajar's abandonment. It was imperative that she survived, and that she helped her child experience a life of prosperity. The mechanisms available for her to create that prosperity are silenced in Islamic law. That silence needs to be broken for the many women who face a similar dilemma. This is one basis for extensive reform in Islamic law, such that community is structured as a network of support for children and families even if, or especially when, females stand alone as heads of household.

Islam is perceived and experienced as a dynamic way of life consisting of praxis and ideology. In order for it to bear positively on the life of African-American Muslim women, then the history and experiences of these women must become a part of the articulation and implementation of Islam in the American context. Reforms in the conceptualization and development of *shari'ah* must dynamically incorporate their experiences. Those experiences denote a sustained effort at survival and familial well-being, despite the number of structural disadvantages resulting from racism, gender, and class hegemonies. The roles played by African-American single, female, heads of household have contributed to sustaining social well-being and moral development. Those roles must be integrated into actual codes and policies that support the integrity of the woman and recognize that the adaptability and flexibility she has demonstrated are beneficial to what can be configured as Islam today. I not only call for de juro or legal Islamic reforms, but also for a de facto cultural climate of mutual support and care toward these women in families. I do not define family only on the basis of a patriarchal matrix, but rather as a collective of human beings striving for survival and well-being no matter what the social context.

Within the framework of intra-Islamic diversity in Islamic thought, I point to juxtaposition between experience and authority. Experiences are ways of unfolding in thought and being. Hajar was a representation of the inadequacy of patriarchal worldviews within the context of religious law and personal status in Islam. She shed light on an ethical aberration that provides a theoretical refutation for the adequacy of historical Islamic law, which failed to take her experience into consideration. It creates a kind of legal invisibility. Although the experiences of women really do occur, they are deviant within a legal construction that is premised upon the patriarchal extended or nuclear family.

An underlying premise in the notion of family as conceived of in historical *shari'ah* is that conjugal relations are formed within the marriage of subjugation. The woman is subject to the man, who is variously conceived as being a degree above her, the maintainer and provider, the lord and master over her affairs. These descriptions are taken as inevitable, natural, or based on divine sources. Elsewhere I have deconstructed each of these presumptions and considered at some detail how erroneous interpretations are associated with the Qur'an.[49] Suffice it to say here, when a presumption already exists, finding what looks like textual support or evidence is no difficult matter. In this regard, I reiterate my belief that the Qur'an is universal in intent, but not in its contextual epistemology. Its intent is commensurate with various lifestyles evolving within human communities so long as the level of moral excellence in the people follows it. Furthermore, social arrangements specified in the Qur'an merely indicate *some* of the possibilities considered appropriate to Islam. Other possibilities exist, and are necessary, good, and appropriate. Most importantly, the Qur'an can be read with egalitarian social, political, economic, as well as domestic arrangements in mind.

Much of progressive Muslim discourse has explicitly challenged hege-monies in social, political, and economic areas, while leaving the family fettered to outmoded models. While some of the foremost thinkers in our time are adamant about the necessity of constructing democratic reforms in all areas of government, "How can there be successful democracy in public life if there is an authoritarian model in the private life?"[50] Since family is a social construction of gender relations, we can construct those families based on the highest ideals that we have as a civil society. We can also develop an infrastructure that helps to sustain those ideals.

To make a case for *more* egalitarian families in the context of Islam and Muslims, I mean when compared to the norm in all Muslim contexts that I am aware of through study or living experience. No Muslim culture that I have ever visited or read about constructs their families around notions of equality. Neither do non-Muslim cultures either, despite various small experiments. Since the moral guidelines for our lives as Muslims must be prefaced upon the Qur'an and the *sunnah*, no matter how variously under-stood, some would not consider non-Muslim models of interest in this development.

Yet in discourse with even the more progressive thinkers, too much equality is seen to violate the "nature" of family. Presumably, family is func-tionally hierarchical and must be restrained by patriarchy.[51]

> Patriarchy defines not just women as the "other" but also subjugated peoples and races as the "other" to be dominated. It defines women, moreover, not just as the other of men, but also as subordinated to men in power insofar as it conceives of society as analogous to the patriarchal household, which was sustained by slave labor.

Such progressive discussions about political equality perpetuate a double standard. Equality can only be conceived of in unequivocal terms when applied to the *natural* participants of the public domain, presumably male. Of course men perceive of themselves as equal, with the same rights, responsibilities, and even capabilities as other men. If they differ for reasons of race, class, national origin, ethnicity, and the like, these are *not* essential characteristics for which they consider themselves in any way other than equal to other men.

But the othering of women from men reduces the possibility that women are seen as the same as men, even if what differs is no more essential than the tremendous variants that separate otherwise still deemed equal men. "Men and women are not simply considered different from one another, as we speak of people differing in eye color, movie tastes or preferences for ice cream. In every domain of life, men are considered the normal human being, and women are 'ab-normal,' deficient because they are different from men."[52] Women *are* different from men. How can we be the same? I whole-heartedly support the idea of women's difference from men. I am grateful for the inspiration I have attained from my very experiences of being a woman. I do not find much in the self-aggrandizing literature of men throughout history that parallels the most important aspects of my experiences.

I do not adhere to a definition of equal that requires some feigned sameness in order to be applied. Sameness is extremely illusive and difficult to achieve. Sameness cannot be sustained with regard to any two people for more than an instant in the course of a single day – let alone in the course of a whole lifetime. While I support the notion of distinctions between women and men unequivocally, and believe those distinctions are worth celebrating – especially for women, who have been compared to and contrasted with men for too much of our life in civilization – I am likewise unequivocal about the notion of egalitarian family.

All family members are equal as human beings. The *worth* of each member is essentially the same as any other. This basic equality is true irrespective of how families are constructed – on the pre-industrial extended model which includes members other than the primary conjugal pair, on the nuclear family model with the primary conjugal pair isolated from other members except for the occasional visits, or on the basis of the various blended family combinations now more plentiful in modern societies. Equality does not require anything and yet each person deserves it because he or she is a human being, created by Allah and given the gift of life with the divine spirit blown within. It means that the worth of every human being – no matter what the circumstances, capabilities, opportunities, motivations, or class, race, and ethnic origins – is equal in worth to every other human being. All human beings are potentially servants and agents of Allah.

However, at the level of function, moral agency, productivity, and responsibility, the disparity that occurs in the context of any collective of people and which obviously occurs in the context of family, however conceived, cannot be ignored. Nevertheless, functional disparity is not a precondition for, exception to, or exclusion from essential equality. The handicapped and mentally retarded member of a human family is as equal as the primary wage earner who is equal to the primary care-taker.

However, some family members contribute more than others to the well-being and mainstay of the very life of the family, albeit in different and yet indispensable ways. Do these contributions make them more equal than others? Does this give them authority over others, such that the others must become subservient to them? No. This is where the term egalitarian flexes its adaptability over the use of the term equal. Where equal is applied to the essential characteristic of being human, equity is applied to functional disparity, incongruence, or inconsistency. Egalitarian is the means by which both the inherent equality of human beings and the equity of responsibility toward other members in the family are reconciled.

Equity is applied to the values attributed to certain types of deeds or actions. The Qur'an describes how recompense should be given in accordance to what one performs. However, recognizing a disparity of deeds and actions for the survival and well-being of the family in the post-industrial era associates greater worth to greater earnings. How can a pop star who gyrates on stage, or a movie actor performing on the screen, be deemed more worthy than a woman in India whose husband and primary wage earner was killed or injured, and who must now carry bricks on her head for pennies a day to provide food and shelter for her entire family?

Systems of evaluations that determine worth according to paper or digital money, or according to what men do, operate on the same distorted scale. One basic flaw in these human worth evaluative scales, which have proven especially arbitrary and yet resilient, is that they require women to contribute in a manner just like men, or to be wealthy in order to merit worth. Hence the effect of global economies, constructed hand in hand with patriarchal privileges, especially victimizes women in families who must continue to fulfill the tasks of primary care-taker and housewife, while being expected to compete against men (who are excused from domestic responsibilities) in measuring his worth in the wage-earning "public" arena, since her family's survival needs her additional income.

While the single husbandless mother who stays at home is chastised for depleting public sources of welfare and social service funds, social service departments viciously attack the single working mother for *not* being at home with the children. It is a double bind that cannot be resolved unless we closely examine how we perceive family and motherhood, and how we determine equality and human worth.

An Islamic resolution to this faulty system of evaluation has already been presented in the Qur'anic scale of evaluation: "Whoever does good, whether male or female and is a believer" shall be rewarded (40:40). Here "good" is not defined, but within the larger context of the Qur'anic world-view and the goal of Islamic ethics, good helps in the development of the person toward *taqwa* and surrender to Allah. That becomes the ultimate basis for valuable consideration. It leads to greater flexibility in measuring the worth of fulfilling whatever tasks are necessary for family continuity instead of stigmatizing those tasks performed in the domestic sphere. On such a scale, we can rethink the value of the Indian woman carrying bricks relative to the gyrating performer – no matter how many people pay exorbitant ticket prices to see the performance. Although she is not *more* human than the performer, the essence and redemption of such an articulation of Islamic value systems acknowledge her contributions as greater in value toward the evolution of an Islamic social and moral order. Such an acknowledgment is not possible through patriarchal materialist systems of evaluation.

In the context of Muslim cultures, men at home with children, for whatever reason, are never taken as primary care-takers or nurturers. Generally this is on a short term or "assistant" basis, and implies that being care-taker or fulfilling these roles is unworthy. Yet the single female head of household is measured both on the scale of her care-taking role and her role in competition within the male dominant public wage-earning sphere, but *never* measured as the contributor of both, and consequently on the Qur'anic scale of good deeds is actually more valuable than anyone privileged to focus on either one or the other for achieving their best in either role. Only an egalitarian notion of family can remove the stigma granted to the domestic responsibility and construct systems to assure equitable measurement of fulfilling that responsibility by leveling the playing field for men and women as principal contributors in both the domestic and the public wage-earning spheres. The place to learn about the necessity of balancing these contributions is in the examples of our modern-day Hajars, the women who have had to do both, while having her role in one sphere make her role in the other sphere invisible or impossible – despite its dual contribution and fulfillment of necessity.

5 Public Ritual Leadership and Gender Inclusiveness

"As Muslims we know the word 'Islam' is the most important part of how we understand who we are. A Muslim or Muslimah is one who surrenders him/herself to Allah. We often translate this word as 'one who submits'; however, the concept is proactive, spiritually ripe and dynamic, and might be better translated as 'engaged surrender.'

"Engaged surrender involves an active consciousness in participation in our social lives, family lives, community lives, economic lives, and political lives, by the heart which is always open to the will of Allah, and which always gives precedent to Allah's will. The concept we have been inclined towards – submission – sometimes gives the idea that there is no will. But the one who willfully submits to the will of Allah is engaged in surrender.

"I will talk about this from a woman's perspective, starting with an important part of many women's lives: giving birth. A woman carries her child under her heart for nine months. What she eats the child eats. As she cares for her health, she cares for the child's health. As she breathes fresh air, she breathes in for the nourishment of the child. As she takes care of her spiritual and emotional states of mind, she cares for the child's well-being. She takes care of all the child's needs. She carries that child for nine months and this is an act of surrender. She is following the will of Allah.

"This is a marvelous example of engaged surrender. The mother cannot take a day's rest. She cannot lay the child down beside her on the bed and say, 'Just for today, I think I will not be pregnant.' But, even more importantly, after the nine months is over, she may not hold onto to that child. She must surrender the child and give in to Allah's will. For, just as Allah commanded her to hold on to that child for nine long months, so must she engage in the act of surrender when it is time to bring the child forth.

"She can no longer hold onto it. If she continues to, it will mean death for her and for the child. So, she will engage in surrender. Each contraction has a duty. As the stomach pulls tight, the cervix opens so that the child might be brought forth into the world. If she resists the contraction, not only will it be uncomfortable for her, it will also curtail the natural motion of the child's gift of life. So she must engage in surrender in the act of labor. She must focus and not be distracted. With her body engaged with the task at hand, her heart and mind must consciously think of Allah in some form of *dhikr*.[1] She must surrender her body into the natural act of the contraction in such a way that the child might be brought into the world without discomfort.

"This image of a mother carrying her child under her heart, then bringing that child forward consciously as she participates in labor, is not only a reflection of engaged surrender, it is also not unlike Allah Him/Her/It Self, who describes Himself before every *surah*[2] (save one) as *al-Rahman, al-Rahim*.[3]

"He is *Rahmah*. He is Mercy. He is the Ultimate mercy. Both His names of mercy, *rahman* and *rahim*, come from the same root word as *rahm*: the womb. Allah thus engages us continually to understand the nature of our surrender. Just as He draws us forth from His spirit, so will he push us out into the world. There is a time when Allah's *rubbubiyyah*, His nurturance and love, will push us out into the world. There is also a time when Allah's *rubbubiyyah* will draw us close (to Him). The best articulation of this image that we have (in this world) is the experience of a woman who carries a child under her heart for nine months and then, must let that child go.

"In Surah Inshirah (chapter 94) Allah says: 'Have We not opened up your heart and lifted / removed from you the burden which weighed so heavily on your back. And raised you high in dignity. And behold with every hardship comes ease. Indeed with every hardship comes ease. Hence, when you are freed from your distress; Remain steadfast and unto your Sustaining Lord turn with love.' Allah gives us the mother in pregnancy and childbirth as a living picture of this idea of engaged surrender.

"We should know that Allah never repeats something for mere redundancy, but to make a point. 'Indeed with every hardship comes ease' is part of the engaged act of surrender that is everyday life. Sometimes there is difficulty and sometimes there is ease. As long as we are on the earth, we will experience difficulty and ease and hence the necessity of engaged surrender. Allah has guaranteed that our lives will be engaged with difficulty and with ease at all times. The nature of one who is truly Muslim is that he/she is constantly engaged in surrender, no matter whether it is difficult or easy.

"This surah also reminds us not to become complacent when things become easy. We should always be conscious, engaged, and we should always keep our hearts open to the surrender to Allah. So that the act of engaged surrender becomes part of our everyday lives, and so that we never take for granted that the ease will go on and on. If we are successful in our businesses, in our struggles against apartheid, etc., it does not mean the battle is over. The battle forever wages on.

"*Marriage:* Marriage is an important part of a Muslim's life. The Prophet (saw) said, 'Marriage is half of faith.' Sometimes we misunderstand this. We think that, if we get married, we don't have to do anything else. But if marriage is half of faith, then marriage is half of what we need to struggle with to engage ourselves in surrender before Allah. When the difficulty is over, we should still be striving. We still strive because our Lord is the goal, as Surah Inshirah says, 'When you are freed [from distress,] remain steadfast, and unto your Sustainer turn in love.' As long as we are human beings, we are always in the struggle to attain some level of understanding and love of the Divine. It is an ongoing process because Allah is our goal, and we can never be finished with our surrender and our engagement.

"Engaged surrender goes on at all times, at all places and for all circumstances. So we should think of our marriages and family lives as part of engaged surrender. We should not perceive of the situation in such a way that when the *nikah*[4] is over, then that part of our lives is over. We should not think that once we sign the marriage contract we can now put all of our attention and energy into our jobs, or into our business and political affairs. Instead, we should look at our family lives as half of our engaged surrender for the sake of completing our *din*[5] on earth.

"Your spouse – your wife or husband – is a new person every day. You should take the time to get to know that person – every day. That is part of engaged surrender. If she or he changes every day, you must engage anew in knowing him or her. It takes a certain kind of consciousness to treat him or her with respect. Sometimes, we think, we already know what she or he is going to say, so we do not listen. Consequently, we do not hear.

"Part of the engaged surrender of marriage is that we must come to our spouse every day as if they are who they truly are – a new person every day. They have not attained their full Islam, they are also engaged in surrender and we must respond to them as if they were. We must not assume they are today the same as they will be tomorrow, because Allah has also challenged and tested them, in the name of Islam, to engage in surrender.

"Perhaps they have been more successful with some aspects of it today than they will be tomorrow. So part of the engaged surrender in marriage, part of fulfilling half of the *din* in Islam, is that we come to that relationship every day, with engaged surrender: with our minds intact and our hearts open. Our minds will engage in accepting that person anew, in respecting that person and honoring that change. Our hearts will open up to loving that person and will surrender and give that person the love and care that is due.

"Allah also says in the Qur'an, 'And among His signs is that He has created from your own selves mates. And He has made between the two of you love and mercy' (30:21). There's that *rahmah* again. *Rahmah* is supposed to be one of the characteristics of how we engage in surrender in our marital lives. We should not take the other person for granted. We should always extend loving care and mercy to him or her.

"Remember the image of the mother – love is both holding and letting go. I must not tell another person how to coordinate his or her life. I, being just another human being, must allow that person to experience life. I must let that person go, and sometimes he or she may fall. This is also what I have to do with my children. I cannot live their lives for them. I must teach them, but I must let them go so that they can also experience engaged surrender.

"We must never assume that marriage gives us the right to dictate the life of another person. It is half of *din*, half of what we have to engage in consciously, as Muslims, to surrender to the will of Allah. It requires more than a few quick commands at the beginning and end of each day. It requires listening and hearing, respecting and honoring, loving and caring. It requires us to be Muslim.

"The idea that we must accept another person unconditionally does not mean we will not make mistakes. Surely, we make mistakes each day, and we ask Allah for forgiveness. And He has guaranteed He has the capacity to forgive. Likewise, others in the path of their own engaged surrender might make errors. If we open our hearts as part of our engaged surrender, as part of our Islam, we will have the capacity to respect and acknowledge that perhaps they have erred, and tomorrow may be able to correct that error. Then again, perhaps I have erred in my judgment and tomorrow I can correct my error.

"So the perspective we have on marriage should be one of engaged surrender. And we should come forward with the consciousness and surrender in our hearts. At the end of the day there is a possibility that this task will be a successful completion of what we know as our Islam.

"I stand before you to remind you and to remind myself that the task of a Muslim is to continually engage in surrender. Sometimes we forget this task. Should we ever forget that we must consciously be engaged in surrender, surely Allah never forgets. He is always available for us, always accepts our *du'a*,[6] and always accepts our effort to engage ourselves in surrender to Him.

"Amin."

These words were given one dreary Friday in August 1994, in response to an invitation to address Muslims gathered for the *jumu'ah* prayer at the Claremont Main Road Mosque, in Cape Town, South Africa.[7] I gave this address as a *khutbah*. In the mosque, some who attended the prayer received and appreciated these words even as they did not escape the intellectual place of gender discourse and the personal politics of power. I submit them here in order to subject them and their context to rigorous analysis for social transformation in the arena of Islamic worship. These words flowed from the center of my innermost yearning for meaning as a woman in Islam. After they were brought forth in full voice in the public domain, the mark of their stature and significance has not been on the basis of their actual substance and particular voice. Condemnation or encouragement was mainly built upon the circumstances in which they were uttered. These circumstances intensely prejudiced the discussions that followed the event for nearly two years. The consequent discussions shifted the focus away from these words as a meaningful form of expression for understanding Islamic identity and attention was given only on the time and place of their utterance. I will bring the discussion back full circle to the words themselves after entering the intellectual rigors of discourse about gender hegemony to analyze them and the circumstance of their utterance for a more comprehensive perspective on spiritual transformation in the context of Islam and modernity. I will not attempt to avoid the multiplicity of dimensions in the gender *jihad* but I will reprioritize those dimensions especially to remove the substance of the female voice and experience from the periphery. For the actual words of this *khutbah*, before what is mostly or exclusively a male collective Friday prayer, have not been given priority in subsequent discussions. My analysis of their substantive importance will follow the narrative leading up to the event, which will be rendered here "the Claremont Main Road mosque event" or simply the "mosque event." To fully remove the displacement imposed on the most significant part of my personal contribution to this act of gender transformation, I first step forward from the place where I was rendered *khatibah,* with multiple aspects of my self sometimes in place and sometimes displaced. In this chapter, I will also clarify the interface and complexities between subversive coincidence and purpose.

There are three possible lines of discourse here, each representing different points of interest in the event. One line of discourse is the content of the *khutbah* itself, which had not previously been subjected to considerable analysis. Another point of interest or line of discourse – the one that has been analyzed most fervently after the event – is to what extent can a woman perform the role of *khatibah?* This line of discourse was always taken up within the context of pre-existing expectations, either for or against the actions of that day. All previous discussions have failed to give full detailed clarity about the circumstance of my presence as *khatibah.* Since I did not participate or contribute to any of the public discussions, my contribution here corrects my absence. The significance of both these discursive lines to the greater gender *jihad* and the struggle for justice in Islam is in the possible final line of discourse, the one I take up here. In the confluence between the previous two lines of discourse – content and context – the public focus on the latter makes my reflections here imperative for a full discourse. It is this comprehensive look at the utterance and nuances of meaning in the *khutbah* that has remained the most hidden aspect, not only of a single story about my participation in the event and the role I was intended to play, but also about gender, Islam, and ritual worship in these times of change and transformation.

A Visit to South Africa

I was initially invited to South Africa to participate in the conference "Islam and Civil Society in South Africa" organized by U.N.I.S.A., the University of South Africa in Pretoria, the location for the conference, and by the United States Institute of Peace. As one of the earlier global gatherings to address progressive Islamic discourse and the notion of civil society, the Conference at U.N.I.S.A. was significant. However, initial plans excluded any consideration of gender and Muslim civil society. It was tagged on as an afterthought. Men as males and humans are allocated space in civil society, through citizenship and civil rights. Men are also the primary discussants on the meanings of citizenship, civil society, and human rights.[8] In many conferences since this one, a single panel is dedicated to women or gender issues. Sometimes, such panels represent mere window dressing, allowing women to be presenters whether or not they contribute significantly to the overall objectives of the conference. Although gender needs to be integrated into progressive and pluralist global discourse, often it still stands uncritically marginalized. No significant attempts have been made to discover a mechanism for the integration of women's participation and of gender to progressive Islamic discourse. When certain voices within South Africa contested this omission and expressed a need to fill the gender gap, the women's panel was added to the program. My name was suggested.

After I accepted the invitation to participate in the conference, the Islamic *Da'wah* Movement (I.D.M.) invited me to undertake a two-week lecture tour throughout South Africa and Namibia. Stops along the tour were organized in accordance with the significance of the *da'wah* movement in modern Southern Africa. *Da'wah* means "call to Islam." It includes both intra-Islamic and extra-Islamic dimensions. The intra-Islamic dimension of *da'wah* calls Muslims to renew their faith. The extra-Islamic dimension, in southern Africa, is a call to non-Muslims, especially Black Africans, to embrace Islam. A similar *da'wah* movement in the U.S.A. between 1930 and the present successfully spread Islam and increased the number of Muslims and Muslim institutions. South Africa and the U.S.A. have comparable histories of extreme forms of racial discrimination. The religion of Islam has attracted many Black followers in part because it is seen as a direct response against racial discrimination. I am a product of the Islamic *da'wah* movement in the U.S.A. The call to Islam has influenced many African-Americans in ways integral to our empowerment, self-awareness, identity reformation, and spiritual wholeness. Islam is the fastest growing religion in both North America and sub-Sahara Africa.

As a Black woman, my self-selection of Islam is not only reflected in my career as an academic – a professor of Islamic studies – but also in my choice of traditional Islamic dress. Both of these were strategically significant to my contribution to the I.D.M. program. Indeed, I.D.M. had previously extended an invitation for me to come to South Africa indicating confidence that I was competent to serve in the tasks set before me.[9] The main thrust of those tasks was reflecting a certain image of Islam as an African-American woman who experienced Islam as a source of gender and racial integrity. Therefore race, gender, or both were often of consequence to the activities selected for my visit, including the people I would meet and the places where I would deliver public lectures. I was particularly expected to address matters of gender, which is the heart of my research and the area in which I have made my greatest personal contribution to modern Islamic discourse. I would make appearances or attend meetings among students, in women's groups, or at Islamic educational institutions. I also was fortunate to meet with other young people from the Muslim Youth Movement (M.Y.M.) and the M.Y.M. Gender Desk, organizations set up to address certain political, socio-economic, religious, and gender dimensions of Islamic activism in South Africa.

When I landed in Johannesburg, I was told that my arrival had been expected for the previous day. Thus, with no time to rest from the journey, I attended a M.Y.M. Gender Desk workshop where I first met Shamima Shaykh (d. 1998).[10] That particular workshop was critically reflecting on the interface between Muslim Personal Law and the New South African Constitution. I was pleasantly engaged by some very intense and bright young minds. I came away with the impression of South African Muslims as both intelligent and forward moving. I responded to their questions and comments without feeling the need to mince my words in order to placate hesitancy and tenuousness over pluralist challenges.

After the meeting, Shamima and I went to a mosque for prayer. A young woman, who had never entered a mosque before, accompanied us. Despite the challenging posture of the young Muslims I had just met, other South African Muslim factions remain quite conservative. There is a great deal of diversity of expression among South African Muslims. Three hundred years after the arrival of Islam, some had come to the edge of radical consideration and others lingered in narrow conservative constraints of neo-traditionalism. At dinner, I met Na'eem Jeenah, then editor of a radical Muslim Newspaper, *The Call*, and Shamima's husband. We discussed many issues of Islamic thought and about the Islamic movement in the New South Africa. I realized that South Africa was an eruption of dynamic energy focused both within the Muslim communities to reinvigorate the faith, as well as toward the larger South African context of new pluralism and democracy under the leadership of Nelson Mandela.[11]

The conference was the major activity in the early part of my visit. During it, I learned a great deal about South Africa's Islamic history and about the importance of the current time marking the successful movement to eradicate apartheid. Muslims had not only been direct and significant contributors to that movement; they were also directly affected by it in developing their articulations of the Islamic experience. I met two presenters in the conference considered the most progressive South African Muslim thinkers, Farid Esack and Ebrahim Moosa. During the conference banquet, I also met Rashied Omar, *imam* of the Claremont Main Road mosque.[12]

What interested me most about South African discourse at the time was the deliberate inclusion of gender equality as an aspect of Islamic social justice. Audiences asked about the idea of woman as *imamah* and *khatibah* on several occasions during my tour. This was the first time I had ever given this matter consideration. I admit a naive excitement about the idea although I had given little or no strategic thought to its impact or rationale. Many of my own rigid parameters were broadened with my encounter of South African Muslims in the Johannesburg–Pretoria area. At the end of the conference, I even exchanged embraces with several of these brothers.

After the excitement of the people and events in Pretoria and Johannesburg, I made my way to Durban. Dr. Ebrahim Dada, the director of the I.D.M., collected me at the airport. He seemed more reticent than I had remembered him from a visit to Malaysia a few years previously. As we toured the I.D.M. office, he was clear about the conservative nature of Islam and Muslims in Durban. I took this to mean that I was also expected to be more conservative in my presentations and responses. Changing Muslim minds is a formidable task. I was whisked off that night for a visit to a Muslim school for the blind in Pietermaritzburg. My hostess had two visually impaired children and the youngest one was among students who recited aloud from the Braille Qur'an. I was deeply moved by his recitation and by the struggles of this family and community in creating a space inclusive of those with physical challenges. I remember reaching over to touch his mother's hand and to express my awe at the struggles with Islam in such various forms: children and adults, women and men, the blind and the seeing, and other handicaps and orientations – all part of the path to surrender.

After I returned to Durban, I delivered several large public lectures. These were interspersed between visits to a local university, Muslim women's luncheons and dinners, and a visit to an assembly at a large Muslim private school. I was beginning to feel overwhelmed by this grueling schedule with sometimes three events in one day, and guarded about the expectation to address such diverse audiences in a manner appropriate to each. Sometimes I felt successful. After one lecture, a young woman came up to me with several others to offer personal greetings. I admired a ring she was wearing; she took it off and, despite my protest, insisted that I have it. I was beset by the graciousness of such people: strangers touched by the simple reminder of struggling to be Muslim and female. In time, however, I felt inadequate to the daunting tasks. On my last evening in Durban, I was in tears as Dr. Dada returned me to the hotel. Addressing the public need is no easy matter. I needed spaces for quiet reflection to balance my inner equilibrium in the face of such diverse expectations and so many outer duties.

The next day I was given just the inspiration I needed to get reinvigorated: a trip to the KwaNobuhle, a Black township in the town of Uitenhage, about thirty-five miles from the coastal city Port Elizabeth. The source of that inspiration was my first opportunity to be in the company of all Black South African Muslims, many of whom were members of M.Y.M. According to the South African apartheid system of racial division into four distinct racial stratifications, I would have been placed amongst the "coloreds." Like most descendents of African slaves, I am now obviously mixed with European and Native American blood. Nevertheless, American categories of racial stratification discontinued its distinctions between colored and Black at the end of slavery; we are all identified as Black. My historical identity felt great affinity with Black South Africans and I surrendered my anxieties into their soulful embrace at this leg of the tour. I not only had a day free to wander through the township, which felt like the comfort of my childhood home in a segregated community, but also participated effortlessly in their program at a small mosque with members of the KwaNobuhle community. This program included children reciting the Qur'an or reading poetry. Following the final part of that program, singing the new South African national anthem, "Nkosi Sikele iAfrica," all members of the congregations embraced each other across age and gender lines with nurturance and affection. That was the spirit of community inclusiveness and compassion that I enjoyed the night before I arrived in Cape Town.[13]

When the sun rose that Friday morning, I was refreshed by my trip in KwaNobuhle and proceeded on to Cape Town. When I arrived, I was presented with the itinerary for the next week but it did not include any information about the day's most historically significant event. I was told I would be briefed later on one additional aspect of the itinerary. I had no knowledge about the event. Before I had arrived in Cape Town, however, flyers had already been circulated, announcing that I would deliver the pre-*khutbah* talk at the obligatory *jumu'ah*, collective prayer, at the Claremont Main Road mosque. I was only informed forty-five minutes before the actual time for prayer about my involvement in it. My excitement about this opportunity rose extremely, although I was left with little time to prepare my remarks.

When I arrived at the mosque the air was thick with excitement. People crowded around the mosque entrance. Women came down from their previously assigned section upstairs and were accommodated in a section next to the men on the main mosque level. The media were obvious by their large television cameras. I made my way through this large number of people and eventually reached the place where I would deliver the *khutbah*: at the front of the congregation.

The Claremont Main Road Mosque Event with Gender as a Category of Discourse

This section begins with an analysis to address the event at the Claremont Main Road Mosque, in Cape Town, South Africa, August 1994. It reflects on the simultaneously groundbreaking nature and reinscription of gender asymmetry. I offer this analysis after having recounted my personal experiences in the previous section in order to draw attention to some of the shortcomings I observed and to utilize its benefits for the promotion of women as leaders in Islamic public ritual. As an explicit articulation for female inclusiveness, I challenge the long-standing historical precedent of male exclusivity in this role. The foundational idea promoted here is the construction of an Islamic ethical rationale for reciprocal relations between women and men in all aspects of society: familial, political, and spiritual functions, roles, and contexts. For me, this reciprocal construct is a reflection of *tawhid*, the unicity of Allah, the ultimate sacred postulate of Islam.[14]

What I have called the *tawhidic* paradigm constructs a metaphysical triangle embraced by a globe within which the relationship between each of three elements are equally essential: Allah, creator of all; one human being (in this case, we will say female); and another human being (in this case, we will say male). Because Allah is creator, however, and not a thing, the function of Allah in this triad is as the tension that holds the other two on a horizontal line of constant equality. Both are of equal significance and neither can be above the other because the divine function establishes their reciprocal relationship. If human beings really are horizontally equal, independent, and mutually co-dependent, each has the same potential for performing any social, religious, political, or economic task. The cultural and historical precedent of exclusive male leadership in the role of religious ritual is not a requirement. Although it has served as a convenience which later became legally inscribed, it was merely customary and should not be prescribed as a religious mandate. Women's *tawhidic* humanity allows them to function in all roles for which they develop the prerequisite qualifications.

Following the "Cape Town Main Road event," discussions were rampant and feverish throughout South Africa. Indeed, some parties moved beyond discussion to violent protest. Eventually the discussions spread worldwide. Even as they reached the global level, I did not enter them. Various factions picked up on the news of the event and responded for or against it, sometimes with extreme intimidation. For example, members of the *majlis-ashura*, Consultative Counsel,[15] at one of my local mosques decided, "if that's what she think Islam is," I should be dismissed from my university position as professor of Islamic studies. No one from that mosque ever contacted me to discuss this matter, yet they collectively decided that they would attack the source of my livelihood as a single parent to four children. Of course they had no power over a secular university in U.S. academia, but the audacity that they even considered themselves able to hold such authority hints at the entrenched nature of patriarchy in Muslim community life and the viciousness with which they will try to sustain it.

I was not only intimidated by the fervent reaction to this event, I was also unprepared to respond and extremely confused about whether my participation in the event reflected mere personal aspirations or larger aspirations for gender inclusiveness. The negative responses included personal slights and direct insults from total strangers. I could not differentiate between whether they were offering their reflections as evidence against female ritual leadership or whether they were merely continuing the double standards about women's agency in Islam and modernity. Guarding the details of my participation reflected both my intimidation and my confusion. Although personal narrative and its critical analysis are indispensable to historical recounts,[16] I maintained my silence perhaps far too long.[17] I share the story here in order to link the personal specifically to the broader, strategic concerns over gender justice in Islam.

Since this event has already been a part of public discussions, especially in the time immediately following its occurrence, what I propose here centers attention less on the dialectics of that discourse, with its exclusive focus on form, and enters into a gender discourse particularly to clarify how the "personal is political." I construct significant and necessary analysis that previous discussions overlooked in reducing certain aspects of this event by giving others an opportunity to pretend they can read my personal aspirations[18] or to address the coincidental. From its very orchestration, I was always a significant part of these events, personally, although completely neglected from the planning discussions. This neglect reveals some ways the event fails as a completely successful challenge to gender hegemony in Islamic thought and practice, despite its best intentions. There is an important interface between the personal specifics and the public generalities. The strategic absence, utility, or tokenism of gender inclusiveness indicates how most progressive Islamic discourse still maintains and supports male privilege and gender hegemony.[19]

The year 1994 marked two important historical developments in South Africa: the end of a long and bloody struggle to eradicate apartheid and the presence of Islam for three hundred years. Some South African Muslims envisioned a corollary between these two to such an extent as to make explicit reconceptualization over notions of pluralism, equality, and liberation in South African Islam.[20] As a woman in Islam, an Islamic studies academic, a learner-scholar, and an activist for women's human dignity, I have struggled for gender inclusion and reform within the Islamic framework. The South African endeavors to include gender in the discourse over social and political justice were especially exhilarating. There were moments during my visit in South Africa when I felt like I had actually found a place where a woman could be truly honored in the fullness of her humanity.[21]

Throughout most of my travels in South Africa, I found that specific aspects – being African-American, a convert (or one in transition), being female, or being an Islamic academic – strategically converged in the public roles assigned to me in different configurations and degrees. Sometimes these intentions were overt on the part of the Islamic *Da'wah* Movement, and I was told directly what to talk about or how to address particular audiences. In addressing a student audience at a Muslim private school, for example, I was directed to emphasize the potential of diligent study as it could lead to success, such as that which I had achieved through my studies. I had a Ph.D. That I dressed traditionally and wore *hijab* also created specific symbolic legitimacy.[22] Later the organizers of the Claremont Main Road mosque event told me that it was of particular significance that I would participate as a *non*-South African. They intended to make a statement about gender inclusiveness, without exposing me individually to the anticipated backlash. While this intention was unsuccessful and I was bombarded for two years with negative backlash, it may partly explain why I was personally inconsequential in many significant ways to their planning. Ironically, who I am was meant to be coincidental. The results would have been different with a different female as the spotlight of their efforts. Organizers of various events where I was invited, whether consciously or unconsciously, randomly intended me directly to confront racism, gender hegemony, and patriarchy sometimes by *being who I am externally, and sometimes by symbolically erasing myself.* Yet these mixed intentions were never articulated to me for an opportunity to make critical analysis, especially with respect to their consequences, both potential and real.

The invitation for actually addressing the Friday prayer, for example, was so subtle and non-specific; I never had any indication that there could be consequences for me. I have a distinct vision of standing between dinner tables during the banquet following the conclusion of the conference at U.N.I.S.A. I was informally engaged in a conversation about some longstanding gender barriers. I do not remember all who were present during this discussion, except the *imam* of the mosque. Neither was I privy to the origins of the idea, which these discussants had thought out, including potential consequences and expectations. After my tacit approval, I was never again consulted about the full logistics of the plans, which were orchestrated with extensive details until forty-five minutes before the actual event. I confess that I accepted the generic idea of participating in challenging gender inequities with full volition. I also admit to a gross ignorance about the full circumstances of South African Muslim gender discourses, let alone to the particular plans that the men who had invited me had discussed at length in order to orchestrate the event. Besides writing a book on alternative gender-inclusive interpretation of the Qur'an and working with a women's organization, I had never directly confronted neo-traditionalists, conservatives, or extremists.

After the conference in Pretoria, my lecture tour continued and all my attention was focused on the events to which I was invited. Likewise I was often privileged to little detail or potential consequences for some of these. They were almost all familiar forms of invitation: meet with various members of Muslim organizations and present formal, semiformal, specific, and generic lectures to various audiences who had extended invitations or were invited to hear me speak.

When it became clear later that several others, brothers especially, had consulted with each other and continued developing the details of the Claremont Main Street mosque event, I realized how important it was that I should have been either consulted on some of those details or, at least, informed. Each discussion they had must have focused on certain expectations, whether directly discussed or indirectly implied. Not without great consequence was I excluded from this planning. Furthermore, had I been consulted the event might *never have taken place*. This is directly related to being a woman. After my tearful outburst in Durban, my menstrual cycle had begun. I was no longer participating in ritual prayer. The organizers did not know this. Yet it will have further consequences for those who thought it was inappropriate for a woman to be in the role of *khatibah*. I expose it here as evidence that even the most "progressive" Muslim male cannot accommodate the relationship between biology, the politics of ritual, and the legal stipulations given historically. They also indicate that the portrayal of public leadership is still exclusively built on the male norm.

Since it is almost certain that this information might have had some consequences on the planning of this event, it exemplifies the need for direct and explicit conversation between men and woman whenever a woman's participation is expected or taken for granted. The absence of this direct conversation is a major indication that the planners were thinking and acting like men in exclusion of women's full humanity, while yet pretending to employ a woman as an agent of gender transformation. They were thinking *for* the woman, rendering her a mere object of their privileged agency. How can a woman be a full and equal human being when the details of her public role are orchestrated without her consultation? This cannot deconstruct gender disparity. When she is secondary to discussions about her particular participation, her own agency is secondary.

From the very planning of this event, selective gender disparities were maintained. Since public announcements had already circulated which stated that I would deliver a pre-*khutbah* talk, why was I informed only forty-five minutes before the prayer? I had to use that small window of time to prepare my remarks for what was supposedly an extremely significant event. Although I was given information about the previous *khutbah* topic with the suggestion to continue my comments along the same theme, informing me at the last minute also indicates that very little value was attributed to the content of my actual *khutbah*. This event was about form. The substance of what I would say was unimportant to how these men saw gender reconstruction. Despite this, the actual content of my brief presentation, as offered above, remains an authentic gender-inclusive public address and the most significant one I delivered throughout the two-week tour, and perhaps ever since. Before I analyze the contents I want to designate a few other places where I felt blatant disregard of my personal contributions to these plans for eradicating gender disparity. I will examine other ways that gender has been decentralized or marginalized even in this most "progressive" consideration of Islam and modernity, beyond this event.

The Transgendered Embrace between Women and Men in Public

After the U.N.I.S.A. conference, Farid Esack asked me if I embraced men. I was surprised that a Muslim male had asked me this question, although the answer was "yes, as a matter of fact I do." Until then, I had only embraced women and non-Muslim males. There in a public setting, in the company of others, for one brief moment, I exchanged embraces with several of the non-*mahram*[23] Muslim males. I felt I was actually accepted as another equal human being. This had a profound symbolic affect on me and surrounded my hopes that somehow it might really be possible to transcend gender disparity within Islam. Now it is much more commonplace for Muslim women and men to embrace.

Muslim cultures have a long history of social embraces. However, except within the *mahram*, an embrace generally follows a same-sex restriction. When two women embrace, it is often close and more sensual. When two men embrace, it is often in camaraderie and affection, but distinctively marked by bravado. Although the embrace is but a mere etiquette not necessarily conveying any depth of feeling, sometimes eye contact is followed with a smile and the embrace is heightened with enthusiasm or lingered over with compassion and grace.

My first impulse was to consider any embrace *across* the gender divide in Islam as radical. Yet, over time, experience has shown me how even this seemingly radical symbol reinscribes gender asymmetry. Many Muslim men who embrace a non-*mahram* Muslim woman embrace her like they embrace each other: like men. If I embrace them like I do other women, with the soft lingering touch, it is too sensual, therefore latent with sexual undertones. It crosses arbitrary gender boundaries. For me to embrace men and be embraced by them, it is not permissible for me to be *so much a woman*. Again, the male is normative and an embrace between a non-*mahram* woman and man requires both *to embrace like men* if they are to be "*human*" in this exchange and avoid implications of intimacy.

Coincidently, since the time of this analysis, I have tried to create greater uniformity in my embrace, regardless of age, gender, or circumstance, except when it seems too much for the other, when I exercise greater restrictions. In addition, despite years of acculturation in my life as a Muslim woman, but especially in general Malaysian public etiquette, I offer my hand for a shake for all Muslim men that I meet, even if rejected.

The Mosque

In both South Africa and North America, the mosque reflects aspects of gender relations and conflict. As a symbol of Islamic heritage and tradition, a mosque is usually established and maintained by local members. It may include a community center where Islamic family activities, educational programs, lectures, meetings, and festivities take place, in addition to the space for ritual worship. Some mosques emphasize traditional Islamic architectural design and other esthetic features. Other mosques in Muslim minority communities are formed within existing building structures with some internal alternation. In both instances it becomes a space marked for Islamic activities and confirmation of Muslim identity.[24] The dominant attitude of the mosque is reflected in both its public demeanor and within the hegemony and authority maintained within it. It is not uncommon for stricter gender separation to exist within the mosque, especially here in the U.S.A. and other minority Muslim communities, than is ever sustained at any other place outside the mosque.

Within the sacred space of the mosque, gender disparity is almost always reflected, and sometimes a mosque seems to prove itself genuine by increasing these rituals of separation, as the young woman who joined Shamima and me at the mosque in Johannesburg had represented. This was the first time in all her twenty years that she had even entered a mosque. Some South African mosques do not permit women to enter, to accentuate that exclusive male privilege in this specially demarcated space and to leave exclusivity unchallenged. Meanwhile, other mosques in the U.S.A. and South Africa, like the small mosque in KwaNobuhle, are designed to encourage inclusiveness for every race, age, gender, class, or physical handicap served in the community. The issue of inclusiveness for the disabled is still grossly under-corresponded to in the vast majority of mosques the world over.

Flexibility in mosque design and usage reflects time and place while ensuring the longevity and advancement of Islam. This makes the mosque an important site to initiate change and mark transitions in the context of the Muslim community. In this respect, the Claremont Main Road mosque as the site for contestation and change is another marked feature of this event. Indeed, after this first *khutbah* by a woman, when the women who had previously prayed upstairs from the men came down to the main floor, they have not gone back up again.[25]

Despite many cultural, ideological, and logistical variants in the degree of separation between women and men in the mosque, there is nothing essentially Islamic about it. Gender separation is neither a matter of faith nor a principle of Islamic dogma and creed. It was never emphasized in the Qur'an, which instead recommends ways for women and men to observe modest limits while *in each other's presence*. The extent to which it has become important today is often more clearly demonstrated in the mosque than is ever observed by Muslim minorities in other pluralist circumstances in societies like the U.S.A. and South Africa. It is a wonder that those who demonstrate such strict gender separation in the mosque manage public streets, buildings, board meetings, informal gatherings, and the like throughout the rest of their daily business in North America and South Africa. Honestly speaking, I think it is a charade, a façade to feign "I am gender pious." Many of the same people who stress such separation will be profusely collegial around members of the opposite sex in non-Muslim public places, especially where wages are earned.

Gender separation in the mosque also reflects gender disparity through space and the opportunities that limit women's access to or participation in mosque activities and especially in decision-making. Likewise, if not complete exclusion, separation in congregational prayer usually relegates women to an inferior place, either *behind* the male prayer lines or invisible to them in the congregational setting. Yet during the *hajj*, pilgrimage, another primary ritual observation in Islam, women and men do not observe gender separation in prayer lines. While some gender discretion in prayer may have been the intention, hierarchy is what is exemplified when women pray in the rear or in a place invisible to the leader of the prayer. Some mosques overcome the hierarchy while maintaining the discretionary decorum of separation by forming equal prayer lines of women and men side by side. For example, at the mosque in Toledo, Ohio, women and men pray in separate sections but they are side by side. Furthermore, there are increasingly settings where intimate numbers of Muslims disregard the archaic gender separations, and pray in the Makkan style of prayer lines, with women and men forming single lines side by side. Some follow a female *imamah* should she be selected.

For the vast majority of Muslims who do not consider such gender inclusiveness permissible, their arguments are selectively grounded on firm religious rationale using only those *fiqh* opinions that support gender separation in ritual worship primarily as reflections of social and historical customs as they developed after the advent of Islam in seventh-century Arabia. There is no single Qur'anic passage to support these arguments and nothing but extensive misinterpretation of the *sunnah* by generalizing exclusive principles or minimizing explicit examples to the contrary. The evidence constructed to support gender separation, especially in ritual worship, is always and only a reflection of social customs and in many cases of social customs as they developed after the advent of Islam in seventh-century Arabia. Since such practices of gender disparity reflect social praxis, not theological rationale, then all legal codification of such rationales were built upon the status quo and can be reformed by the collective and conscientious alterations in the status quo.

Hijab: Women's Traditional Dress and Head Covering

Along with the other matters not discussed with the organizers of the Claremont event, I had no indication of their specific concerns at that time over Muslim women's dress and their decision for me to participate in this event. I am not altogether convinced, however, that my conservative style was inconsequential. In my general observations over the matter of dress and Muslim leadership, I note a certain modest formality symbolizes the seriousness of the ritual setting. In addition to this, Muslim women's dress, particularly the head covering, remains significant to the politics of gender *jihad*.[26] At the time of the Claremont Main Road event, I always observed the more traditional *hijab* in the public roles I played in the struggle for gender justice. I am certain this preference was of some facility to the organizers as well. However, while I recognize that some consider the *hijab* as a public declaration of identity and ideology, I do not consider it a religious obligation, nor ascribe to it any religious value per se. The paradox – that I had consistently worn *hijab* for over thirty years while not considering it obligatory – does not remove its appearance of conformity with the perspective of neo-traditionalists and conservative Muslims: it makes me *look* safe. It has been a double-edged aspect of my public role and representation that figures strategically in the debates over Islam and gender. My dress choice has radical, self-inscribed meaning – not apparent to an outside observer.[27] While it appears to confirm to the fixed and uniform position of a Muslim woman's persona, it also defies that position. Reinvesting new meaning into old symbols is a necessary part of Islamic progression. The articulation of the distinction between these two meanings of fixed uniformity and radical personal reinscription cannot be obvious by form alone. It can *only* be heard by the voice of the woman who wears it.

Khutbah, Pre-Khutbah, and Congregational Prayer

Muslims are obligated to pray five times every day. In addition, according to law and tradition, Muslim males are required to cease their worldly affairs and gather for the midday prayer in congregation once a week, on Friday, *yawm al-jum'ah*. This gathering, referred to as the *jumu'ah* prayer, has been attended by women throughout Muslim history, and they continue to attend, but their attendance is inconsistent, reflecting other aspects of community and mosque politics.

Irrespective of women's attendance in the mosque or the degrees of gender separation, a Muslim male has always been the public prayer leader, *imam*, and the one who delivers the obligatory *khutbah*, sermon that precedes the prayer when both women and men congregate. The single notable exception to this practice historically was when the Prophet Muhammad assigned Umm Waraqah as *imamah*, in her *dar*, community or household.[28]

Another issue about congregational prayer had been a matter of debate in South Africa for some time. Could the *khutbah* be delivered in local vernacular or must be it be delivered in Arabic? Some mosques had resolved this matter by dividing the two parts of the *khutbah* between local vernacular and Arabic. Some of the male leaders made a decision to rename the two parts, using "pre-*khutbah*" for the first part when delivered in local vernacular. Then the second part, when delivered in Arabic, was designated *khutbah*. In Claremont, depending on the Arabic capability of the particular *iman*, either both parts are in vernacular or the second part is in Arabic. However, this community never distinguished between the *khutbah* and a pre-*khutbah*. How then could they advertise that I would give the pre-*khutbah* talk?[29] It was another subversive strategy employed in progressing Islam and contributing to the gender *jihad*. Like the *hijab*, certain semblances reflecting the patriarchal conservative norm are maintained to allay traditional sensitivities, while attempting to challenge other aspects of the status quo.

While such a subversive strategy has efficacy in the evolutionary process of advocating and presenting change, it can also have negative results. First, this subversion resulted in the mosque reneging on its position that there should not be a pre-*khutbah* presentation followed by the *khutbah* itself. Secondly, the woman who delivered the address was not given the status of a *khatibah*. Instead, her *khutbah* was relegated to the status of lecture. Despite this tactic, many, including myself, would acknowledge my address as the *khutbah*.[30]

I intended to give the *khutbah* before the Friday congregational prayer – technicalities aside. I expected this invitation was intentional to break the gridlock of gender disparity in Islamic public ritual. It was part of my overall interest in breaking the gender disparity in mosque attendance, governance, and other public spaces, as well as in ritual, including congregational prayer itself with its history of nearly exclusive male leadership.

Substance in the Khutbah or Form of the Khatibah

The content of the presentation at the Claremont Main Road mosque is the only place to retrieve my full identity as a Muslim woman invited to symbolize the need for gender transformation in ritual leadership. Yet on my way to the *imam*'s office when the service was over, I asked Farid Esack what he thought of my presentation. He said, "Honestly, I didn't listen!" Some would later say this reflected his enthusiasm for this overt outward form of gender inclusion – even as it ameliorated the particularities of actual substance in the presentation. I felt displaced by this, but then worried that my desire was self-serving. On the one hand, I want to see leadership as service to the collective; on the other hand, I was troubled by this reduction. Does the leader have no individual qualities other than a formality of ritual, such that all it takes to deconstruct male hegemony is simply to input a female form, whether or not she makes any substantive contribution?[31] For a genuine female-inclusive reconstruction over the male hegemony in leadership, a woman must be present in both her particulars as a woman and her shared aspects with men as a Muslim person. Moreover, for a woman to contribute as a leader in the role of *khatibah*, she is required to present a substantive *khutbah*.

In contradistinction to this response, two women affirmed the particulars of the *khutbah* over the form. Sa'adiya Shaikh said, "It made me feel good to *be* a woman!" The other, my hostess Najma, who was, incidentally, seven or eight months' pregnant with her fourth child, commented, "I can be who I am. I don't have to be anyone else: I am a Muslim woman." Here, womanhood as uttered in the words of the *khutbah* and in the role of leader was stressed, not the coincidental form of her female body in the place heretofore exclusive to men as leaders.

What could cause such a divergent reading between a Muslim progressive male and two Muslim females except the distinction between focus on form and focus on substance? I applaud those South African male progressives who were bold enough to orchestrate such an event. Clearly there would have been no event without these brothers, because no woman had the authority to introduce a female into this male sacred space. Nevertheless, over time, I was disappointed by the emphasis on form.

In his 1997 book, *Qur'an, Liberation and Pluralism*, Esack refers to this as a revolutionary event in South Africa. I appear in his account as the form of a female who stood where male forms had previously been exclusively privileged. In reading his account I did not feel I was offered the privilege of being a full human being with any of my particulars as a woman with certain experiences intact. Some of the most momentous particulars can only be retrieved from my actual words, which his exhilaration over the "event" had eclipsed. However, two pages later, he shows he can listen when he gives a detailed account of another woman who shared her story in the form of a lecture after the *salah* at the Claremont Main Road mosque. Sitty Dhiffy, one of many monogamous wives, had contracted A.I.D.S. from her husband. Esack assessed the substance of her presentation as a "most moving initiative . . . Many of us wept openly, for Sitty, for our own ignorance, for the many Muslims who cling to their prejudices and yearning for control, for those who are terrified of shedding their negative images of the Other, images that succeed not only in blocking out the Other but also of imprisoning the self."[32]

In this sensitive and detailed account, Sitty Dhiffy appears as a whole person – female in form, with substance and content.[33] Her particularities are only known by the voice in which she renders them to public space. No attempt was made to have these removed, for they are the basis for her specific presence. Not only is she both a woman, she is also the victim for being a woman: having contracted this disease by submitting to an unfaithful husband. Although she remained a victim who cannot be ameliorated by our platitudes, her wholeness as a female Muslim was not left in the shadows or margin. She gives a genuine reflection, claims a place – even if only to generously facilitate our enlightenment about her plight. Her speech does not call to radical change or reform of gender disparity and the problems of male control over sexuality. The public response is to show proper sympathy toward her plight, not to make any changes in her marginal "place" among us as a living Other.[34]

Here, platitudes serve as metaphors against true engagement. As such, the genuine experience of the *other* is so particular it remains outside the norm. The true embrace of women's marginality can only be within the shadows of the margin itself. When women's stories are brought into the center, they do not recast the center story. There is no substantive change, since the marginality in which women live is still unreformed. This position of women's lives *in the margins* must be redeemed from where they continue to experience it. No mere performances in the center will reconstruct status quo. Therefore the task is not so much for women to claim that center space as legitimate for female agency. Instead, the whole of the community must enter into the margins with women to affirm the place where women's lives are experienced. It is the only way to create alternative placements as central and to wrench the meaning of center from its longevity as the male experience of privilege and hegemony. Such a privilege has presumed that the center of attention must continue to be focused in one fixed place, which has coincidently been defined by one characteristic: masculinity.

To symbolize this transformation, again consider St. Augustine's metaphor with the idea of God as a circle, the center of which is *everywhere*, the circumference of which is *nowhere*.[35] In addition to an unspecified boundary or circumference, the center is at *every* place that a human being exists. For each articulation that captures the essence of Islam is the center point. The center is not a fixed place. The margin story may be the center. Women's stories and experiences have been cast to the side by male definitions of public space. Women most often speak from that place of patriarchal dislocation; the tale is a vital and real articulation in the reality of human meaning and the essence of Islam. We must shift our focus to allow multiple locations of life in service to plurality as legitimate and authoritative without rendering one location as final and ultimate. Just as the mind shifts to the spot of the story that encapsulates the divine center, it shifts to allow new realities continuously. That shift is crucial to the process of freedom and gender.

Esack's active listening and response to the story recounted by Sitty Dhiffy testifies to this analysis. In his two accounts, one voice has substance and the other is insignificant and therefore still silent. My participation at the Claremont Main Road mosque event was only a formal act, not a substantive one. To persist with these inconsistencies will not remove gender disparity, or shift appropriate attention on the marginality of women's lives. I once thought my vision too personal. However, the experience of leading prayer in New York in 2005 has confirmed that it did not matter what I said.[36] I take a stand regarding how heavily this weighs against gender and justice. My presentation fell along the same lines of the historical silencing of female voices, and invisibility of their particular experiences and contributions. This marginalization of the full spectrum of female experience still persists among some progressive thinkers who never focus on the margin experiences. Any reality away from the center stage of Islamic public discourse and praxis are measured according to an exclusive male standard of evaluation.

Since this event, the substantive content of my presentation was circulated internationally and received some consideration (although not as much consideration as the form where these words were delivered!). Other male Muslim progressives, intellectuals, and activists confirmed that what I said was appropriate in Islam.[37] By accepting the content, they indicate how a woman can make legitimate contributions in Islamic public discourse. Their acceptance is housed in the language of "appropriate." But separating that language act from the time and place of its deliverance also falls short in fully considering whether or not the place and time in which it was presented was appropriate. Thus the discrepancy between the oversight of some South African progressive males over the content to focus only on form is still inverted, fragmented, and irreconcilable when the contents are analyzed outside of its contextual boarders. Although a woman may have something of substance to say, she must still face limitations with regard to the circumstances under which she says it. For complete gender equality, this dichotomy between form and substance must be bridged.

The Content of This Sermon

Perhaps having been informed that I would stand as *khatibah* only forty-five minutes before the *jumu'ah* service is evidence that what I would say was of little consequence. Nevertheless, had I known about the event with sufficient time to haggle over what I would say, I do not think I could have come up with anything better. I consider what I said to be my best presentation, not only in South Africa during those hectic two weeks, but also in terms of many other public forums since then. The actual substance of the talk resulted from primal inspiration, not only from a source beyond my own conscious construction, but also from a place where I feel intuitively the greatest confidence through a unique, female place of experience: Islam as engaged surrender from the perspective of being female, mother, and wife.

The text of the sermon uses this female, particular reality as public discourse to construct and configure the normative articulation of what "Islam" means. Here, experiences particular to a female define and determine the generic. Here, a woman's particular reality is normative for Muslim identity. If this articulation seems unusual for public discourse, then it reflects the normative status of the Muslim male to define for all others, male and female, what it means to be *human*. Hence, Islamic public discourse has always focused on the male experience and rendered that experience not only appropriate for men in public spaces, but also for women.[38]

The Islamic tradition has the habit of sustaining the normative Muslim as a male. This is the challenge we need to address in our struggles to break through gender barriers. If women only demonstrate and exemplify their ability to be "like men," or to be victims of patriarchy, then nothing is learned from them over and above men in the pulpits, at the head of the line, as well as in the parliament and bedrooms. If the only women permitted to be "leaders" are those who cease to be overly identified with the experiences of the majority of Muslim women, the *ummah* gains nothing. The voice of a woman must also include something about herself, particularly as a woman, and this must then be incorporated into what it means to be human in the world. If she only offers herself in the public role like a man, what is the advantage? A single model of normative Islamic leadership persists, whether in male or female form. This single model of what it means to be human has consequences within ambiguities of the lives of Muslims today. When the boundaries of identity are no longer so clear, we can benefit from new stories and new centers of attention actually located in the margins.

Women do not have to act just like men in order to be leaders. Martha Minnow[39] seems to suggest that the right to be one's own particular and unique identity while sharing a group identity must not become a contradiction. One neither loses individuality by identifying with aspects of group membership, nor does one lose group affiliation by distinguishing oneself from the group. Identity is not so fragmented or singular. Identity is a composite of all its fragmented parts. As the *khatibah,* I am not either a leader or a woman – I am both a leader *and* a woman. "If I should be for myself as a unique and separate person, I should also be for myself as a member of groups."⁴⁰ The struggle to eradicate the formality of gender disparity in Islamic public ritual leadership in this event in South Africa was orchestrated with some cost to my womanhood. I am *not* more human because I am like a man. I am woman; I am human and my humanity is female. I accepted the opportunity to give the *khutbah* at the Claremont Main Road mosque to deconstruct gender hegemony both in form and in substance.

I felt qualified to serve as *khatibah,* because in addition to being a woman, my qualifications also include study and training in Islam as well as knowledge of and dedication to Islam. Despite limited precedent, Muslim women can enhance public discourse by offering what is peculiar to them as women as well as what is similar between them and men. Although both these aspects reflect woman as *khalifah*, full moral agent, women's public roles in this enhancement have not received its full equality through out Islamic history. Instead, the major canon of Islamic public discourse and ethical articulation makes the male experience and articulation the norm and the standard measurement for what it means to be human in the public arena. That which is explicit to being woman has been prohibited from public space and discourse.

Many modern efforts at gender reform allow women to enter the public space only in the secular realm, or only through the non-presence of their sexuality in the context of Islamic ritual, i.e. if they display what men have determined is worthy of precedent.⁴¹ While honoring precedent is important in Islam, women must also contribute not only what historical precedent has lacked but what has also been neglected or silenced in public space. The insights drawn particularly from women's experiences – as women in Islam – must be rendered legitimate contributions to *general public discourse*. In modernity, this will expand the breath of meaning for Muslim identity and enhance the perspectives of the entire community.

It is in this way that some progressives and conservatives actually embrace the same paradigm: to be fully human, a moral agent, and a public leader, one must be male. For the conservatives this means a woman is allowed to maintain her womanhood, as long as she does not draw attention to her marginality by rendering it fully human. For the progressive this means a woman is fully human and can therefore act in roles heretofore exclusive to men, as long as she is not too much woman. Given such a choice, I reject both limitations. I am fully human; I am fully woman. If gender bias in Islamic practices is ever to be genuinely removed, then we women need to articulate from the center of the marginality of our lives. The stage needs to be reset and women's stories need to become models for the overarching process of Islam as engaged surrender, no matter where it occurs.

Until this event, I had maintained a dichotomy, a conflict between some of my thoughts and my actions. This dichotomy played itself out in my role in this event. It also stuck a blow to a survival tactic in Islamic gender battles, where prudence is demanded in diverse ways despite leading to misinterpretations and misapplications of symbols. This can have dangerous consequences when given a proposal to directly confront gender inequality in a role even I had not dared to confront. When I was introduced to this cluster of radical Muslims in South Africa, I revealed more about my intimate reflections on various issues than I had ever done in public. After years of silent deliberation, this event and all its aftermath also inspired me toward greater fervor and a more boldfaced public engagement to break the gridlock of gender hegemony once and for all.

Still, despite some radical challenges presented in this event, genuine equality and parity were missing at other levels. Just because female and male bodies are in the same formal role does not always mean that equality has been achieved; sometimes it is mere form. To move beyond form, there must also be celebration of what is peculiar to women in leadership over men and women, just as there must be celebration of what is peculiar to men in leadership over men and women. Otherwise, some women will come to the front only to reproduce the priority of the male norm, or act androgynous.

Does the female leader, and worshipper, have to ameliorate all that is peculiar to her as a woman in the roles heretofore exclusive to men? Do men ameliorate their masculinity when fulfilling the role of leader? Is pluralism the melting in an illusive pot that transcends diversity in order to become an anomaly called human? How do we maintain all our particularities while not being limited to or judged exclusively by them? While I think we can transcend the politics and inequities of particularity, I do not think we can transcend the particulars – nor do I not want to. As Minnow suggests above, members of a distinct group do not lose their right to their own particular and unique identity. Indeed, sharing in a variety of group identities should not present contradictions. An individual is neither fully distinguished from nor exclusively identical with his or her various group affiliations. There are many crossroads between group and individual affiliations. Nor can one's unique self-identity be restricted to exclusive membership in any one group over another. In particular, I must claim myself as woman in public and private. I am *both* individual *and* woman, not *either* individual *or* woman. Only with all aspects of myself intact may I be the full *khalifah* Allah intended for all humanity.

Although public ritual leadership in Islam still remains nearly exclusively male, from an ethical standpoint it should not continue that way. Maybe we cannot rewrite the history of women's experience as part of female particularities because of the legacy of silence and exclusion. Therefore we cannot look only to history for precedent, to provide us with historical examples of women as leaders. Their lives were too private. We can draw precedent from our current knowledge and developments. In addition, I argue on the basis of a Qur'anic principle as an ethical precedent to construct an intra-Islamic rationale for reconsidering gender in leadership of Islamic ritual. It is built on the *tawhidic* paradigm, as the highest principle of the Islamic worldview, which supports the idea that continued gender asymmetry is against Islam. A new future of integrity in all aspects of the *din* is outlined on the basis of this oldest principle of Islamic thought.

Islam is only possible with *tawhid*. More than mere monotheism,[42] many nuances of *tawhid* have been and continue to be the subject of much Islamic discourse pointing toward the same essence. *Tawhid* is the operating principle of cosmic harmony: true justice. It operates between the metaphysical and physical realities of the created universe, as well as within them both. On a theological level, *tawhid* relates to the transcendent and yet eminent divinity or ultimate reality that is the unicity of Allah.

As an ethical term, *tawhid* relates to relationships and developments within the social and political realm, where it emphasizes the unity of all human creatures under Allah, the one Creator. If experienced as a reality in everyday Islamic terms, the Muslim *ummah* would be a community with no distinction between humankind for reasons of race, class, or gender. Their only distinction would be on the basis of *taqwa* (49:13) or moral consciousness, which is not an external matter accessible for human-to-human judgment. All of nature is interconnected under the rubric of *tawhid,* which reinforces the golden rule of reciprocity as articulated in many faith systems and just philosophy.

This Qur'anic system of correlated and contingent pairs at the metaphysical level is further emphasized at the physical level, especially in social-moral terms. The basic construction of human pairs is the male and the female. Then the *tawhidic* paradigm becomes the inspiration for removing gender stratification from all levels of social interaction: public and private, ritual and political.

Conclusion

That *khutbah* in the Claremont Main Road mosque did make a mark on present-day Islamic history – whether or not understood or approved by some Muslims. However, I suggest here that the basis of judgment of my participation in the event should include whether I said something in violation of the integrity of the Islamic tradition or supported it, especially by augmenting it by adding the historically marginalized or silenced female voice and female experience. If I had violated any Islamic principle, then I was not a worthy candidate. On a purely practical level, leadership must always be elected on a case-by-case basis, with the consensus of those who are actually participating in the act of worship: neither any woman at any time nor any man at any time, but on the basis of established qualifications, character of person, and with respect to the needs and temperament of the communal circumstance. Since the basis of Islamic history has been patriarchal, we must make a concerted effort to correct the imbalance this has caused in the *ummah*. We need to give ear to women and women's experiences, not only forming a new consideration of Islam, but also forming a new public voice and establishing new public policies.

Nothing remains sacred and above reproach unless it functions to preserve the integrity of Islam and to allow for the continuity of Islam equally for women and men, in a future that is beginning to look distinct from the past, especially in the area of gender praxis. With this in mind, I submit that the brothers who invited me to participate in the role of *khatibah* at the Claremont Main Road mosque in Cape Town were attempting a radical but legitimate Islamic act. I have considered both weaknesses and strengths because I certainly owe them my gratitude for this opportunity to participate as a central figure in this noteworthy contribution to reform Islamic futures. In particular, I acknowledge that Rashied Omar, as *iman*, offered up his place of privilege, unflinchingly demonstrating the sincerity of his aims to deconstruct gender hegemony. The questions I have had to answer here, both for myself and for others interested in these issues, simply reflect the push for transformation that he courageously made possible for me first to experience and then further investigate.

6 Qur'an, Gender, and Interpretive Possibilities

> Say, "If the sea were ink for [writing] the Words of my Lord, the sea would be exhausted before the Words of my Lord, even if we brought another [sea] like it in addition."
>
> – Qur'an 18:109

There's no getting around it. Muslims have been struggling through an identity crisis not only as a consequence of colonialism's infiltration and corruption of Muslim complacency, but also in response to the globalization of ideas like pluralism, Western secular human rights universals, and their sheer backwardness – as recently reported through an internal study of the state of the Arab world/Middle East (read: Muslims, despite actual demographics). I entered this struggle with my own peculiar identity concerns as well, as a woman.

I concluded early in my research that one way to resolve my questions about gender was to direct myself to Islamic theology rather than Muslim social contexts or commentary, present or historical. Using the Qur'an, I proposed ideas about the Muslim woman's full human agency and dignity despite Qur'anic interpretations, juridical codes, and practices to the contrary. The irony of this ivory tower approach, however, is that it led me directly into social praxis and issues of social justice and reform in Muslim cultural contexts. In this particular matter, theory was put to the test of Muslim women's lives and the still rampant patriarchal control of not only praxis, but orthodox interpretations as well. Meanwhile, after more than fifteen years of research on the Qur'an, it has proven to me without a doubt that patriarchal privilege still continues with increments of success in secular and Western contexts despite the lack of particular claims of religious legitimacy. So unraveling the binds of patriarchy in the context of Muslim cultures, including that religious component, will still take more time, and solutions to practices of inequality must come from multiple strategies simultaneously.

Given the odds against the success of a mere theoretical strategy of alternative interpretation of the Qur'an, Islam's primary resource, I have taken up the charge to both articulate the relationship to and the movement through the Qur'an to social justice for women and men. Despite my book, *Qur'an and Woman*, and its revolutionary contribution at the time of its formulation, the idea of alternative interpretation of the Qur'an from a female-inclusive perspective is by itself insufficient to bring about all gender reforms necessary for the multiple dimensions of Muslim men and women's lives. This points to the need for a more radical synthesis of strategies and struggles toward the end of gender equality.

I compare this need to the movement that brought about the eradication of slavery in the global context. Muslims and Islam were catapulted into the global reconsiderations such that they eventually came out as one voice among many. No distinctive Islamic voice was raised either for or against, to such an extent as to leave a significant historical mark on the movement. It mattered little if the evaluation of the treatment of particular slaves was inhumane or beneficient; the conclusion of this movement, including the ulterior motives invested in it, was the recognition that slavery itself was inhumane. Consequently, the institution is now illegal. It remains to be seen if a particular "Islamic" contribution would have been a major contender in this movement to eradicate such a practice. Yet discussions of Muslim women's full human equality seem impossible without a comprehensive intra-Islamic transformation. I continue to see the Qur'anic text as a central means for that transformation provided the hermeneutical implications are accepted to the extent that both the historical intellectual tradition and the current intellectual considerations are seen as integral to that centrality and prerequisites to actual social reforms.

Gender Justice Through Qur'anic Hermeneutics and Beyond

Qur'anic hermeneutics from a gender perspective was a novel idea when I proposed to move toward it almost two decades ago. Now I accept the critiques of moving beyond my apologetics. In some ways, this has been a legitimate challenge and one that I was prepared to take on as early as the first publication of *Qur'an and Woman* in 1992. In other ways, this challenge is not so much directed at my work as it is at my position vis-à-vis certain issues within the context of gender reforms in Muslim societies. I have been dubbed a "gender fundamentalist" – as if the name should deter me from the root source and inspiration of my efforts, the Qur'an, or away from the moral imperative to not only maintain my dedication to survive the gender *jihad* but also to insist even further that gender is a category of thought ill-respected in even the works of many male intellectuals of Islamic reform. Most are progressive and reformist on anything but class and gender. Unfortunately, the challenges to my positions in *Qur'an and Woman* have remained deconstructionist in nature, with no crucial reconstruction offered – even as lead-ins to assist me toward greater possible alternatives in my own work. In *Progressive Muslims,* Ebrahim Moosa specifies "Muslim feminists" for his critique of making "too much of a few verses of the Qur'an that suggest reciprocal rights and duties between *unequal spouses* and then hastens to suggest that the Qur'an advocates egalitarianism as a norm."[1] No mention is made of the comprehensive mandate for female-inclusive readings not only of the text *as revealed* and now writ, but also to the fullest implications of this inclusion, philosophically and theologically. Women's readings of the Qur'an are either expected to be perfect and comprehensive, or they are inadequate. Therefore, rather than finding encouragement from others with prior privilege in engaging in textual analysis, they are castigated for their efforts at contributing, however inconclusively, to new understandings of the Qur'an. Those understandings reveal possible roads toward finding new conceptions of what it means to be *human* in a religion that has had a history of this very same kind of castigation from the male elites, who were so entrenched in their own struggles for understanding the divine–human relation that they took for granted their androcentric basis as in fact a reflection of the totality of the divine intent. In the final analysis, this critique without recommendation only reiterates the significance of the quest of Muslim women, whether feminists or not, "to explore and develop new ways of interpretation of especially the revealed text."[2]

This circular argument, with its feigned perspective as an objective critique, draws no attention to the significance of gender as a category of thought by reducing the overall agenda of Islamic feminist research and theories to "a few verses." Meanwhile, it unabashedly reinscribes the male privilege of "generations of scholars" despite their being exclusively male and with their specific "patriarchal norms."[3] Simultaneous with this explicit demonstration of retaining male scholarly privilege is the articulation and practice of the utility of "unequal spouses" such that women's domestic roles that have permitted the continued masculine privilege in public arenas of intellectual and philosophical discourse focuses mainly on the politics of the political, while boldfacedly ignoring the personal as political. No insight into the reconstruction of authority rests in this reiteration because *unequal spouses* both facilitate male privilege by "standing steadfastly" by their "side."[4] Meanwhile, they continue masculine self-aggrandizement at the same time as they construct a public persona of being liberated. This is evident in the empty articulations combined with simultaneously rendering selected female scholars and activists as tokens for public window-dressing and by limiting other women, even their own family members, to roles which provide the glue for sustaining their image as proper family men. Therefore, women must either cater to masculine standards of evaluation as either facilitators or be castigated as adversaries. Obviously female autonomy in engaging with the entrenched practices and ideologies of male privilege cannot at one and the same time rely upon male progressive scholars unless these men advocate, as does Khaled Abou el-Fadl, that women further pursue their own learning in order to acquire competence in greater self-reliance instead of this continued reliance upon men's expertise for epistemological, philosophical, and ontological full agency.

To my own deep disappointment I had naively believed that progressive male thinkers and activists would actually be principal catalysts in helping to transform Muslim women's identity. Instead I confronted the paradox of the double bind. Unless and until women want full agency for themselves, they will always find opportunities to be co-opted to support male authority, either in the public or the private sectors. "Men and women are not simply considered different from one another, as we speak of people differing in eye color, movie tastes or preferences for ice cream. In every domain of life, men are considered the normal human being, and women are "ab-normal," deficient because they are different from men."[5] Nevertheless the challenge remains an opportunity for me to reflect further on those alternatives that move toward new answers to even yet unasked questions beyond Qur'an and gender and – in a manner of speaking – beyond the literalist Qur'anic readings asserted as if in fact divine, rather than mundane expressions of divine Self-disclosure.[6] I am continuing my research in hopes satisfactorily to demonstrate how the challenge to a "gender fundamentalist" approach to the Qur'an is ultimately, still, merely a matter of interpretation and hermeneutics for the sake of egalitarian praxis, but especially in the private sphere where it remains sequestered to obscure its popularity for male exploitation.

I have always felt positively inspired by the Qur'anic worldview and this inspiration assists me in addressing these challenges and in researching the works of other scholars.[7] This scholarly transfertilization is instrumental in helping unveil possible paths *through* the Qur'an as a consolidated utterance – or fixed text – as well as an utterance or text *in process*. One important aspect of this challenge confronts the possibility of refuting the text, to talk back, to even say "no." What happens when the text actually states something unmeaningful from the perspective of current human developments and understandings? Two choices result: either face the particular statement as unacceptable regarding current levels of human competency and understanding, and therefore reconsider textual meaning in light of further interpretive development, or reject the particular text. Both choices are often misunderstood as one and the same. To stand up against textual particulars is therefore to be charged with heresy – an ever-present threat in the background to assuage our progress toward gender justice.

The executive director of Sisters in Islam, Zainah Anwar, once asked, "Why can't we say we are working for gender justice from a human rights perspective" instead of our earlier claim of working from a gender-inclusive Islamic perspective? Quite honestly, I understand the frustrations. My response, however, was, "I refuse to leave the definition of Islam to the neo-conservative extremists." I also refuse to leave the definition to the hypocrisy of progressive Muslim males who do not seek to internalize the inherent reciprocal equality as it flows to all levels of the human being and in all human interactions and actions through engaged surrender. I propose to her that we are "working in a partnership between the will of Allah, as revealed in text, and the confirmation of Allah and divine principles through human agency." As much as this partnership confirms the primacy of the Qur'an as the *word*, one form of Allah's Self-disclosure as an ineffable reality, it simultaneously explores the implications of revelatory experience with its inexplicable transcendent nature that must intercede into the mundane realm in order for guidance to actually lead to social justice at all times, in all practices, and in all places.

Zainah proposed a workshop organized around that theme in Malaysia, 2002. It was my first public attempt to present ideas about this divine–

human cooperation, especially as one might perceive a structure of gender relations in Islam in terms far more egalitarian than readily understood from basic reading of Qur'anic text or from the historical androcentric construction of divine principles into explicit legal codes in the discipline of jurisprudence. In one sense, anything beyond literal Qur'an can be deemed supra-text, a refutation of the text, post-text, or a way of saying "no." In another sense one might see the opportunity this allows human beings to act as Allah's agents, responsible for making the meaning of the Qur'an implemental as universal guidance and not mere history.

Personally, I have come to places where how the text says what it says is just plain inadequate or unacceptable, however much interpretation is enacted upon it. Besides, the Qur'an never overtly advocated the eradication of the institution of slavery and concubinage, but confirmed the existing practices of slavery while offering thirteen ways to free slaves, reducing the acquisition of slaves through prisoners of war, and promoting just treatment of slaves as the lesser of two evils. There are two gender examples that have always been of some concern. One of these examples I will treat only minimally here until I have sufficiently developed my research. The other example revisits verse 4:34, with its potential abuse for perpetuating violence against wives. I have dealt with the content of this verse and its harmful consequences in practice quite extensively by now. Thus it will become the basis of demonstrating three aspects of "textual intervention" by way of interpretation and the potential of refutation of certain explicit verses of the Qur'an. Those three are: (1) similar interpretive projects have proceeded throughout Muslim intellectual and legal history in order to explicitly restrict the abuse of the textual statement; (2) we can promote the idea of saying "no" to the text, while; (3) still pointing to the text to support this, as part of hermeneutics and interpretation. It is therefore neither un-Islamic nor heretical to the same extent as it might be deemed post-text in this post-revelation social, cultural, and philosophical context.

An Inquiry into the Qur'an and Sexuality

While on the one hand the Qur'an seems to operate within a structure of linguistic taboo about sexuality and matters of intercourse altogether, on the other hand it promotes male sexuality in particular with the following three citations: (1) polygyny, housed in the language of desire, "Marry those who please you, *maa taba lakum,* of the women: two, three or four"

(4:3). However polygyny is permitted in the text, it is also *conditioned* upon almost unachievable terms of justice. (2) Women are designated as *harth*, tilth, or something to be cultivated or tilled: "Your women are a tilth for you to cultivate . . . as you will, *nisa'ukum harthun lakum fa'tuw harthaku, innaa' shi'tum*" (2:223). Whether this is a discussion of sexual position or permissible times of male sexual satisfaction, according to different jurists, it is still directed toward men and men's sexual desires, while women and women's sexuality remains passive. (3) The notorious virginal *huris* for men – even after they are dead, men's pleasure should not be forsaken! (52:20, 55:72, 56:22). It's hard to take any of these affirmations away from their explicitly male sexual predilection "Where nowhere are extolled the virtues of their earthly wives."[8] In fact, the Qur'anic statement about "*al-qawaa'idu min al-nisa'*, usually taken to mean post-menopausal women," includes that such women will also "not hope to marry *la' yarjuna nikaahan*" (24:60) and "can cast aside their outer garments."

Research on human sexuality verifies that women are not only still active, capable, and willing sexual participants past menopause, they reach the peak of their sexual desire and enjoyment in their forties and fifties just as menopause most often occurs. Is this verse inaccurate about women's sexual desires, as it seems to claim? The necessary interrogation of the term *nikah* is key to understanding this statement. Since the jurists designated the term to mean "sexual intercourse" as one and the same as "marriage," the difference between these two designations complicate the simple reading. Women may at one and the same time "desire sexual intercourse" while "not hoping to be *selected for* marriage," the only legitimate Qur'anic space for intercourse outside of being a concubine. Paramenopausal women and post-menopausal women in many cultures even until today are not considered the best choice for marriage.

There were several reasons why I have not addressed such glitches in my earlier works. First, I recognize that the Qur'an addressed its primary audience, within the context of revelation's social, historical, and cultural circumstances, and as Fazlur Rahman describes it, "through the mind of the Prophet." These necessarily affected its linguistic construction and even its reaches for meaning.[9] It had to have *contextual* meaning or it would fail at its stated method of being "plain Arabic" (16:3). This is acknowledged within Qur'anic interpretive sciences and part of the prerequisite knowledge for understanding text. Some verses are *'am* and some are *khass*. *'Am* means general. Whether general and universal are one and the same is a subject requiring even more extensive interpretive consideration. Because "general" can be relative to the general context of its revelation, there is space to re-examine those verses considered 'am against general contexts outside seventh-century Arabia.

I am influenced by the Qur'an's claim to offer universal guidance for *insan*, humankind, to conclude that even some verses classified as general are relative to the revelatory context. That context, seventh-century Arabia, was not only thoroughly patriarchal it was relatively isolated from most of the rest of the world, as well as mostly obsolete to our current realities. Unless these verses are rigorously examined vis-à-vis their context, the universal meanings could be lost by their modes of articulation. The general understanding of family at the time of revelation, as I discussed at length elsewhere in this book,[10] is not universal because family is a social institution and subject to change relative to social development. The question of universal was not fundamental to early exegetical works, hence the use of the word "general" rather than something equivalent to universal, which was not yet a part of human reason due in part to the role of particularities in constructing meaning and understanding. If something was generally understood, it could be totally irrelevant to other societies; as the idea of "global pluralism" did not exist, general was limited to the immediate space and time of the revelation.

Still, Muslim scholars and laity believed in the universal intent of Qur'anic guidance, even when certain times and places had exclusive perspectives on universal relative to the general understandings in context. Thus universal, at the time of revelation, was not globally comprehensive. Indeed, the Qur'anic categories of human belief systems was focused on those prevalent and known in seventh-century Arabia, inclusive of *ahl-al-kitabi*, people of the book, or members of the Abrahamic faiths: Judaism, Christianity, and Islam. There were also *mushrikun*, polytheists, at that time, but polytheism in Qur'anic discourse did not include any direct references to Hindu or African traditional religious polytheism, which have both the concept of numerous gods as well as the concept of the sacred as Ultimate. These sacred traditions relied upon this Ultimate sacred nature as facilitated by enactments or articulation of other "gods" to redefine multiple theophonic attributes while still adhering to their intrinsically unified – i.e. *tawhidic* – nature with regard to the sacred as universal.

There were also idol worshippers present in the context of the Qur'anic revelation, which are conflated as one and the same as *mushrikun*, because of their multiplicity. There were no animists, believers in the sacred manifestations throughout creation, as in many indigenous religious traditions, like native African, Australian, and North and South American pre- and post-Qur'anic traditions. These are not directly spoken to in the Qur'an. Furthermore, all forms of Buddhism, Taoism, and Confucianism, with unembodied or non-personified concepts of the sacred, were excluded from Qur'anic discussions of faith or religion, despite their existence prior to the seventh century in other parts of the globe. Popular Muslim thinking does not interrogate the subtle relationships between the idea of a universal divine essence, the concept of the sacred, and the various manifestations of these already recognized and practiced in other parts of the world, while the general context of Arabia and its surrounding areas are taken as the comprehensive arena for considerations of the meaning of the divine. Instead of coming away from the universal intents of the Qur'an against its general audience at one time and place, the global realities of divine–human relations are often reduced to some simple aspect of the Qur'anic contextual discussion – if not totally ignored. Consequently, the *shari'ah* prohibits intermarriage between Muslims and members of these world faiths, and acknowledges the Qur'anic marriage of female subjugation to permit men to marry *ahl-al-kitabi* women.

Nevertheless, I continue to believe in the Qur'an's universal intent while armed with comparative religious studies in the twentieth and twenty-first centuries. Each measure of human understanding of the totality of the divine nature is more like a window, through which a person or a community can have a view of the totality. I cannot defend the notion that the window itself represents the total sacred potential. It is a framework or a viewpoint, limited to the ones who look through it. Therefore, *'am* verses are not one and the same as universal. What I consider universal in the Qur'anic statements can only be understood in light of the transcendent. Transcendence does not adhere to mundane limits. In fact, its definition is best articulated in negative theological terms, by stating or focusing on what the sacred or the divine is *not*. "Allah is one" compares to an unlimited possible articulation of what Allah, or Its "one-ness," is not. It is not multiple gods, idols, and literal prescriptions to its manifestations throughout creation, especially in nature. The multiplicity of human responses to the idea of the sacred or the ultimate have been and continue to be expressed in terms relative to all these negated qualities despite their apparent correlations.

Put another way, if Allah has 99 names, characteristics, or *sifat*, attributes, then focusing on any particular one of these is neither separate for Allah's *tawhidic* totality nor the same as Allah's comprehensive reality which embraces all 99 without mutual contradiction. This is one reason why both the *jamal*, feminine attributes of Allah, and the *jalal*, masculine attributes, are related integrally to the totality of Allah. To accept Allah's mercy requires acceptance of Allah's wrath. To focus on that mercy is not a negation of the wrath, it is a human predilection influenced by very mundane, and not transcendent, universal or ultimate potentialities. Thus the second reason for my responses to seeming glitches or even contradictions in even the Qur'an's *'am*, general utterances, was their historical necessity in a particular time and location while the comprehension of the transcendent reality of the divine cannot be discussed in the boundaries of any human language as a symbolic meaning-making system. "Language is intrinsically unfitted to discuss the supernatural literally." Words about God and the Unseen "must be used analogically because these matters 'transcend all symbol-systems'."[11] Therefore, I have never been locked into a literal meaning of Qur'anic text when I explore the Qur'anic intent of universal guidance. This frees human agency to grapple throughout all points in history with what is actually stated in the Qur'an and to observe the deficiencies of all statements in language over meaning let alone divine potentiality.

As to the matter of Qur'anic *khass*, specific statements, I consider it direct and simple; for example, when the Qur'an addresses the people of Madinah and the wives of the Prophet Muhammad are prohibited from marriage after his death (33:53). This statement's restricted application to these particular women has no general, let alone universal, intent. One cannot derive any meaning from it to be applied outside the *khass* of its utterance. *Only* the wives of the Prophet, now fourteen hundred years deceased, have any relationship to the verse although it is a literal part of this universal text of guidance. In fact, to derive general, let alone universal, intent from such a statement would so obviously misread the statement it would violate the Qur'an. It is the overt and obvious nature and utterance of this statement with its extremely limited terms of application that should easily alert all readers of the text that the Qur'an does indeed *have* a specific context, but also that the Qur'anic text *was* responsive to that context.

I was not deterred by these nuances. I moved beyond its particular linguistic confirmations and limitations *in* context and looked through it as a window toward the transcendent – toward its potential, as if the words were *ayat*, signs, that point beyond themselves to ultimate meanings for transformation. It requires readers of the signs to invest their human agency, as free-willed and rational beings – aspiring to surrender to the divine will. Agents investigate the relationship between Qur'anic statements with their potential trajectory to point all humankind to divine guidance rather than to literal application of verse after verse to extremely confined or limited implementations as in the seventh-century Arabian context, as if these could fulfill universal guidance.

After all, Qur'anic interpretation is about the human search for the meaning of God. It is not just in our most fundamental belief in the Qur'an as the word of Allah, or God's Self-disclosure, but in the sense that Allah is and always was and therefore cannot be contained or constrained by text – let alone by the search for meanings of that text by any human being, with all his or her flaws and inadequacies. The Qur'an is, as it were, a window to look *through*. A doorway with a threshold one must pass *over* toward the infinite possibilities that point humanity toward a continuum of spiritual and social development. I could never allow its substance to succumb to the patriarchal audience of its time, nor to the scope of its readership – then or now. I accept that even my own reading is dwarfed by my context in history as well as by human incompetence and lack of understanding. This acceptance frees me from defending any understanding I develop or meaning I find as the *only* right understanding. This leads my understanding to unlimited change as I grow and encounter both the whole of Allah's creation, the whole of the book, and the whole scope of human meaning-making under sacred guidance. I am not afraid of my efforts to understand the text, to act upon my understanding, and to share each stage of development in that understanding as part of the human love, belief, and surrender to the Author of the text, however I might encounter Allah from one moment to the next. The substance of the Qur'an cannot be constrained by its particular utterances, let alone by the narrowness of its readers. Indeed, as Ali Abu Talib asserted in the famous dispute against the *Khawarij* (extremists), "the Qur'an is written in straight lines between two covers. It does not speak by itself. It needs interpreters, and the interpreters are human beings."[12] As Muslims we have always been, and always will be, only human. With our human development of postmodernist and deconstructionist disciplines of meaning, we accept the fact that we are potentially guided by the text, even if not limited to its particular utterances.

The text is silent. It needs interpretation, and has always historically and currently been subjected to interpretation. We make it speak for us by asking of it. If we are narrow, we will get a narrow response or answer. If we are open, it will open us to even greater possibilities. Contexts make particular interpretations dominant and others inadequate. We are subjects of our own history in the making, as well as to the historical past upon which we rest, knowingly or unknowingly. "Human nature [is] created historically through a dialectic between human biology and the physical environment. This interrelation is mediated by human labor or praxis. The specific form of praxis dominant within a given society creates the distinctive physical and psychological human types characteristic of that society."[13] Therefore, even our capacity to conceive of any kind of God is prefaced upon our individual as well as civilizational context and the conceptual constructs at our disposal. As civilizations develop so does the human capacity to understand both its own nature and the nature of God.

The revelation of God is unfortunately also constrained by the minds of the men and women for whom it was revealed. When we do perceive of the Ultimate in Its infinitude, for whatever glimpses or theophonic awakenings we might experience, we are left to integrate them into our own identity as it may yield to and yet be limited within our specific contexts. Then it's back to the drawing board, to chisel out other less finite possibilities. I do not say that God is in Herself constrained by us. However, our conceptions of God are at best where the Hindu yogi recognizes as the sixth *chakrah*, the place of our "notions of God." We cannot linger everlastingly at the seventh *chakrah*, or the crown, the place of "God beyond all names and forms," except for a twinkle of an eye. Or else we be gods ourselves, and though ultimately there is truth in that, our corporeal forms will only allow us intoxicated glimpses of this Reality. Afterwards we are tumbled back in a hangover of separation, yearning, and despair. Our earthly form confines us, and all that is left to us in the wake of that moment of epiphany is a deep sense of alienation.

Verse 4:34 and Implications of Literal Application of Hudud Ordinances

I have used the Qur'an's contextual patriarchal circumstances with predominant focus on male experiences, including male sexuality, to begin my research on the complexity of both uncovering meaning from the Qur'anic text as well as for implementing the Qur'anic intent for universal guidance. While Muslims accept the Qur'an as universal guidance, the predominant method for achieving that universal in mundane context has resulted overwhelmingly in the practice of literally applying specific utterances. In

Qur'an and Woman, I considered this to have potential contradictions to the spirit of the Qur'an. This reference to the word "spirit" I had concluded from studying Fazlur Rahman's work in conjunction with my research and experience with gender and transcendence. But the ambiguity of the word also required elaboration.[14]

The existence of so many exegetical works (*tafasir*) indicates that, with regard to the Qur'an, the interpretation process has existed and will probably continue to exist, in a variety of forms. It is essential that the adaptive nature of interpretation, from individual to individual and from time and place to time and place, should continue unabated until the end of time – on the one hand because it is natural and on the other hand, *because only through such continued interpretation can the wisdom of the Qur'an be effectively implemented. This implementation will be specific to the varying experiences of human civilization.*

No interpretation is definitive. I have attempted here to render a reasonable plausible interpretation to some difficult matters. The basis for this plausibility is the significance I draw from the text with regard to the modern woman: the significance of her life style to her concerns and interactions in her context.

I believe the Qur'an adapts to the context of the modern woman as smoothly as it adapted to the original Muslim community fourteen centuries ago. This adaptation can be demonstrated if the text is interpreted with her in mind, thus indicating the universality of the text. Any interpretations, which narrowly apply the Qur'anic guidelines only to literal mimics of the original community, do an injustice to the text [now and in the future]. No community will ever be exactly like another. Therefore no community can be a duplicate of that original community. The Qur'an never states that as the goal. Rather *the goal has been to emulate certain key principles of human development: justice, equity, harmony, moral responsibility, spiritual awareness and development. Where these general characteristics exist, whether in the first Muslim community or in the present or future communities, the goal of the Qur'an for society [and piety] has been reached.*

(emphasis and additions mine)

Besides the imbalanced expression of human sexuality in terms most specific to masculine, heterosexual dominance, the second place of dissatisfaction when grappling with textual inadequacies is verse 34, *surat-al-nisa'*.[15]

Men are [*qawwamuna 'ala*] women, [on the basis] of what Allah has [preferred] (*faddala*) some of them over others, [and on the basis] of what they spend of their property (for the support of women). So good women are [*qanitat*], guarding in secret that which Allah has guarded. As for those (women) from whom you fear [*nushuz*], admonish them, banish them to beds apart, and scourge them. Then, if they obey you, seek not a way against them.

There is no getting around this one, even though I have tried through different methods for two decades. I simply do not and cannot condone permission for a man to "scourge" or apply *any kind* of strike to a woman. Because of the extensive time I have examined this verse, it is the best place for me to demonstrate the diverse interpretive and implementive possibilities as they have been applied through some historical examples and conditions, including my own attempts at interpretative manipulations. This leads me to clarify how I have finally come to say "no" outright to the literal implementation of this passage. This also has implications in implementing the *hudud* (penal code) ordinances. This verse, and the literal implementation of *hudud*, both imply an ethical standard of human actions that are archaic and barbarian at this time in history. They are unjust in the ways that human beings have come to experience and understand justice, and hence unacceptable to universal notions of human dignity.

I have had what Khaled Abou Fadl[16] calls a "conscientious pause" regarding the application of the *hudud* ordinances and the verse on wife beating.

Every adult Muslim, man or woman, is obligated to understand and implement the *Shari'ah*. Accountability is personal and individual, and *no single person or institution may or can represent the Divine Will.* Hence the individual is directly responsible for seeking and learning the way of God – the *shari'ah* . . . or the truth.

   Truth here relates to the object or purpose of the Divine Will. God, it is argued, does not seek an objective or singular truth, God wishes human beings to search and seek for the Divine Will. Truth adheres to search – the search itself is ultimate truth. Consequently, correctness is measured according to the sincerity of the individual's search.

   The mark of the search for the Divine Will is the dalil (pl. *adillah*). A *dalil* is the indicator, pointer mark or evidence of the Divine Will. *God, for the purpose of edification, and in order to test human beings, and as a sign of His mercy and compassion, demanded that human beings exert an effort in seeking the evidence of His Will (badhl al-juhd fi talab al-dalil or talab al-'ilm).* (emphasis mine)

Then he elaborates further on those things that might "require a conscientious pause." If by the standards of age and place, or the standards of human moral development, traditions lead to *wakhdh al-damir* (the unsettling or disturbing of the conscience), the least a Muslim can do is to pause to reflect about the place and the implications of these traditions. "Can I, consistently with my faith and understanding of God and God's message, believe that God . . . is primarily responsible for this . . . or that such and such can be true?" "Everyone . . . is functioning in the realm of the possible and probable while struggling with indicators (pl. *adillah*, sing. *dalil*). To claim full or perfect knowledge of God's will is to challenge the singularity and uniqueness of the Divine perfection."[17]

However, if all determinations take account of the indicators and evidence, what do we make of morality, or a basic sense of right and wrong? Is all right and wrong only derived from the divine text and nothing but the text? The text is not the only representative of the divine.

A person develops knowledge of God, *not through textual indicators alone*, but through a complex matrix of relationships that are collateral to the text. A person develops a direct relationship perhaps through prayer and supplication, and might develop an understanding of the Creator by reflecting upon creation, or might observe the work of God and Satan through reflecting upon history. These various avenues to the knowledge of God exist apart from the indicators of the text, but they work in conjunction with the text to formulate a conviction about the nature and normativities of the divine. Although the text plays a role in forming these convictions one cannot exclude the possibility that the conviction which has been formulated might come into friction with certain determinations of the text. A person can read a text that seems to go against everything that he or she believes about God and will feel a sense of incredulous disbelief, and might even exclaim, "This cannot be from God, the God that I know!"[18]

When such frictions occur between textual utterances and collateral evidences, one must assert a "diligent and comprehensive"[19] investigation of the text. I elaborate this through my investigation of verse 4:34 including an historical consideration of the possible means for both understanding and implementing the particular text toward fulfillment of the principles or "spirit" of the whole of the text. There are four stages of this historical development.

Stages in Textual Interpretive Development

One might say that the first stage of textual interpretive development would be at the time and in the context of its revelation. The simple response to this statement for a husband to strike his wife seems to be, *yes*. Despite this simple response, however, we also know that the Prophet's response to this revelation was, "I wanted one thing and Allah wanted something else." He *never* implemented this text in his life. He never struck a woman or beat a slave. It would be easy to say that the reason for this is that every one of his marriages were without incident. After all, these were the "Mothers of the Faith," exemplary companions to the time of revelation. On the contrary, the Qur'anic *khass* descriptions of more than one conflict between the Prophet and one or more of his wives confirm this was not so. Not only did the Prophet retain severe doubts about the sexual fidelity of his wife A'ishah when rumors were implying the contrary, but also those doubts were not alleviated by any direct exchange between him and A'ishah. These doubts persisted until a *khass* verse testifying to her innocence was revealed. This passage goes on to provide an *'am*, commandment to avoid slander and rumors, and even instates a *hadd* punishment for those guilty of speaking such rumors without corroborating their suspicions with reliable eye-witnesses or other evidence (24:4–25).

The Qur'an also elaborates on another occasion, when the Prophet vowed a month-long seclusion from all his wives after they schemed against him over something he had done with which they were unpleased. The *khass* revelation even went so far as to offer to replace all his wives (66:3–5). This month-long separation can be viewed as a demonstration of the second solution recommended in 4:34, to "remain in beds apart."[20] If the Prophet remains the best exemplary of Qur'anic meaning, then he should have moved from the separation to beating his wives. The Qur'an instead speaks of the possibility of divorce (66:4), and the Prophet demonstrates the additional condition of interpretation and application, self-reflection.

The second stage of interpretive development is demonstrated continually and in diverse ways during the two or three centuries following the revelation as *fiqh* develops and provides other interpretive responses. It was a practical *intervention* between literal textual application and *conditional* application. Most significant of this intervention is that *fiqh* restricts such a "strike" to "*ghayr mubah*, without harm." Furthermore, *fiqh* interprets the strike as only "*ramsiyun*, symbolic." This confirms a textual understanding against the use of it for unabashed spousal abuse or domestic violence. The jurists seem to be arguing within their existing sociological context and asserting an understanding of textual intent – perhaps also based on the precedent of the prophetic example. This is nevertheless *an intervention opposing literal application*. It could be seen as proposing *"yes," "but"* with conditions. It is no reductionism to believe that the conditions also stem from interpreting the Qur'an on the basis of the Qur'an, with "justice" the overarching concern for human interaction of *mu'amalat*.

In *Qur'an and Woman*, I intentionally worked on a third potential stage of development inspired by reading in my own context. Multiple meanings can be deduced from the various uses and definitions for the word *daraba* as in the Qur'an and elsewhere. This wide spectrum of linguistic nuances, and the extensive lists of definitions supplied by the Arabic dictionary and lexicon *Lisan al-Arab* indicate that there could be much more to meet the eye and subsequently apply in trying to understand this verse. It was plain to see how this multiplicity allows room to manipulate multiple meanings to determine multiple possibilities for application. I concluded with an alternative interpretation that the Qur'an meant to restrict unbridled violence. This intervention utilizes the linguistic space for manipulating meaning and promotes a *"perhaps not"* possibility. Perhaps the Qur'an did *not* intend to emphasize the narrowest reading, since violence against the innocent and oppressed is strongly discouraged elsewhere in the text. Perhaps the seventh-century application of this countered the practices of female abuse and violence towards women, but twenty-first-century standards have shown us other possibilities as well as the clear negative consequences of violence in the family for all members, the abused, the abuser, and the witnessing members.

The last stage I consider here in the context of our current knowledge and explicit data regarding domestic violence takes into consideration information gathered from research on, and women's experiences with, abuse – that is, using the "various avenues to the knowledge of God (that) exist apart from the indicators of the text."[21] Here I argue against any notion that it is acceptable for a man to beat his wife. Any kind of a strike, or any intention to apply the verse in that manner, violates other principles of the text itself – most notably "justice" and human dignity, as Allah has led humankind to understand today.

Therefore the application of the verse as permission for a man to strike his wife must be rejected. To say "no" to this verse now simply exemplifies the process or trajectory throughout the history of textual interpretation and application. From the cultural context of the text, with the precedent of the Prophet – against such a practice – through the restriction of *fiqh* conditions, and the manipulation of interpretive multiplicity, we finally arrive at a place where we *acknowledge that we intervene* with the text. The next step is to admit that we are continuing the process of intervention between text and meaning, as believers in Allah and in revelation. It provides a means to reject literal application of this text and certain other textual particulars altogether.

What I am proposing is that the collective community has always manipulated the text in concert with civilizational, or, better still, human development. We must now simply acknowledge that it has always been done and accept the responsibility of agency in doing so openly and in consultation with the community. Since we live in the time when at least the conceptualization of women's complete human agency and equality between women and men is conceivable, then we must dance the delicate dance between text and agency to assert a movement of complete gender justice. I have already argued significantly that the text *can* be interpreted with egalitarianism in mind; I now propose one step that some consider as beyond even that. *We are the makers of textual meaning.* The results of our meaning-making is the reality we establish from those meanings to human experiences and social justice. We need to make the text mean more for women's full human dignity than it has been conceived to do or applied toward at any other time in Muslim history. Our motivation to do so, however, is fully within the framework of Islam as a meaning-making system of social justice with the text as the *dalil*, primary indicator of that meaning, while acknowledging that no one text can ever completely disclose the full nature of Allah and therefore can be the complete and exclusive articulation of it.

As believers in the faith tradition of Islam, *we cannot rewrite the Qur'an.* As an historical record of the words revealed by Allah to the Prophet Muhammad, those words are unchangeable. In addition, those words have always been subject to multiple meanings and to various interpretations. The goal of interpretation is to unveil the meanings that reflect the spirit of the very idea that Allah, the Ultimate, Who is ultimately unknowable, intends for human agents to *apply* the meanings they are able to unveil in a manner most reflective of the principles of the message. The jurists, the poets, the Sufis, the dialecticians, the philosophers, and the linguists, women and men, *all* took part in interrogating textual meanings to build a global community of balance or equilibrium – a just society.

We can rewrite the law, the *shari'ah* through *fiqh*. In fact, we must rewrite the law. The *fiqh* of earlier times, just like the *fiqh* of our time, only has meaning as *fiqh al-waqi'ah*, the *fiqh* of lived reality, that assists in establishing codes of conduct to facilitate the achievement of a just and moral social order as mandated by Qur'anic principles. At the time of revelation, gender was not a category of thought, examined in light of diverse, relative living realities. The absence of such a category of thought was not sexist at the time of revelation, but it is palpably so today. Whatever sexism might be found in the words of the immutable Qur'an is a reflection of the historical context of Qur'anic revelation. Today, sexism is rejected in all its expressions of asymmetrical theories and practices where men are privileged to the detriment of women by deterring them from reaching their fullest potential as divinely assigned full human agents. By rewriting the legal codes, through distinguishing their sexist reflection, we can achieve an Islamic reality more meaningfully reflecting Qur'anic principles in a harmonious equilibrium.

Just as there are medical ethics, where we must rely upon specialists in other areas, in this case, we have particular specialists in social and psychological fields of human knowledge, to help augment our continued arrival to where the Qur'an can potentially lead us. Clearly, we were able to stop practicing the institution of slavery and never charged ourselves with violating the text. Even the most conservative of Muslim fundamentalists do not argue to return to the Qur'anic position of accepting slavery under the seventh-century practice. What more impetus to correct gender imbalance than the Qur'an's own tenacious insistence in dealing with the issues in a most despicable and despised context of pre-Islamic patriarchy? There are more verses in the Qur'an regarding the full human dignity of women than any other social issues. Surely the Qur'anic trajectory as universal guidance should not be made into retrograde patriarchal standards and practices.

Ultimately, we can exercise the continued progression of human agency and rewrite the basic paradigmatic core of what can be considered Islamic ethics by a multiplicity of means now available to human understanding about what it means to acquire, practice, and assert how we live as ethical beings and moral agents of the divine will. Gender, as a category of thought, is one of the most significant aspects of this development of human understanding and is essential to raising the level of an Islamic ethos to more closely resemble the universal intent of the divine message as contextually disclosed in the revelation of the Qur'an.

On Linguistics and a Hermeneutics of Gender Justice

Instead of trying to change the immutable words, we grapple with and challenge the inherent sexist biases of the historicity of words. As agents we surmise what are particulars and what are universals to establish general mechanisms for achieving the fullest justice of our time. Muslim scholars help point us toward the theoretical foundations of that justice. Legal scholars must represent the people's need for full justice, unhampered by its relative reflections during past historical movements but rather inspired by their relative potential, and consolidate these with today's historical realities, without narrow authoritative intolerance, so that we can lead toward the many possible futures of Islam, when surely new circumstances will require freedom in achieving the continuity of the interrogative process toward the goal of a just social order.

While researching and compiling *Qur'an and Woman*, as an agent, African-American, female, believer, transitioner, and thinker, I occupied a place of extreme anonymity. This allowed me a freedom to examine our tradition through my mind and my heart. I have lost that freedom once the ideas made a public début. On the one hand, this has forced me to broaden my research perspective of what "Islam" can be, and what it means to me, through various areas of study like progressive Islam, feminism, and postmodernism, Third World, and Western political theory and politics, liberation theologies, the new globalization, and of course, through experiences. On the other hand, I have lost the protected insulation around my heart and mind when I was free to focus solely upon how an open heart moves toward understanding the divine through text. Now that I know more, my heart is burdened more. I am painfully aware of the need to manage multiple audiences, as the Prophet advised, by "speaking to the people in the way they understand." This is the challenge I must meet, and I can no longer work solely from or for my own spiritual inspiration, but must acknowledge the complexities of the entire Muslim world, including those who have a predilection for divergent opinions, let alone those who are violent against the innocent.

Without the luxury of solitary heartfelt inspiration, I am responsible for engaging in discussions of interpretive possibilities and making comparative analysis about the Qur'an's centrality as a prerequisite to all intellectual discourse, and yet still as one indisputable core of spiritual realization. As the primacy of the underlying spiritual inspiration of the Qur'an is almost wholly lost in textual analysis, my initial discussion was more at liberty to highlight that aspect as a river running beneath the intense layers of liberal and progressive thinking about language, context, and hermeneutics. Allah is, has always been, and will always be, present. Allah has endeavored to assist free-willed moral agents of Her presence through many *ayat* – in the text and everywhere in the universe. Revelation can be seen as an *ayah* of crisis intervention as well as *dhikr,* a reminder, and a *furqan,* criterion, of Allah's continual presence, continual creation and/or continual Self-disclosure. For language-dependent human minds, revelation is the ultimate sign of Allah's presence or Self-disclosure to guide human hearts in the surrender to Its divine will. Through extensive analysis of the text, we have learned how language is a most unique gift imbued to humankind with immeasurable power and potential, while paradoxically one of the most fallible. In human language, we can lie. What is more, we can become trapped in our own lies through denial or blatant hypocrisy. When the Qur'an says, "Why do you say that which you do not do? It is a grievous injustice to say that which you do not do" (61:2), humans can stand forward to speak on the very issues of human well-being that they privately violate. As long as the truth of our actions is kept secret from our public personae then we can wear this false persona as easily as we can violate truth through our private actions. I want to mean what I say, and say what I mean. Even more, I want to be the Muslim I aspire to be as best as I understand and attempt to articulate in the context of the human language facility.

Yet this language facility is also applied to understanding the transcendent nature of the divine. *Within* the paradox of multiple meanings of the language medium, to say nothing of the direct lie, there can be huge gaps rather than mutual understanding between Muslims as one group among many recipients of revelation. God's disclosure through text in the fallible human language medium can never completely disclose That Which is also disclosed through countless other mediums, signs, or *ayat.* Complete disclosure can never be contained by any means, least of all the heavily flawed means of human linguistic communication.

This has already been addressed between the Mu'tazilites and the Asha'rites by trying to decide definitively whether the Qur'an is *eternal* with God or *created?* There are other questions to ponder. Is Allah multilingual, so that She can reveal in Hebrew, Aramaic, and Arabic, or is Allah *meta-lingual*, not constricted by any language? Every language is a constraint on complete divine Self-disclosure. Is Arabic preferable, divine, or just the most convenient tool to use with an Arab prophet? Is the divine message limited to (or by) words – of any language? Do Muslims truly recognize the presence of Allah in words, or deem themselves gods by enforcing their understandings and misunderstandings of those words? Is recognition of the presence of Allah limited to reading the words of the Qur'an? Since the majority of Muslims are non-Arabic speaking can they know the presence of Allah?

I have heard the recitation from many a *hafiz* (Qur'anic memorizer) who cannot render comprehensible phraseology in their recitation, but instead only parrot the sounds they learned by rote memorization, and it sounds like gibberish, not meaningful communication. Meanwhile, a *hafiz* who has specifically learned the Qur'anic linguistic worldview can bring tears to the eyes of a comprehending listener. Is Allah's presence so limited? No. Allah's presence is everywhere as He continues to create and recreate at every second sustaining the universe in the bosom of His love. And like the infant child *knows* he or she is loved in the arms of the mother or the father, so the believer knows the presence of Allah, before, during, after and without reading the Qur'an. In other words, whatever "the word of God" means, the Qur'an is not God. Words are fallible. Hence Muslims can and have used it for justice and as well as despicable violence. It is "Muslims" in response to their own hearts and minds in interaction with the words that determine the results. The Qur'an is the source; people are the resource. That is why I stress not only the significance of interpretation, but also the relationship of interpretation and actions.

The Sun neither Rises nor Sets

When we read the words "*gharabat ash-shams*" in the Qur'an, literally, "the sun wests," sun is the grammatical actor, the subject of the sentence. The basic sentence structure requires a subject and a predicate. The predicate is the grammatical act, indicated by a verb. The action of the subject in a sentence is articulated as a particular verb. Here, the sentence contains a verb that does not exist in English, "*gharaba*." Etymologically this verb can be traced to the word *gharb,* which means *west*. The Arabic sentence in the Qur'an depicts the place of the sun at the end of the day – in the west. But it cannot be literally translated into English as, "the sun wests (itself)." To "west" itself, as this sentence states, despite the absence of an

English verb equivalent to "west," makes the sun as the subject/actor, and *west* as the verb or action.

In another sense, this sentence might be describing a movement somewhere in the universe, which results in the location of the sun's evening appearance in the west. From the perspective of earthly creatures the sun appears in the west. With no English equivalent for the verb "west," translators use the idiomatic English equivalent, "The sun sets." The English sentence has subject and verb as well. In it, "the sun" is subject and "set" is verb. Whereas it is insignificant in the Arabic sentence whether the verb here implies that the sun, a star in the universe, actually moves itself, vis-à-vis the earth, to the west, the action of the English sentence is very significant. The results of the Arabic sentence is that the subject, "sun," is connected to its location in the west, as indicated by the verb. It is a logical and scientifically accurate statement, whether we know or not from the verb how the action of "westing" is achieved. Some movement of the sun could achieve it, or some other movement, like the earth turning on its axis could achieve it. The result, however, is that the sun is west with respect to human perceptions on the earth.

Unfortunately, the absence of a verb "to west" in English requires the translator to reduce the sentence to the only semantic English equivalent, literally "the sun sets." We accept this translation based on the absence of a verb "to west" in the English language. We stick to the translation, "the sun sets," with the implication that the sun performs the act of setting, even though the sun actually makes no motion. The earth moves on its axis until the sun appears in the west. Our English sentence reflects the time when human knowledge actually thought the earth was the center of the universe and the sun's appearance in the west meant that it was the sun itself that had moved west resulting in sunset. But the sun does not set. No English statement exists to reflect the reality about the workings of the earth in relation to the sun. "The sun sets" only expresses the limitations both in prior human knowledge as well as in the resulting articulation *in language* to the limitations of human perspective historically. Oddly, this linguistic limitation persists until now, despite our subsequent development in scientific knowledge, which has taught us that the actor is really the earth. So still today, we say "the sun sets," making no reference to the sun's persistent location vis-à-vis the movement or action of the earth.

Although a word equivalent to "set" exists in Arabic (*nazala*, to descend), and actually occurs numerous times in the Qur'an, it is a technical term of special semantic implication and most frequently refers to the action of divine revelation. With it are other implications: that the source of revelation, which Muslims say is Allah, is above, and that the recipient of the revelation, the Prophet Muhammad, was below, in a descending direction from Allah. Yet above and below are also potentially metaphoric, as I explained in the *tawhidic* paradigm. Coincidently, the same metaphysical direction, whether directly to the Prophet's heart, mind, soul, being, or via the archangel *Jibril*, Gabrial, "*ruh-al-amin*," the reliable spirit, a physical direction is also implied. The source is above; the receiver is below. Thus, when we say that the Qur'an was revealed "through the mind of the Prophet," the combination of Allah's transcendence as source of the message, onto or into the Prophet, a mundane human being selected for the receipt of revelation, we rely upon mundane or human language alone. We can only conclude that we do not and cannot know if the Qur'an was created or eternal with Allah, since we cannot know how it can actually be both at the same time. We do not, however, have the language to express this transcendent simultaneity.

I might note in passing other references to *nazala* or *anzala* used with a metaphysical downward movement, such as it is principally for revelation. For example, actions, like peace descending to the hearts of frightened soldiers are mentioned in the Qur'an. There are other physical actions of descent, or going down, that the Qur'an mentions when describing actions from this world – notably rain descends to earth from the sky above. But there is no term for a downward movement of the sun that occurs in the Qur'an. It never says "the sun *sets*," or the sun goes down. The semantic "westing" of the sun is more scientifically accurate, and no attempts are made to show corollary between the downward movement of the sun vis-à-vis the earth, despite the limitation of human knowledge and in the present limitation in the English human linguistic formulation.

Conversely, the Arabic grammatical construction for sunrise has the same limitation as the English. This complex nuance discloses more emphatically my point. For example, in *surat-al-Kahf* (18), the Qur'an actually uses the verb *tala'a,* to rise, with reference to the sun. For example at 18:17 and 18:90, *tala'a* is used as verb attached to sun as subject. In addition, *matla'i,* the passive participle of the verb, is also used with reference to the sun. However the verb *tala'a* placed as a direct action of the sun, in this case "*tala'at ash-shams*," means the sun ascended, or the sun rose. The English grammatical construct, "the sun rises," articulates the phenomenon in the same way. Again, from the perspective of an earthly inhabitant, the sun does *appear* to rise, but sound or correct scientific knowledge of the universe has proven otherwise. It is the earth that acts vis-à-vis the sun, by turning on its axis, until the sun appears in the east.

Although the Qur'an talks about both the east and the west, locations relative to human perceptions on the earth, its language does not strictly adhere to the scientific reality that the sun's appearance in the east only results from earthly movement. It refers to the movement of the sun as "rising," although physically it neither rises nor sets. From the perspective of an earthly inhabitant, the sun does appear to rise, but through sound or correct knowledge of the workings of the universe, we know otherwise. It is the earth that acts, by turning on its axis, and gives the sun its appearance in the east and the west. But the sun neither rises nor sets. Regarding sunrise, the Arabic phrase is fossilized like the English phrase. Both accurately reflect a perception on reality from the perspective of human experience and the epistemology of human language. This in turn leaves an effect on the human mind. Neither phrase expresses what actually occurs in nature. Although the Qur'anic phrase "the sun wests (itself)," which is technically closer to the physical reality, exists without the "sun set" equivalent to the English, it is ambivalent in the Arabic whether the sun achieves its "position" in the west by its own movement or the movement of the earth. It is through the absence of a scientifically accurate articulation that such linguistic inadequacy occurs. This points us toward an elementary exploration of the primary function of human language. Language is a meaning- making facility only relative to human perception.

Sunrise and sunset are so standard in English, with at least one of them standard in Arabic as well, that we no longer question the imprecision of their articulation. On other occasions, the development of human scientific knowledge was so radical that the language used to articulate it had to be altered. For example, the relationship of the sperm as the agent of human procreation and the egg as a passive recipient: we now know the female egg is the actual seed which begins cell division when penetrated by the male sperm for ultimately achieving a complete, new, and unique human being. Other linguistic and semantic derivations easily cross the threshold from the strict technical circumstances in which they were constructed into everyday English parlance. One of my favorites is the statement "on par." It infiltrated mainstream English while only a small minority of golf players existed. Indeed, I even "understood" the meaning of this term twenty years before I even knew its origins in golf.

Revelation and, in our particular discussion, the Qur'an, is accepted as "the direct words of Allah" to the Prophet Muhammad. For simplicity's sake, let us begin with Allah's omniscience. The Creator of the Universe knows and has always known the actual reality of movement of the matter in the universe. When human scientists discovered and confirmed the evidence that it was the earth's rotation causing what appears as "easting"/ "rising" and "westing"/"setting" of the sun, they exposed evidence to a reality that had already existed, and was therefore already known by Allah, but new to humankind. Before human research provided evidence to verify that previously existing reality, human language had formulated grammatically sensible articulations to express what they perceived. Ironically, the English phrases "the sun rises" and "the sun sets" have not been adjusted to reflect these newly recognized realities.

This investigating into seeming linguistic discrepancies between Qur'anic language and scientific fact directs us to a necessary encounter with the createdness of revelation, the linguistic means of divine disclosure. Although the divine is not created, the only means for humans to receive a revelation in "clear Arabic" was for the Qur'an to utilize the linguistic constraints of Arabic as it strove to express the full nature of the divine. But it did not merely give meaning relative to human linguistic competency, it also guided humanity toward new meanings relative to human experiences, experiments, and perceptions yet still containing numerous pointers beyond the moment and circumstance of revelation, to help us as we develop and make new discoveries of reality. The most immediate task for a self-described text of "plain Arabic" (26:190) was in fact the imperative of the Qur'an to adapt the language of revelation plain or clear at the time of its revelation.[22] It did not and, as it says directly, could not exhaust the knowledge of Allah through language alone. "If all the trees on earth were pens, and the seas [were] ink, with seven [more] yet added to it, the words of Allah would never be exhausted: for verily Allah is all might, wise" (31:27).

Simultaneously, the Qur'an must speak the Truth as it intended universal guidance. This only leaves open the idea that one feature of universality is its eternal reality. In this way I have said "the Qur'an is constrained" not only by language, but also in particular by the Arabic language, especially in its seventh-century context.[23] To achieve this dual purpose – contextual clarity and eternal or universal guidance – the Qur'an has necessarily left clues that allow the explicit Qur'anic linguistic compliance to human reasoning, while challenging the limitations of the reasoning present in an inevitable preparation for newly verified historical and scientific developments in human continuity of civilization. I have referred to this as a Qur'anic trajectory, pointing us to higher moral practices even if not fully articulating these because of the context.[24] The whole of the Qur'an as guidance points toward the directions of moral excellence and ethical propriety. These are not static through time, place, and circumstance, but are relative and continue to require alterations in order to serve the highest values and principles.

The term *ayah* provides another clue to this reasoning. An *ayah* is a sign, a pointer, or an indicator. It points humans toward a certain direction. That pointer is a guide, but only inasmuch as it continues to be followed. The Qur'an uses this word often. It reveals that certain circumstances, certain people, certain discussions, and certain occasions are signs guiding or pointing to understanding or comprehension of the Truth. As it said, it also proclaims itself as universal guidance (2:2) pointing all who have moral consciousness in the direction of an ethical basis for living. But ethics inevitably develops, transformed by the constant makeover of human knowledge, experience, and change. If all there is to the Qur'an was its grappling between human linguistic competency in seventh-century Arabia, we should not only all still ride around the desert on a camel and live without air-conditioning, we should also still enslave other human beings, accept silence as a woman's agreement, and think that the sun moves around the earth each day until it rises in the east and sets in the west, while the earth stands still as the center of the universe.

The moral, technological, economic, social, and ecological context at the time of revelation, including its linguistic utterances, was necessarily constrained by the limits of that context. The expansive and eternal intent of universal guidance toward right actions, as known to an omniscient divine, whose Self-disclosure as revealed in seventh-century Arabia, was not properly rendered but was particularized within the parameters of the social-cultural, moral, legal, and linguistic constraints of that context. If one truly believes in the eternity of the divine, then one cannot accept that Allah begins or ends with the particulars of Qur'anic utterances. Indeed philosophically, limiting Allah to the utterances of the Qur'an, a specific text, would also limit Allah to seventh-century Arabia. The extent to which Allah's particular textual exposure is equated with Allah's totality in Its transcendent and unknowable reality is the same extent to which some think that Qur'anic patriarchy reflects Allah, rather than that context. One scholar expressed the idea that the god of the Qur'an *is* patriarchal, reducing Allah to the patriarchal contextual articulation and nothing else. That is a kind of *shirk* (violation of *tawhid*). It holds the seventh-century Arabian conceptual framework of Allah, and the epistemological constraints of that context as equal to Allah. Such thinking, which concretizes Allah to the limitation and literalism of the Qur'an's revelatory context, parallels the Christian discourse that literally takes the notion of God's incarnation as the body of Christ.

Therefore, it would appear that the limits of linguistic epistemology, formed as a reflection of the human mind and in correspondence to human experience, is incorrect vis-à-vis astronomical science. Allah's knowledge could not be adequately or accurately expressed in the existing Arabic epistemology. This process of adjustment of truth, fact, or Allah's knowledge to the contingencies of human language is a hint at the formidable task of revelation in the human language medium. Human language limits Allah's Self-disclosure. If revelation through text must be in human language, in order for humans to even begin to understand it, then revelation cannot be divine or Ultimate. This is distinguished from the idea that revelation is from a divine source: rather, it indicates how the source availed itself of the limitation of human language to point toward the ultimate direction for human moral development, otherwise known as guidance.

Furthermore, the Qur'anic revelation constantly hints at and opens up to new meanings. The extent to which these hints were possible to more fully achieve or be understood is directly proportionate to the facility of perceptions in the human being, and to the potential they have to extend their perceptions by indicators both in language and elsewhere, which lead toward such meanings, despite the limits by, or constraints of, structural coherence in the existing language used for the revelation.

I return to my particular interest in the patriarchal implications of text and language as a representation of the limiting constructs of semantics, despite Qur'anic attempts to both work within the seventh-century limitations and to reach beyond them. In this case, the mind of the Prophet acts as a filter through which divine disclosure takes place. Just as "Islam" reminds us that the Prophet was an ordinary, albeit exceptional, human being, he was also an ordinary, albeit exceptional, male. He was also a member of seventh-century Arabia, chosen as the context of this revelation because of the absence of the message of truth. The aberrations of behavior, etiquette, and thought were chastised in no uncertain terms by Qur'anic revelation itself. The arrogance, misogyny, and unfair business practices along with the misguided political forms were all reprimanded. It cannot be accidental that more Qur'anic passages about social justice are directly related to the treatment of females in that society. It was obviously one of the areas most in need of reform from corruption and abuse.

I am reminded of the extensive attention given to women's social, moral, spiritual, economic, political, and intellectual potential, while the social context of seventh-century Arabia was still prone to certain practices of gross gender inequity. Despite the tedious amount of attention given to gender and to the reform of social praxis, the most prevalent ideas of that time form only the starting place from which to begin the movement toward fulfilling of the eternal nature of guidance which the Qur'an points humanity toward. I consider it integral to Qur'anic intent to continue to reform. Not only does the Qur'an squarely address patriarchal privileges, it repeatedly implies, suggests, and commands change.

The Qur'an constantly made special address to those in whose hands were the power and privilege to establish social justice, albeit with varying degrees of success and failure even during the process of revelation all the way up to the Prophet's death. They are the ones held accountable and the ones with the greatest responsibility to change. There is less futility in addressing the weak and oppressed elements of the community about their autonomy and dignity except as part of the whole of community. This aspect of the Qur'an forms the core of its ethical framework. If justice is the dispensation of the strong granted toward the weak, then the Qur'anic address is a proper assessment of foremost means for where change needs to take place. While it was just as easy to address the oppressed, rendering them principal actors in their own liberation, it was certainly the more privileged and powerful who held the greatest responsibility. Such focus on the oppressed as the central actors in a movement to end oppression has only been so well articulated and advocated in the last few centuries, helping to expose the wisdom behind liberation theologies and recent grass-roots movements against oppression. However, in both the direct Qur'anic address to the privileged and the more subtle and yet pervasive address to all humankind, oppressed and oppressors, I see divine wisdom. The less disruptive option for social reform calls those with the most extensive access to rights and privileges to grant greater rights to the less privileged, to establish full human equality, and then to articulate this within the fundamental attributes of faith or belief. As with the previously cited *hadith* of the Prophet, "One of you does not believe until/unless he or she loves the other what is loved for self."

So the Qur'an addresses the men more than the women and deliberately reprimands the men more than the women, and expects obedience from men and women with regard to its commands. Instead of affording themselves the opportunity to become true servants and agents of Allah's will,

Muslim men throughout history have lavished more attention on the language directed toward them than upon attaining the goals of justice directly commanded of them. It was not until women, in the modern era, began the task of publicly indicating the Qur'anic pointers that men were so careless or flippant about – rather than agents toward – that this tendency, which had prevailed for over a millennium, was blatantly exposed. Since the significance of gender as a philosophical and epistemological category of thought has only become pronounced in modernity, it is really no surprise that gender implications of all fields of Islamic intellectual thinking has overlooked this. To persist along the lines of its continual negation by insisting that women continue to surrender the reformation and re-examination of Islam's paradigmatic foundations through its primary sources to male elites is to demonstrate willful denial of the eternal divine potential in justice.

7 Stories from the Trenches

In the battle for gender parity, those who stand guard at the gateposts of Muslim status quo have sometimes reacted vehemently against claims for justice. The trenches are deep and the fighting often unfair, but the motivation for my entry into the struggle is nonnegotiable. One of the special merits of Islam as *din*, or, way of life, is that establishing and re-establishing orthodoxy set an agenda for Islamic praxis. One cannot stand on the sidelines in the face of injustice and still be recognized as fully Muslim, fully *khalifah*. I have accepted the responsibility and continue in the struggle.

– Amina Wadud[1]

Introduction

Most of the ideas presented in this book have been in development over the more than three decades of my life as a Muslim who, in my early life, grew up in the shade of a role model, my father, a man, and a believer in God. He exemplified the integrity of being unconstrained by limitations of poverty and race in a world full of unbridled greed and sanctioned arrogance. After two decades, since my research began for the book *Qur'an and Woman*, I have continued researching while interacting with both the academic and activist communities of Muslims and non-Muslims through conferences, workshops, and other collaborative forums, locally, nationally, and inter-nationally. I continue to engage in consideration of the major issues for each of the chapters that stand independently. Yet several other issues of popular or strategic interest have not been covered in detail in this book. There are other topics as well, which were sometimes of lesser concern in my research goals yet were ignited with intense significance in public debate.

I consider these stories from the deep trenches of the gender *jihad*, which I will address here, in order to speak my own voice vis-à-vis these issues. I will not attempt to acknowledge the vast number of generous responses and long-term affects or significance of these stories while they are still part of the ongoing debates and activities. Nor will I react to the many unwarranted accusations that have been launched at me by global strangers in these debates. These events are open game for those who wish to begin name-calling, to cry heresy for perspectives different from their own, with little direct concern of the issue. However, when the issues addressed also reflect a long-standing interest, invested research, or experiences that I have either dealt with in detail in this book or am investigating further through my research, it is at least worth outlining my major standpoints by referencing the details as included or giving a brief overview. Just because an event has brought about considerable public response has not meant that those responses reflect the scope of my work, my views on multiple issues related to the event, or even a minimal knowledge of who I am vis-à-vis the controversy. Indeed, I am still in transition and not even I can say how much my perspectives will change, resume at an earlier place with a whole new set of rationales, or just repeat themselves. I mention select events here, with as much detail as seems appropriate at this time. In even briefly responding with some details to the events that precipitated a public outcry, I mostly hope to provide notes to point at their relationships to other themes and topics addressed elsewhere in this book. In one case a controversy was raised regarding an important issue, which will be addressed in a separate volume. The issue of ethnic relationships and the persistent tendency for transnational Muslims in North America to condescend transitioning Muslims of African-American background is worthy of a lengthy critical analysis. Although I have more than a little experience of this problem, I have not done sufficient academic research on its multiple reflections from the scholars who have presented detailed analysis on the history, development, and present manifestations of these forms of prejudice. So I am not sufficiently equipped to do more than raise a few points to clarify the controversial context of my experience in addressing this issue in a public forum. Much more work is needed to extend the state of my own scholarship in this area and I will not jump to hasty conclusions here, only to regret the exposure of my limitations.

The formulas for addressing both these controversial events and the other topics in this chapter might seem to be mere structural consequences, but in planning to include this chapter I had in mind an opportunity to include some vignettes from the "trenches" of struggling for gender justice. These struggles are not isolated from other experiences in my life as a Muslim but some of the issues are difficult to locate and integrate with the topics I have addressed elsewhere in this book after lengthy research. It matters very little how or why certain issues ended up here rather than elsewhere. It does matter that the issues be discussed at least in the light of fulfilling one of my objectives in writing this book – to make available to a larger audience some pro-faith, pro-feminist ideas from an inside experience of the gender *jihad*.

Hijab

"If you think that the difference between heaven and hell is 45 inches of material, boy will you be surprised." This is my *hijab* mantra. I have repeated it so often over the years, I am no longer certain of the time of its origin. Often, when I say it now, I also remove my own *hijab* from my head and drape it over my shoulders. Over the past several decades, the *hijab* has been given disproportionate symbolic significance both within and without Muslim communities. Like a *sixth pillar*,[2] we cannot discuss Islam and gender without discussing the *hijab*. While overloaded with multiple meanings, it is often the single marker used to determine community approval or disapproval. Although sometimes random and coincidental, it is also burdened with different levels of volition by Muslim women.

I have recognized and lived the idea that *hijab* is a public declaration of identity with Islamic ideology. I do not consider it a religious obligation, nor do I ascribe to it any religious significance or moral value per se. It is certainly not the penultimate denotation of modesty, as mandated by the Qur'an, "the best dress is the dress of *taqwa*" (7:26). While the *hijab* can give some semblance of a woman's affiliation with "Islam," it offers no guarantee of respect or protection. Those who reduce women to their sexuality will continue to do so, whether or not admitting this eases their consciousness. Reducing women to their sexuality, rather than affirming that sexuality is part of the whole of women's human make up, is not going to be transformed without raising that consciousness.[3] In reality, the *hijab* of coercion and the *hijab* of choice *look the same*. The *hijab* of oppression and the *hijab* of liberation look the same. The *hijab* of deception and the *hijab* of integrity look the same. You can no more tell the extent of a

Muslim woman's sense of personal bodily integrity or piety from 45 inches of cloth than you can spot a fly on the wall at two thousand feet.

Paradoxically, I consistently wore *hijab* for my first thirty years as a Muslim woman, including covering my face for four years when I lived in the U.S.A. and in Libya. While I do not consider it obligatory, my own devotion to wearing it appeared to conform to neo-traditionalist or conservative Muslims' perspective. This made me *look* safe to some and dangerous or unworthy to others. It is a double-edged aspect of my public role and representation that figures strategically in debates over Islam and gender. No matter how stringent or coincidental my own intentions throughout those three decades, or today, I cannot escape, determine, or image what it means to others.

My dress choice and preference for *hijab* has radical, self-inscribed meaning – not apparent to an outside observer. I am certain my conservative dress with simultaneous radical thinking was part of the incentive for the invitation I received in South Africa in 1994 to deliver a sermon at the Friday congregational prayer.[4] While it appears to confirm the fixed and uniform position of the "good" Muslim woman's persona, it can also defy that position. Reinvesting new meaning into old symbols is a necessary part of *being a woman* in the context of Islamic progression in the global community. The articulation of the distinction between these two meanings of fixed uniformity and radical personal reinscription cannot be obvious by form alone. It can *only* be heard in the voice of the woman who wears it.

Before Islam embraced me, I was already wearing long dresses and covering my hair. Long clothing fascinates me – the flowing shape of fabrics that move together when I walk are like gentle leaves on a tree-branch bending to yield unto to a blowing breeze. In fact, I am part of a still ongoing trend in the African-American community, where women carry their bodies with dignity and express their sexual integrity through more modest dress fashions than the ones in popular white American culture. I adopted clothing that would cover my legs at all times in public and began various styles of head wrap before I entered Islam.

Before that time, I had already been duped into the pull of the pornographic tendencies of Western culture regarding female fashions. They continue to run amok in exploiting the minute details of the female body. Even female toddlers are dressed in these popular exposing styles – shirts with one arm bare, the other covered by a single strap, shirt buttons open from the waist to the ribs, shorter and shorter skirts and pants, some cut so low that they exposing those bottomless panties called thongs. I remember once, while a teenager, I wore a dress so short it didn't have enough material to cover my underwear when I sat down. I had to remain standing to "look cool" in this skimpy outfit. Meanwhile, I must admit that my eldest daughter taught me something unexpected about such choices. They could also be self-motivated, with no connection to the weak provocations of male libido. It is my oversensitivity to men's inability to control their lust that influenced both my choices of exposing or modest garb. Such lack of control exists despite women's choice of dress. If a man respected a woman as an equal human being and not as an object of his sexual fantasies, then even a naked woman should be safe from male abuse. Furthermore, with regard to the particular items of Muslim women's dress styles, including the *hijab*, when a Serbian soldier in the rape camps can rip a two-year-old girl's body apart by raping her, it is obviously naive to assume that any amount of head-covering would have made any difference or created any real change in deep-seated male sexual aberrations. Furthermore, when African men, Muslim and non-Muslim, who have A.I.D.S. accept rumors that sex with a virgin is a cure, and then rape a female infant, talking about head coverings does not lead us very far at arresting this violation.

The Agency and Cost of Choosing Hijab
As a descendent of African slave women, I have carried the awareness that my ancestors were not given any choice to determine how much of their bodies would be exposed at the auction block or in their living conditions. So, I chose intentionally to cover my body as a means of reflecting my historical identity, personal dignity, and sexual integrity. When I entered a mosque the first time to inquire about the Islam of books I had been reading, I was already dressed in long clothes and my head was covered. I suspect this influenced the (only) men present to skip over giving me information and instead say, "If you believe that there is no god but Allah and Muhammad is his Prophet, you might as well state the *shahadah*, first pillar of Islam, the declaration of faith." The particular mosque I had chosen to visit was one block from my mother's house in Washington, D.C. It was convenient to me although I had no way of knowing how heavily influenced they were by the works of the Pakistani scholar, Maulana Mawdudi, and all the women associated with the mosque dressed in face veil as well.

Caught up in the momentum that Thanksgiving day in 1972 at the age of twenty, I agreed to become a member in a global collective with an intellectual legacy and complex multiple cultural manifestations although I was really too ill-informed to actually make a fully conscientious transition. Once I made the declaration, however, I began to follow the ritual practices as described in a booklet they provided me. I also continued my independent reading and research.[5] At that time, I begin to wear only the traditional *hijab* style as head covering to identify this transitional moment.

My preference for *hijab* has also exposed me to other aspects of its debate. In academic and conference settings, women have avoided me, perhaps with preconceived notions about the relationship between *hijab* and intellectual competence. The *hijab* means silence and conformity, so I could not possibly have any independent thoughts to contribute to the upcoming forum. It was unnerving after my presentation how frequently the same women who had avoided me would clamber around me to engage in continued dialogue. In Egypt and Jordan I also experienced how *hijab* in the Arab world carries some class implications. The women of established wealth and inheritors of liberal discourse during the days of nationalism did not dress in *hijab*. When I encountered them at foreign gatherings before, during, and after conference or workshop events there was a note of condescension in their voices. Class privilege was associated with Western-style dress.

Likewise the allure and exoticism of the invisible beauty is also associated with the veil, as so well articulated in eighteenth and nineteenth century *harim* literature.[6]

A former dean of the School of the Art, and well-known black artist, once told a non-Muslim friend that he would like to paint a picture of me – wearing a bikini. Undressing the covered woman still lingers like Hollywood images from the sit-com *I Dream of Jeannie*. Meanwhile, other threats are even more ominous and violent. On September 11, blaring car horns harassed me while returning to my office from class.[7] Since that time, I have had a multitude of airport double and triple security checks – supposedly random. Once in Pittsburgh, I sat on a small plane while the captain announced that a security breach in the airport would delay all flights. Not two minutes later, I was escorted off the plane for a special search by the head of security. I was told a tale fabricated by military officers at the airport from my point of origin. Muslim men had blown up the buildings – overtly dressed Muslim women receive the backlash. Finally, after leading the New York congregational prayer on March 18 2005,[8] several learned traditional scholars made extensive commentary that a woman leading congregational prayer was a distraction to the men's ability to control themselves sexually and thus impeded their ability to concentrate on the prayer performance. Unfortunately this is true, but not because of the woman herself; rather, because of distorted masculine sexuality, which public discourse insufficiently targets for improvement – instead, it is accommodated, by forcing women to assume the responsibility to curtail male temptation. This is another all too common double standard with insufficient attention given to correct men about their own impropriety and lack of human dignity. Personally, I worry what that says about Muslim men if even in worship they cannot keep their minds on Allah and away from their lust.

Even though dress may seem coincidental, it is laden with significance in the gender *jihad*. Women observe or ignore the traditional head covering or *hijab* with or without full intention or volition. Despite my *choice*, wearing *hijab* has *never* been free of the tremendous symbolism given to it within and without Muslim communities over the past several decades. It is not coincidental. Dubbing it the *sixth pillar* only shows its ability to divert attention from the issue of substance regarding modesty and relations between the sexes, like unrestricted male libido. The *hijab* is also a significant marker for community approval and disapproval. The paradox of my choice and devotion to wearing *hijab* without considering it obligatory means a significant duality of some strategic consideration for my various roles and experiences in the gender *jihad*.

Now that I am past the age when the Qur'an says women can lay aside their outer garments (24:60), I am less inclined to wear my *hijab* at all times – especially when cutting the grass in 90 degree summer heat! No longer do I grab for that 45 inches of material whenever the doorbell rings, when I walk to take mail out of the box at the end of my driveway, when taking a ten-minute drive to transport one of my children, or running a local errand. I still prefer to wear *hijab* as part of my more public participation and do so whenever I dress for campus, for professional or public engagements, business meetings, community affairs, and interfaith forums. I also remove the *hijab* in less formal dinners after the explicit conference to avoid a rigid stigma. Now, my quest is to achieve modest integrity over formulas and symbols. I once thought that by simply wearing modest dress, especially styles explicitly identified with Islam, like the *hijab*, I would be addressed for my mind and my overt humanity. Too many experiences to the contrary have stripped me of this narrow sense of security. It is just as easy to be reduced to my sexuality while wearing the *hijab* as when not wearing it.

Despite this, in context of Muslim confessional collectives, the *hijab* is still the primary marker that allows a woman to speak her voice. She is still too often prejudged by this symbol. Although I prefer to wear the *hijab*, it has never made the articulation of my radical observations more palatable. It did afford me opportunities to be heard. At the International Muslim Leadership Consultation,[9] those who heard my voice and recognized the radical nature of my observations actually called me a "devil in *hijab*" and demanded that I take the *hijab* off. On several occasions that week, I did wear hair wraps other than the traditional *hijab*, allowing my hair to be exposed.

Interestingly, as a woman of African descent, wearing the traditional *hijab* has increased my ethnic anonymity in many countries, including the U.S.A. It has hidden my African origins, allowing others to identify me with several Muslim ethnicities. When I began exposing my dreadlocks, I was more readily identified as African-American. This has gained greater personal and political significance. It affirms both my cultural history as well as my transitional status. Despite global notoriety, it is surprising to some Muslims from generations of Muslim culture, who still assume that "Islam" is explicitly and rigidly non-Western. Hence Muslims from the West or of Western origins cannot be major players in the movement to reform Islam, with due respect for the traditions, as well as astute reflections and obvious experience in modern pluralism and current conflicts.

September 11, 2001

The events of September 11 have changed our world forever. The complacency of the American citizen to ignore the ever-present human tragedies of intercultural political devastation and even its own foreign policies was violently confronted. This exposed them to the fear and vulnerability continually experienced by many of the world's population. The arrogance of safety replaced by the reality that many people already know or directly experience on a regular basis could have led to awareness that no one is safe until we alter our quest for global hegemony. The official American response to this fear has been to multiply the perpetuation of violence. The consent for retaliation at the level of the general American population is only slightly less abhorrent than the profiling and acts of terror perpetuated against Muslims living in America. Therefore, feelings of safety and security have become even more distant in the face of global havoc, chaos, and brutality. Unfortunately, the escalation of violence since the end of colonialism has not been a symbol for the necessity of working more radically for peace and reconciliation. That day not only negatively affected American victims and their families, it caused latent disrespect to become more overt for Muslims both in the U.S.A. and abroad. That event caused displacement and pain to be permitted in the public space without the etiquette of reciprocal respect for citizenship or of shared humanity. I wrote one short story about 9/11 as an African-American Muslim woman, dressed in a manner openly recognized for its association with Islam. Who I am inside the veil became subject to what others wanted to acknowledge or ignore based on the media frenzy to provide exotic news coverage and tidbits of info bites. I live in Virginia, the state whose position as capital of the Confederacy bears the burden of past evils and cruelty its inhabitants have done little to transform. Richmond was also the landing place of the first Africans to be forced into slavery. Racism and xenophobia is still so thick, it seems displaced at this time in American history. Since coming here with my children, in 1992, from multi-ethnic, multi-religious, multi-lingual Malaysia, I have begun to feel what it is like to be on the auction block. If I should step at the wrong time, in the wrong place, or with the wrong attitude, all of my inherent being and human dignity will be stripped bare, and new forms of chastisement have whipped me.

This is the only essay I wrote about 9/11.

* * *

Erasures

I chose the title from a *khutbah*, or sermon, delivered at a local mosque a few weeks after the event. The *khatib*, orator, referred to the way that the "identities of the victims as loved ones had been erased" for those left behind in bereavement. They would never call again, no matter how recently their voices might have had been heard. They would never visit anyone again, no matter how recently they had been in the company of family and friends. At the end of the *khutbah*, the main point was to challenge the faithful to persevere in the face of adversity, and to remember Allah's presence at all times – not just during those moments when one feels Allah's glory and grace in good times. Part of belief is to remain grateful, even in the face of tragedy.

I understood this metaphor of erasure since certain boundaries of my own being had been shifted and reconfigured from that day of destruction. I had to struggle to retain my dignity and regain wholeness. I recognized the particular metaphor of erasure in the collective experience for African-Americans and Muslim women in the immediate aftermath of 9/11. As the unique consequence of extreme forms of ethnic profiling became standardized, defended by verbal justification, the modern movie-going response to the evil and violence practiced by the bad guy is applauded when the hero, or good guy, turns and beats the bad guy to a bloody pulp. Movie endings of reconciliation do not make blockbusters. They are not good entertainment. How can Americans aspire to intense conflict resolution when the major images generated in popular culture justify extreme revenge?

On September 11, like most people, I was shocked, confused, and totally unable to believe the breaking news. This was followed by horror and dismay. As an Islamic studies professor, I could only get random glimpses of the news from campus media sources that day. In my class, I read an official statement issued by the Center for American-Islamic Relations (C.A.I.R.). They attested to total disapproval of such terrorist acts, whoever the culprit. Not clear on the extent of the catastrophe, but aware that it had been linked to extremist Muslim factions, I still assumed my responsibility was to maintain things as normal. After my first class I was walking through campus to return to my office. Suddenly a car horn blared beside me. I work in a city, so at first I thought nothing of it. When it was repeated, I looked up to notice that there were no traffic problems. In fact no other cars or pedestrians were in proximity to this vehicle. Although I was dressed in the traditional Islamic *hijab*, it never occurred to me at the time that this car horn had anything to do with me.

However, when I arrived at my office, the secretary hurried up to me with several phone messages including two from my daughter in another state. There were several more on my voice mail, all voicing concern for my safety and well-being. The secretary had been watching the news on a personal portable television in her office. She was worried for me too, and suggested I wear a hat or something instead of my *hijab* when I left the office. I found the suggestion preposterous at the time. Then the university president cancelled classes for the rest of the day. As I drove home, I did become frightened. I slipped my scarf off my head and wore it draped over my shoulders. I could not trust what an angry driver might do to me in the state of heightened panic and loss of control. That was my first erasure – the loss of choice.

As an individual, I lost my feelings of safety in making options about my own dress. As a Muslim woman, human rights' activist, I advocate a woman's right to choose whether to cover or not. As discussed above, I do not see *hijab* as a religious mandate or a significant indicator of faith. As an African-American Muslim woman, I had chosen a form of cover most recognized as a symbol of Islamic identity to express my camaraderie with Muslim women worldwide.

When gripped by fear for my personal safety on 9/11, I was also stripped of my agency to choose, and like my slave foremothers stripped of my garments of self-integrity in order to survive. I drove past the expressions of animosity by drivers with an American flag on the front and the Confederate flag on the back. One S.U.V. praised the N.Y.P.D. and F.D.N.Y. while promising to "get even." I prayed that I would not be the target of that promise at the moment my vehicle drove past. American flags proliferated, with or without "God bless America" stickers, and labels took on the ominous meaning that God could bless only America and American interest, with no regard for blessing anyone else in the world.

When I got home on September 11, more messages concerned for my safety awaited me. The next day C.A.I.R. warned women in *hijab* to be careful and advised us not to go out if avoidable. I took personal leave from classes. Forget maintaining things as normal – a new norm of extreme risk for being noticed as Muslim was being acted out. When I did go out, I tied a scarf short around my head, avoiding the distinctive *hijab* and its "Islamic" association. All of Islam was under fire. All Muslims had been reduced to this one extreme and violent action. All Muslims were open game for the required revenge.

By Friday that first week, this first erasure was beginning to impinge upon my self-confidence and the integrity of my chosen identity. This was erasure for being Muslim – coincidently female in *hijab*. To start reclaiming my wholeness I also needed to reaffirm this symbol in my own Islamic right of choice. I moved out of that erasure by selecting to attend spiritual ceremonies and interfaith-based activities focused on healing the whole of humanity. Still I felt ambivalent about this overt symbolic expression exposing my Muslim identity in an Islamaphobic context.

The period of mourning was followed by weeks of responding to public and professional service calls. One call came from the Internet women's newsgroup called E-news.[10] Their web page describes their mission:

The mainstream media too often neglect the public policy stories that concern women and that impact our lives. They too often overlook women as sources and experts for news. And when the media do cover women's issues, the stories are too often stereotypical and simplistic or answer the wrong questions. Women's E-news fills that void by offering solid, serious, well-researched news about and for women. Women's

E-news asks the intelligent questions that women want answered. We probe the implications for women of events, policies and practices.

The contact person confirmed, "all we hear are men's responses" to the crisis. She later quoted my assertion that men perpetrated these events in response to actions men exclusively had decided upon, planned, and orchestrated. Indeed, "men make war while women and children are victims as well as other men. Yet, we do not hear women's voices with regard to these events." This E-news interview included some of the details I have described here about my experience on September 11.

For several reasons, this interview caught the interest of someone from the Public Broadcasting Service (P.B.S.). "We are so keen to bring you to New York for a special program about the September 11 events and Muslim women. Your comments were so insightful." Ah, here was a "fresh angle" for the media to exploit. Somewhere in this conversation I informed her that I am African-American. Within 24 hours, I was erased. I was Muslim enough to be harassed, woman enough to have insights on collective female marginalization, but since I was *not* Middle Eastern I could not speak as either Muslim or woman for P.B.S.

Although other reasons were feigned in the next telephone conversation when the invitation was withdrawn, I intentionally followed the logistics. When asked if I could help fulfill their request by naming other Muslim women, they made inquiries into their ethnic origins. This would eventually clarify their parameters for who was deemed appropriately Muslim – exclusively Middle Eastern women. This erasure was humiliating. I could be threatened *as a Muslim*, but I could not have a legitimate voice as a Muslim. I had insights *as a woman* but I could not provide a female voice. More importantly, someone outside Islam was determining my place inside Islam.

I began to observe in earnest the post 9/11 politics of representation of Islam in American media. African-Americans form the largest single ethnic group of Muslims in America, yet their voices were the least represented. Women, one-half of the Muslim population, would form none of the major spokespersons. Yet women remained the most easily identifiable and most vulnerable for random acts of retaliation in the aftermath. Erasures from outside the community of believers might be dismissed as part of the larger agenda to erase Islam. The internal erasures on the other hand were equally problematic and more disconcerting.

Later that month C.A.I.R. confirmed that women in *hijab* had been increasingly subjected to harassment. The spokesperson for this announcement and its detailed implications was male. Were we to believe that no woman was available to comment? Or is it simply that no woman could represent this concern as well as one who never had and never will wear a *hijab* himself? When the television program *60 Minutes* dedicated one segment of its program to "representatives" of the American Muslim community, four Muslim brothers were present: one white American, one African-American (who remained nearly silent throughout the program), and two transnational brothers, one a long-time immigrant to the U.S.A., but the fourth member was a South African academic, who, despite having visited the U.S.A. before, on this occasion had only been here for six weeks. Yet the program organizers considered him more eligible to represent Islam in America than the selection of at least a single woman for the program.

Despite the blatant ethnic reductionism of Muslim voices after 9/11, the silence of the female voice continued to recast the patriarchal perpetuation of destructive actions, but also revealed the privilege of their perspective on human events – only enhancing the negative consequences for all humankind. It cannot be said to have divine sanction. I think about this whenever I present a talk about Mary, mother of Jesus, as explicitly reflecting the gynocentric voice in the Qur'an. The voice of Allah, the originator of revelation, speaks through Mary at a most womanly moment – the labor pains of childbirth. All else is eclipsed for the sake of her care-taking. If that voice was present in the planning of conflict resolution we would surely be less likely to conclude the matter by choosing war, terror, violence, and retaliation.

Before she died, Olive Schreiner of South Africa wrote,

There is perhaps no woman . . . who could look down upon a battle field covered with slain, but the thought would rise in her "So many mothers' sons" . . . No woman who is woman says of a human body, "It is nothing!" On the day when the woman takes her place beside the man in governance and arrangement of external affairs of her race will also be the day that heralds the death of war as a means of arranging human difference.

It is not because of woman's cowardice, incapacity nor, above all, because of her general superior virtue, that she will end war when her voice is finally, fully and clearly heard. Rather her voice speaks from the center of her reality, and that reality brings forth life, so it cannot promote the destruction of life as the objective for a humane and dignified future. It is past time to include the voices of women in all matters public and private to bring about greater truth and harmony in organizing the affairs of humankind.

Three Public Controversies in the New Millennium

Having a public role resulted from taking a stance on issues of concern to my goal of growth and development as a private individual struggling to establish my identity as a Muslim woman and a member of the collective community and within ongoing historical traditions. This public consequence of my primary goal was never my intention and I continue to feel ambivalent about it, often resorting to long periods of isolation and retreat to try to maintain personal balance and spiritual equilibrium. Once it was established, however, I neither lost my goal of personal and spiritual identity development nor refused the consequences of and responsibility to the public role.

I have been accused of seeking the public role that has been thrust upon me only by those who do not know me and hence do not recognize my own priorities. Such responses have also allowed my primary goals to be reduced to particular statements or to certain selective sensationalized events. Thus others, who do not know me, who have never read my works, or do not consider my decades of involvement in the gender *jihad,* concoct judgments on the basis of the reductions that best suit their own opportunism to justify their opposing views.

In effect, all of Islam, including my participation and aspirations, is focused on a false presumption that defending particular interpretations by openly opposing those who express other interpretations is a requirement for being inside the Muslim *ummah.* As one essay describes it,[11]

> If a stone's dropping into a pool of water represents revelation, and the subsequent concentric waves that radiate from the point of entry represent tradition, then modernism could be visualized as a ring floating above (or below) the farthest periphery of the waves that is disconnected both horizontally from the water and vertically from the trajectory of the stone.

I do not agree that all modernism as so graphically described is "disconnected" from Islam and Islamic tradition. Its real position as a continuation of the concentric circles from the divine center must be properly acknowledged. This is recognized with only a minimum amount of insight. In the future, it will surely become the characterization of today's diverse Islamic expressions, which are part of the Islamic intellectual continuum. Muslims have always grappled with their current contexts, as agents building upon the principles of revelation vis-à-vis the universal potential of those principles in explicit application to diverse contexts. There is an even greater need for this continued grappling with our tradition in our present circumstances. Otherwise, the move of the concentric circle will enter rigor mortis.

Certain particular public events have been enshrouded with aspects of misrepresentation that unfortunately might never be corrected. As modern media has proven, people seek the sensational. The following treatment in response to three particular public events are provided in order to satisfy those who may have questions about the events, despite the way they were sensationalized, used for demonization, or reported by other sources most often without my input. Nothing is recanted or denied about my participation in the events, my approach to the issues, or to other people's opportunism. This book elaborates my perspectives on a wide range of issues. These summaries are provided only to locate them both within their particular time and place of occurrence and within my primary goals, the principles underlying them, and as part of my personal and spiritual identity intimately connected to interpretations and implementations of Islam. They will be presented in chronological order.

* * *

Second International Muslim Leaders' Consultation on H.I.V./A.I.D.S., Malaysia, 2003

The Second International Muslim Leaders' Consultation on H.I.V./A.I.D.S. was held in Malaysia. Some of the conclusions drawn from the First Consultation in Uganda, one year before, indicated a more conservative approach to H.I.V./A.I.D.S. and to "Islam" than the approach taken by the organizers in Malaysia. For example, the word "leaders" was given a broader meaning (previously exclusive to neo-traditionalist authorities) to include community activists working on H.I.V./A.I.D.S. issues and Muslims who are H.I.V.-positive or have A.I.D.S. themselves.

The conference format was meticulously organized by the Malaysian hosts, divided between plenary sessions with a panel of speakers, followed by breakout workshops inviting in-depth discussion by all attendees. The invited speakers would circulate through each of the workshops after their presentations, ostensibly to answer questions and address comments raised by the attendees. The secretariat provided rapporteurs at both the plenary sessions and the workshops, with scheduled sessions to report back to all conference attendees. This format was not only carefully thought out and orchestrated, it was more inclusive than running five days with "talking heads" lecturing a passive audience, who may or may not ask questions during a Q&A session, unduly extending the plenary and often intimidating the more reticent attendees from speaking. The first indication that the Malaysian hosts were not respected in the meticulous and inclusive planning started the second day when certain participants didn't attend the breakout workshop sessions. Instead, a few started shouting after the presentations of invited speakers during plenary sessions. This shouting rose to the level of total disruption during the plenary on "How Can Islamic Teachings Reduce Vulnerability?" My presentation was the spark igniting a fire.

Under the pretence of the demand for a Q&A session to follow all presentations, a group of eight people not only disrespected the careful organization of the hosting committee for the three hundred international attendees and participants, but also used the opportunity to directly insult me: "devil in *hijab*!" and cries of "heresy" followed. I had never experienced such an extreme lack of decorum and remained silent under the assault. The detractors walked out of the conference room. When a transgendered victim of H.I.V./A.I.D.S. stepped to the podium after me, other attendees also walked out. Eventually, the secretariat restructured the forum in an attempt to placate these eight visitors, despite their extreme lack of etiquette. More than fifty supporters organized a petition to have the disrupters removed from the conference and read several statements at other sessions. In light of the situation, the secretariat allowed me to make a statement announcing my decision to withdraw my paper. Although I had hoped to help demonstrate my respect for the organizers who attempted to placate the detractors without challenging their rude behavior, I had also hoped it could help bring the forum back on track and help regain the momentum of the consultation. But the damage was done, and it would therefore be clear that inclusive discourse on H.I.V./A.I.D.S. was impossible for those intolerant of difference.

The version of my presentation that follows has only been edited for minimal structural repair. All of the contentious statements are retained, some with endnotes or elaborations when deemed beneficial.

Vulnerabilities: H.I.V. and A.I.D.S.

Introduction

The spread of H.I.V./A.I.D.S. within families brings up an interesting concern with addressing inconsistencies between intent and experience within the family: how do certain family structures create greater vulnerability? The first part of this presentation will look at an interesting paradox: the family, that institution through which human beings expect and receive their greatest nurturing, is the same institution that can create the greatest vulnerabilities in the spread of H.I.V./A.I.D.S. for women and children. When the structure of family itself causes vulnerability, critical examination is even more in order to construct ways that civil society can empower family members to challenge the abuses that occur within families. However, some see the very idea of challenging "family" as a disruption in social well-being. Ultimately my question is: How can families empower all members equally despite vulnerability due to age or gender?

The first part of this presentation will examine the terms and experiences of vulnerability to H.I.V./A.I.D.S. for women and children as members of existing family structures in the context of Islam and Muslims. My objective is to disentangle or demystify "family" by focusing on both its supportive and destructive aspects. Family as a construct must be subjected to a rigorous analysis as part of any agenda that seeks to fight against the spread of A.I.D.S. As such, combating A.I.D.S. will also contribute to reforms in Muslim Personal Status Laws. One goal of these reforms will be to help the family structure function as a comfort and support for all its members equally. I will review some of the underlying assumptions about family in Islamic law inasmuch as these historically constructed assumptions are still implemented in Muslim societies while allowing undue privilege for men and male desires. This presentation uses the H.I.V./A.I.D.S. epidemic as evidence of dangerous and untenable double standards in the face of modern social change and experience. I will consider structural inconsistencies that often go unchallenged when the word "family" is introduced. While seeking to retain the family ideals of nurturance and support, I will also focus on the way some family structures provide for particular vulnerabilities.

The second part of this presentation will begin to think about theological implications of combating the spread of A.I.D.S., increasing public awareness, and empowering both direct and indirect victims of H.I.V./ A.I.D.S. Some family members have directly contracted the virus through abuses and misunderstandings of other members while some family members find their lifestyle and future indirectly affected by members with H.I.V./A.I.D.S.

Thinking about H.I.V./A.I.D.S: Gender and Family in an Islamic Perspective

In 2002, I had my first encounter with constructive organizational level efforts to respond to the A.I.D.S. epidemic at a meeting in Nairobi, Kenya. The World Conference on Religion and Peace (W.C.R.P.) convened as part of the H.A.C.I. program (H.I.V./A.I.D.S. Children Initiative) launched specifically to address the needs of increasing numbers of orphans of A.I.D.S. The Secretary General for W.C.R.P., Dr. Vendley, will give a keynote later in this conference and can no doubt provide details on W.C.R.P.'s particular project related to utilizing community-based religious organizations for information, advocacy, and support.

My experience at this W.C.R.P. meeting was important not only as a context for learning but also as it sparked my interest in the work needed in the context of Islam and Muslims with A.I.D.S. On that occasion, African religious leaders also gathered for a summit. The Muslim participants convened one morning to discuss the initiatives and Islam. One of the *imams*, religious leaders, dominated the first half of that forty-five-minute meeting by giving a *khutbah*, speech or sermon, on the importance of avoiding *zinaa*, fornication. This *khutbah* was insignificant to our development of a clearly articulated "Islamic" position on the particular initiative regarding A.I.D.S. orphans. Indeed, the whole tenor of the speech was useless as a framework for developing an Islamic theological response to H.I.V./A.I.D.S. Yet such a response might be useful if developed in the future. During the time since that meeting, I have begun to think about an Islamic theological response and the problems that it might pose.

H.I.V./A.I.D.S. and Vulnerability

In effect, what I present here emphasizes the ways that "Islam" and Muslims exacerbate the spread of A.I.D.S., as well as offers my critique of the neo-conservative traditional Islamic theological response of reducing it to "*zinaa.*" Such a reduction can never cure A.I.D.S. A.I.D.S. exists as an immune deficiency syndrome. It has spread to epidemic proportions: over forty-two million people are affected with an estimated three million deaths per year. Of particular interest to my thesis is the consequence and spread of

A.I.D.S. among children under the age of fifteen, with additional infections of over one half million annually. In addition to its fatality, consequences here include children who become orphaned each year due to the death of their primary care takers from A.I.D.S. The estimates are fourteen million children orphaned by A.I.D.S. What does a theological premise, "*laa taqrabuna al-zinaa*, Do not approach *zinaa*" (17:32) avail these children? How has Islam in particular assisted them toward living a life of dignity and how has it prevented them from experiences of dignity and worth, unstigmatized by our ostrich theology and law?

My experiences at the Nairobi meeting included a visit to an orphanage run by a women's church group. To be sure, these women were also concerned with the spiritual health and development of the children in this home. What happens when religious groups, Muslim or otherwise, take such an afflicted child into such homes and orphanages? What if the child had Muslim or Christian parents? Do we only take in those children who are members of our own religion? Can we raise any child with true religious choice once we take them in? It presents an interesting case vis-à-vis the concerns for these fourteen million children. If we save an endangered child is the child then further endangered by loss of religious choice?

The other group, of even greater concern to my work, is monogamous wives, especially in the context of Islam, where a Muslim wife is not only expected to be, but defined in terms of her being unconditionally sexually available to her husband. Properly fulfilling this role of wife is fatal to some women, with estimates as high as 80%. That is, 80% of the heterosexual women with A.I.D.S. are monogamous and have only ever had sex with their husbands. These percentages come from all H.I.V./A.I.D.S. infected women. My suspicions would be that the percentage would be even higher for Muslim women. What does a theological premise, *laa taqrabuna al-zinaa*, avail these women? How has "Islam" in particular assisted them toward living a life of dignity and how has it prevented them from experiences of dignity and worth, unstigmatized by our ostrich theology and law?

Ultimately the solutions to the problems of A.I.D.S. will not be limited to victims in the two particular groups in my examination. However, I am interested in how these two groups demonstrate the emptiness of such religious platitudes, like *laa taqrabuna al-zinaa*, in addressing the problem. Even when those responses are based on the Qur'an and *sunnah*, they are ineffective in resolving the problem of women and children's vulnerability.

H.I.V./A.I.D.S. and Sexuality in Islam
With regard to the 80% of heterosexual women who contract A.I.D.S. in

monogamous relations, a direct look at Islam and sexuality is called for. According to *shari'ah*, if a Muslim man desires intercourse with his wife, she must comply. If she does not, she is guilty of *nushuz*, recalcitrance. Such a recalcitrant wife, *nashizah*, is no longer eligible for *nafaqah*, maintenance or financial support. In addition, in various degrees of interpretation and application, verse 4:34 of the Qur'an asserts that the husband of such a woman may beat her. In the face of this, the vast majority of Muslim wives, those with gentle husbands, husbands of polygyny (open or secret), husbands of violence and abuse, upright husbands of moral standing, and husbands of A.I.D.S., open their legs to their men as they are not only expected, but commanded to do by that which is most popularly understood as "Islam." Women turn toward men who have contracted A.I.D.S. and open their legs to their own death and destruction. Since the overwhelming majority of Muslim women with A.I.D.S. are monogamous wives, the statement *laa taqrabuna al-zinaa* is not applicable to them. Yet they will become the one stigmatized and even shamed, while Muslim authorities continue to support the unbridled sexual license of the male libido. It matters little if the men have contracted A.I.D.S. by either legal and moral or illegal and immoral means. By legal and moral means, I refer to the husband who has contracted A.I.D.S. by marrying a younger, more sexually virile female carrier to confirm their own masculine sexuality, and then spread it to the demure and compliant wife of longer standing. In turn, if she gives birth, their innocent child is also in danger of being infected. What has this woman done to deserve the single theological solution, *laa taqrabuna al-zinaa*? The consequences for the *muhsinat,* married virtuous women, and the *qaanitat*, religious and morally devout Muslim women, are the same – they will die because they did what they had been taught was "good." How does a statement, *laa taqrubina az-zinaa*, apply to them? How does "Islam" resolve this problem?

Sexuality

One of the underlying concerns for fully addressing H.I.V./A.I.D.S. is a hard and fast look at sexuality in Islam. To do this, I remind us first about sexuality and gender in general. My references here are to research by Western feminists. In particular, I am interested in work done on the tyranny of patriarchal domination through heterosexuality or the sexual politics of domination. For the most part, marriage in *shari'ah* is marriage of the woman's subordination. Whatever choice she may have in contracting marriage to a particular prospective husband, her choice is then limited within the structures of marriage and family that prevail once the marriage is consummated. There is a considerable lack of reciprocity vis-à-vis what happens in the marriage itself.

A prime theoretical contribution of the contemporary analysis of women's oppression can be captured in the slogan "the personal is political." What this means is that the subordination of women by men is pervasive, that it orders the relationships of the sexes in every area of life, that a sexual politic of domination is as much in evidence in the private spheres of the family, ordinary social life, and sexuality as in the traditionally public spheres of government and the economy. The belief that things we do in the bosom of the family or in bed are either "natural" or else a function of personal idiosyncrasies of private individual is held to be an "ideological curtain that conceals the reality of women's systematic oppressions." For the feminist, two things follow upon the discovery that sexuality too belongs to the sphere of the political. The first is that whatever pertains to sexuality – not only actual sexual behavior, but sexual desire and sexual fantasy as well – will have to be understood in relation to a larger system of subordination; the second, that the deformed sexuality of patriarchal culture must be moved from the hidden domain of "private life" into an arena of struggle, where a "politically correct" *sexuality of mutual respect* will contend with an "incorrect" sexuality of domination and sub-mission."[12] (emphasis mine)

In addition, according to another article[13] on sexuality, Muslim scholars apparently were already ahead of the feminist here:

In comparison with many other religious traditions, it has often been noted that Islam is a religion that has evaluated sexual life positively. Articulating the integral relationship between spirituality and sexuality is one way that the Prophet Muhammad challenged his society. It remains for us, today, to continually struggle with that challenge. The system of norms, rules, and laws created by Muslims in the past (a collective body we call *shari‘ah*) does not absolve us of this challenge. It may, in fact, create complexities that drive us to reinvestigate the topic while pre-senting obstacles to a just resolution of those complexities. Scholars in the contemporary period have not lived up to the standards and frankness of pre-modern Islamic scholars, and much work has yet to be done on the question of sexuality in Islamic scripture, law, and society. Many scholars and Islamic leaders in the present shy away from honest discussions of sex and sexuality, with all its promise and problems. Muslims in pre-modern times certainly were not shy about discussing matters of sex and sexuality, so why should we be so prudish? The most basic goal of this essay is to return to us, the contemporary Muslims, the "awe and bewilderment" that al-Ghazali felt when considering sexual pleasure.

So sexuality is connected not only to spirituality, but to politics as well. What is required of us in political situations is an acute sense of justice. But Muslim neo-conservatives often ignore or obscure justice when it comes to matters of sex, gender, and sexuality. We need to think more clearly about "intimate citizenship," how personal, emotional, and sexual dimensions of our lives, which are often locked away as "private," actually have very public and often political consequences.[14]

Coincidently this article cited above takes a thorough look at the issue of homosexuality and presents the reader with various classical interpretations of the story of Lut from the Qur'an. Yet even in the new territory being forged by this article, Scott Kugle never manages to disentangle his compliments of the past and critique of the present from the extent to which even his struggle to look more affirmatively at sexuality at that time was still only based on male sexuality. What he does consider here is Islam's lack of prudishness in the classical period, when the predominant notion of human being was the male human. Furthermore, the Qur'an itself, as well as the *shari'ah*, is founded upon male sexual experience. In addition, I have looked at a few places when the Qur'an *seems* to affirm masculine pleasure and experience. I point to three specific incidents that give a cross-section of male sexuality and fantasies without ever responding in an equivalent manner to women and women's sexuality.

Foremost, however, is the Qur'anic affirmation of marriage in general, which should be considered gender-neutral. The underlying assumptions, of an overwhelmingly heterosexual social order, are that women and men should be engaged in and enjoy healthy sexual exchanges. However, the first indication that there are disproportionate elements in this general gender-neutral formula is in the attention given to men's "right to satisfaction" from the several places in the Qur'an: the verse on women as *tilth*, then to the conditional permission to multiple wives, and concluding in the afterlife with meticulous details concerning the *huris* of paradise. Not only do no equivalent articulations exist in the Qur'an about women's sexual satisfaction, the Qur'an refers to post-menopausal women as being "beyond want" despite ample evidence to the contrary. Following closely upon this, the emphasis on sexuality in the law is overwhelmingly on male heterosexual satisfaction.[15]

An H.I.V.-positive woman is not an indictment of the promiscuity of the woman, since: "Men are *qiwamuna*" (responsible, though to many this is taken as "in charge") (4:34) can be seen as recognition of the unequal power dynamics of masculine and feminine sexuality. It is not in the command form, implying perhaps the idea that it is an edict, to be fulfilled by the mere nature of being a man. It is stated in the form of an active participle recognizing agency and being. A man may fulfill *qiwamah*. Therefore women must yield sexually to this *Qa'im* (responsible male), whether he is acting in a manner *mustaqim*, straight, or crooked. An analogy could be made between the sexual moralities of an H.I.V.-positive married Muslim woman and pregnancy in an unmarried Muslim woman. Neither is proof of a woman's sexual misconduct or indiscretion. With today's fertilization sciences, pregnancy is not even proof of intercourse. Further evidence shows multiple causes of pregnancy without a woman's consent. However, both the case of women with A.I.D.S. and unmarried pregnant women lend themselves well to the idea that women are more vulnerable in Muslim societies. Hence, some efforts greater than veiling, isolating, and silencing them are ethically mandated. The simplest suggestion: have men confront other men about their sexual misconduct and the thought patterns underlying them, in order to distinguish such misogyny from being misappropriated as "Islam" or surrender to the divine will.

Vulnerability and Gender

Much of my information in the following was taken from the World Health Organization.[16] "In most societies, girls and women face heavier risks of the H.I.V. infection than men because their diminished economic and social status compromises their ability to choose safer and healthier life strategies." Gender roles powerfully influence the course and impact of the epidemic and affect the extent to which A.I.D.S. affects vulnerability. Gender inequalities, the different attributes and roles assigned to women and men in society, affect their ability to protect themselves and cope with its impact. "Reversing the spread of H.I.V. therefore demands that women's rights are realized and that women are empowered in all spheres of life,"[17] especially sexually. The factors that increase the vulnerability of women and girls to H.I.V. "include social norms that deny women sexual health knowledge and practices that prevent them from controlling their bodies and deciding the terms on which they have sex." In addition to this are "women's limited access to economic opportunities and autonomy, and the multiple household and community roles they are saddled with."

The proportion of women living with H.I.V./A.I.D.S. has risen steadily. Women are often affected at an earlier age than men. Girls are five or six times more likely to be infected than teenage boys. There is also growing evidence that a large share of new cases of H.I.V. infection is due to gender-based violence in homes, schools, the workplace and other social spheres, to say nothing of situations of civil disorder and war where women and girls are systematically targeted for abuse, including sexual abuse.

H.I.V.-positive women are also discriminated against when trying to access care and support. Meanwhile the burden of caring for ill family members rests mainly with women. Discrimination in care support and women's own indispensable support roles often mean that many will seek assistance for their own illness much later than will H.I.V.-positive men. Without women-specific programs being integrated with other services such as ob-gyn, social support, substance abuse, nutrition, and the like, women's particular needs and vulnerabilities will be hopelessly problematic in formulating any agenda effective enough to assist in the reduction of the spread of A.I.D.S. and will render it null and void.

The *laa taqrabuna al-zinaa* agenda is one such problematic agenda. It does manage to increase the stigma of all H.I.V.-positive cases. Muslim women who are described in the Qur'an in terms particular to their sexual virtues especially feel the concern for moral propriety. The significant role played by stigma in reducing the gains of a battle against H.I.V./A.I.D.S. needs its own attention. Like with rape, women are more clearly the ones most victimized, but they are also the ones more likely to be stigmatized by its occurrence and as such will more than likely hide their experience in order to avoid the negative social and spiritual consequences of such a confession. On the other hand, when a woman stands forward to pronounce her opposition to those factors that increase women's vulnerability, she herself may be cast in *a negative light with suspicions about her morality* being whispered behind her back.[18] In this force of stigma, it is no wonder that women are still among the minority of those who have worked comprehensively to help construct a more compassionate paradigm, including an "Islamic" religious paradigm, to confront such an issue.

Yet only with women's full participation and empowerment can the disease actually be arrested. In this regard, an Islamic perspective on H.I.V./A.I.D.S. is impossible without simultaneously addressing women's empowerment, including their sexual empowerment in the context of the patriarchal paradigm that still predominates our notions about sexuality in Islam. A new paradigm is needed that promotes women's rights to know, i.e. be informed; to say no, i.e. refuse; or otherwise independently determine the exact nature of their full sexuality, and to offer their responses to the predominance, not only of male-pleasure-oriented heterosexuality, but to the tyranny of it against women.

How does "Islam" Resolve this Problem?

There are no Qur'anic verses on epidemics, whether of the immune-deficient or S.A.R.S. type. Yet Muslims must address these problems. Furthermore, if a Muslim is efficient at bringing about a cure, or resolving issues about the spread of these diseases, we might want to associate his or her "Islam" with the consequence of the research or medical findings. If we do make this association, however, it would at best be indirect. Even if the successful researcher makes an explicit or direct statement that the work was accomplished as a result of his or her being Muslim, it will be impossible to refer to a specific Qur'anic verse or prophetic *ahadith* that could stand as the foundation of the technical skills, medical know-how, or research methods that could actually prove to bring about solutions. In a sense this gives us, as Muslim, the greater freedom in participating fully and responsibly in the search for a cure. If we fail, we cannot be indicted as bad Muslims. On the other hand, if we are successful, we cannot associate our success explicitly to Islam, even as we take inspiration from it.

Likewise, we cannot blame a failure of Islam as the cause for A.I.D.S. If we address shortcomings within family law, as conditional upon the safety and security of those whose lives suffer from existing family structures, then we can help to reconstruct the law to remove those factors which help the spread of A.I.D.S. Although these structural problems may be seen as secondary causes of the spread of the virus, the process of reducing the spread of it has shown the need to address all causes. Furthermore, these structural changes have other positive results in formulating more egalitarian families and society.

As a non-medical person, and one who does not contribute to disease research, I am clear that I cannot propose a solution to H.I.V./A.I.D.S. My concern here is to address the ways that hollow Islamic theological rhetoric is made hallow or sacred by authoritarian means. Religious leaders, scholars, and medical personnel cannot resort to these empty platitudes to excuse them from dealing directly with a problem of this catastrophic proportion.

H.I.V./A.I.D.S. and Zinaa

If H.I.V./A.I.D.S. was merely the result of immoral or un-Islamic behavior, then non-Muslim countries should consistently have higher percentage rates of cases. However, highly industrialized countries like the U.S.A. have more active measures to curtail the spread of the disease perhaps *because* they do not resort to such an equation and reduce the problem to morality. When the emphasis is on reducing the spread of A.I.D.S. and not on taking a moral high ground, then more effective means for its reduction have resulted. Again, the underlying presumption that this disease can be directly linked to some un-Islamic level of moral behavior precludes the efficacy of other factors to determine the actual spread or safety and protection from its fatalities. The U.S.A. began its campaign against the spread of A.I.D.S. without the religio-moral high ground that Muslims have allowed to thwart effective responses to the epidemic. Without persisting in the earliest name-calling, isolation, silence, and denial, the U.S.A. actually took up means and strategies to address the spread of the disease. Simultaneously, they also launched the first ever such public campaign to promote celibacy among American youth. Commercials show popular and sophisticated young people occupied in a number of activities – going to school, earning and saving money, or creatively engaged in sports or the arts – articulating their reasons for abstaining from sex until they are married. It has promoted a public discourse that more effectively advocates for abstinence, without requiring it to be limited to religion.

H.I.V. and Shari'ah

My concluding remarks are based on the impossibility of an exclusively Islamic theological response to H.I.V./A.I.D.S. I don't mean to sound pessimistic or un-Islamic here, but I have already stated that:

> If a Muslim is efficient at bringing about a cure, or resolving issues about the spread of these diseases, we might want to associate his or her "Islam" with the consequence of the research or medical findings. If we do make this association, however, it would at best be indirect. Even if the successful researcher makes an explicit or direct statement that the work was accomplished as a result of his or her being Muslim, it will be impossible to refer to a specific Qur'anic verse or prophetic *ahadith* that could stand as the foundation of the technical skills, medical know how, or research methods that could actually prove to bring about solutions. In a sense this gives us, as Muslim, the greater freedom in participating fully and responsibly in the search for a cure. If we fail, we cannot be indicted as bad Muslims. On the other hand, if we are successful, we cannot associate our success explicitly to Islam, even as we take inspiration from it.

Indeed, I see Islam as inspiration for making my comments here as forceful and hard-hitting as I can in order perhaps to jolt my own soul out of any tendency toward what has been called the "ostrich approach" to Islamic theology in the face of seemingly insurmountable odds that do seem to find an explicit and simplistic textually based solution. In his book on *shari'ah*,[19] Abdul Rauf reminds us that *shari'ah* is the "operative formula by which the Muslim determines what is good and ethical." What is good confirms to divine intent. "The primary focus of the *shari'ah* is on human-kind's journey towards intimacy with our Creator," it protects the religion from the vicissitudes of history. He goes further: "it is the law of Islam that is arguably the most important element in the struggle waged between traditionalism and modernism." He recommends that we draw our temp-oral into the eternal and "think about the morality of issues that were not posed to us before." Indeed, if the "Islamic point of view" has not yet been established, regarding certain issues that Muslims will have to encounter, then, he asserts, it "ought to be."

Yet he refers to the three responses by Muslims to modern dilemmas. Number one is the "ostrich approach": bury our heads in the sand, and quote isolated *ahadith* and Qur'an, especially those which imply Muslims are on a moral high ground and thus unaffected by these new dilemmas. The second is to build a Muslim society by establishing standards adhering to divinely ordained values. The third is to develop a methodology to integrate us into the global society at large without losing our religious integrity and identity. Clearly this third option will be the most affirmative one in response to H.I.V./A.I.D.S.

The nuts and bolts of any affirmative action on legal reforms will be drawn from a variety of sources of Islamic law, textual and *ijtihadic*. How they have been used and can be use vis-à-vis H.I.V./A.I.D.S. is not fixed, yet using them is essential. Differences in their usage need to be plainly spelled out, showing the ways and means of using various criteria and one's own sense of moral imperative to achieve optimal opportunities to benefit H.I.V./A.I.D.S. sufferers and to prevent further spread. We must be honest, however, that this is a process. For something like H.I.V./A.I.D.S. there is no simple precedent. A.I.D.S. is an indiscriminate, equal-opportunity killer: it matters little if you pray every day or never pray at all. Therefore we will not be able to resolve the problem by the ostrich logic that pretends good Muslims don't contract A.I.D.S., let alone die from it. How relevant is such a stand in protecting millions of children with H.I.V./A.I.D.S.?

With respect to legal reforms I intentionally defer to those experts on matters of jurisprudence with this one important caveat gleaned from my experiences addressing issues of Islam and gender for several decades. No interpretation, application, or positive development can proceed without every effort to include the ones whose agency is most directly affected by the case presented. H.I.V.-positive persons and victims of A.I.D.S. from all sectors of society must be included in the process of resolving the problem if we hope to achieve effective results. In this respect it is the reality of the ones who experience it which determines not only the nature of the experience, but the positive responses to it for the goals of education, curtailment, and control.

*　　*　　*

The "I Am a Nigger" Controversy, Toronto, 2005

The Noor Cultural Center in Toronto teamed up with York University to extend an invitation for me to give two presentations in Toronto in February 2005. Both institutions were particularly interested in ideas about textual interpretation. As I understood the email communications, I planned to focus on issues of gender and Qur'anic interpretation. I also wanted to indicate complexities of interpretation and implementation within complex changes in circumstance. The experiences of North American Muslim movements, like experiences of other Muslims in the diaspora, include interactions between Islam's intellectual heritage, diverse cultural traditions, and the contexts of secular modern nation-states in the West. A great deal of attention has been given to these multifaceted dynamics both from official government agencies within these Western nation-states as well as by the diverse population of Muslims now residing in them. This is an important discourse and there are so many contributions already available I could never do justice to its complexities in this brief section. However, it is well worth the attention given to it.

Here, I refer to the important discourse only to indicate two ways in which my experience with the Noor Cultural Center is only one event reflecting on-going complexities. These two aspects of the dynamics are selected here only to allow me the opportunity to simultaneously respond directly to this experience and to reduce it from the sensationalism that it precipitated. The Noor Center is part of an important post-9/11 development in Muslim communities in North America. More *members* of the diverse Muslim communities have worked together outside the mosque congregational context to create organizations that address Islam and Muslims. I have been invited to several of these new extra-mosque Muslim enclaves and all of them have a refreshing response to the reality of being a minority within a context that has tremendous power to affect the lives of Muslims here and worldwide, despite adequate diversity of Muslim self-representations. All of them are explicit about the need for greater tolerance toward the diversities that exist among Muslims in North America as well as the need for building greater networks with non-Muslims. If the mosque organizations are focused on preserving the boundaries of Islam to such a level as to give more attention to constructing and preserving those boundaries, then where will Muslims, whose lives are not so narrowly defined, go for furthering their knowledge of Islam and for affirming their identity as Muslims? Furthermore, how will their identity as Muslims *in America* be integrated with their lives in close interaction with non-Muslims in America? Only protecting narrow boundaries is a deterrent to such agendas.

More Muslim Americans are creating institutions that promote this dynamic interchange rather than prescribing and protecting narrow boundaries. The audiences in the variety of functions organized in these extra-mosque institutes are composed of both Muslims with active mosque participation and those who have felt excluded from the mosques. In accordance with the emphasis on greater tolerance, these institutions have also addressed attention to controversial issues and perspectives while not confining the speakers or invited guests to conform to any one particular definition of Muslim, as well as inviting and interacting with non-Muslims. These new institutions are one of the best things in North America that have resulted from 9/11, and hence one of the important aspects about the event that deserve more attention.

The second aspect of the controversy that followed my presentation at Noor is much more complicated, requiring more attention than is provided in this book. By focusing on the gender *jihad*, I have introduced aspects of the ethnicity *jihad* that is manifest in the context of North America in distinct ways from its manifestation in other Muslim majority and minority contexts today. The issue of ethnocentrism and racism will have to be the subject of a future project on being Muslim within the arena of scholarly and political debates. My treatment of this aspect out of the only two that I consider worth attention will be reduced to the following observations.

How could a three-hour marathon of lecture and formal questions and answers intended to discuss ideas about interpretive possibilities get reduced to a single statement, which I uttered after at least two-and-a-half hours in this marathon? Unlimited answers are appropriate to this question and many of them have been dealt with in public debates following the publication of the article entitled "I am a Nigger" on *Muslim Wake-Up*.[20] Another answer is simply to point to the obvious: if any single line uttered in a three-hour forum should capture so much attention, it is a *clear* indication that being a Niggah is a matter of extremely strategic importance in the context of North American Islam. Indeed, this response reflects a long historical precedent in dealing with racism in America. It is *not* the role of the racially oppressed to *help* the oppressor to come to terms with his or her racism. The author of the article failed to mention how this statement was in response to *his* question about why there is so much internalized racism among Muslims. As the victim of racism, the Niggah is not responsible for the racist's oppression, or its solution. Despite the emergence of publications, presentations, workshops, confrontations, and efforts to investigate this issue, the continued perpetuation of tension between transitional African-American Muslim experience and transnational American Muslim experiences is not only alive, it is of strategic importance in any ways that Muslim American identity will be determined both within and without the Muslim communities. Either Muslims in America investigate the multiple dimensions of this strategically important matter, or it will continue to prove that it can bring all discussions and interactions to a full stop.

How any issue is treated in the public frenzy that the media might help to enflame is not a reflection of the actual context, commitment, complexities, or intentions of those who were participants in the forum out of which the media frenzy grew. Public access to information is a much better goal of all aspects of free press and publicity than the role that the media now seems to play in the lives of people seeking information. The media shapes those issues, which are being presented in accordance to the currency of their sensationalism with complete disregard for the actual events being reported and the extent to which the events are located within the trajectories of Islamic history and experience for over fourteen hundred years. This leads me to the final controversial issue in this chapter.

March 18, 2005: A Woman Leads Congregational Prayer in New York

My theoretical reconstruction of historical male hegemony in public ritual leadership in Islam need not be duplicated in order for me to address the particulars of the prayer service on March 18, 2005. That it was sensationalized in the media, and therefore open to a frenzy of global responses, reiterates the point I just raised above. Therefore, it has already been given extensive public attention and anyone interested in the twists and turns of the debates has more than ample access through these various publications.

The completion of this book with its discussions on multiple aspects and experiences inside the gender *jihad* is a clear indication that the roles I have played in this struggle are neither limited to this one symbolic act nor concluded by performing this act. To many people, worldwide, I am only known through sensationalized controversies. That is understandable. I hope they will eventually come to understand that sensationalist responses to certain public actions are not the basis of, and never can be the goal of, my identity quest as a female in Islam. For this reason, I rejected all invitations to do further interviews relating to the congregational prayer in New York City when those invitations were clearly expecting to gain more attention by publishing articles and presenting news programs focused on the event *just because* it had gained such attention. That is an unfortunate consequence of addressing issues of gender within today's climate of sensationalism. There are, however, a few points about this particular event that only I can tell. These are offered here, as a matter of public record, in order that my participation is reconfigured along the lines of my lifetime experience within the struggles for justice and Islam.

In the fall of 2004, I was one of several invitees, recognized for participation in progressing Islam from its various aspects of stasis and stagnation, to join the advisory committee to a newly forming group who chose the name "Progressive Muslim Union." Despite the existence of a plethora of organizations worldwide who use the word "progressive" in their name, and despite the number of self-identified progressive Muslims who were among the invitees,[21] lengthy discussion over ownership of the word "progressive," including the exclusion of some members of the existing P.M.U. governing board, managed to consume a great deal of time. The organization has been established, the name has been retained (with "in North America" added), but a number of the invitees, myself included, are not affiliated with P.M.U.

Until the prayer, I tried to remain with the group as an advisory board member. The organizers expressed their hope to organize a conference through the Harvard University Diversity Project during the March 18–20 weekend. I was invited to lead congregational prayer the Friday of that conference. I accepted. The conference was not successfully organized, but several months later I received a new invitation to lead congregational prayer on the same date as previously scheduled. After looking into the logistics (I had committed myself to do a presentation at Auburn University Seminary in New York the Thursday evening before), I asked the Auburn organizers if they would arrange the return flight to Richmond in order to allow me to stay in New York throughout the day on Friday. This is the simple logistical background for my participation in this particular event. The organizing committee would occasionally contact me about the developments in planning. One of the organizers, Asra Nomani, who was on a tour for her recent book publication, was able to secure needed funds from her publishers, in order to actually assist the plan to come to fruition. I gave most of my energy to considering both the content of my Thursday evening lecture, and the substance of the *khutbah*. I had not forgotten the extent of the controversy that had followed the previous public announcement and participation in a similar invitation in South Africa more than a decade before. Thus, I was especially keen that I concentrate on the nature of public ritual as a performance directed toward Allah, rather than an act of defiance against those who have created the necessity for a gender *jihad* by simply denying women the full human dignity with which Allah has created us. My conclusion was to keep the prayer service as close to the normative male privileged procedure, while contributing from my own female perspective, and encouraging greater gender parity in public ritual leadership.

When the organizers began to publicize the intention to have "the first" female-led Friday congregational prayer service with me as its leader, the climate also began to heat up. This increased the tension for me between potentially competing intentions. I deliberately chose to turn away any media attention focused my way. I agreed to participate in a press conference before the prayer as requested by the organizers. My comments included the comment that "The only thing different about this for me was that I do not do press conferences before prayer." I followed that by saying, "After this, I would not be giving any more interviews." For several months, I did not. However, in the first two weeks following the prayer, the requests flowed in with other responses to the prayer at a rate of about fifty a day.

When I left the press conference to observe the quiet time I needed before the actual prayer, the organizers fielded questions from the media and tried to get the prayer space set up. I had reminded them of a few details about the ritual format even as a break from the male exclusive format would occur simultaneously. I explicitly mentioned that the second call to prayer should be given *after* I had walked to the front of the congregation, faced them, and pronounced the greeting: "*As-Salaamu Alaykum*, Peace be Upon You." The young woman giving the call to prayer started to make that second call while I was on my way to the podium. To cover up this break, I had no recourse but to sit on my prayer rug facing the congregation with my head bowed until she finished. I then stood up to take the podium, facing the congregation using only handwritten notes. I will give a brief overview here, noting that between the large portions given in Arabic then translated into English, and the portions only in English, it would be cumbersome to attempt a whole reconstruction for inclusion here, as requested. All those parts recited in Arabic were followed by English translation, nearly doubling the delivery time (while here I refer to their having been recited in Arabic). The text provided below is a nearly all English reconstruction for general readership.

*   *   *

Another Stand at the Podium, Khutbah to the Salat-al-Jumu'ah on March 18, 2005

(The beginning was recited in Arabic and translated into English.)

Praise be to Allah, Lord of all Worlds (or all alternative universal possibilities). I begin in the name and praise of Allah *ta'ala*. I bear witness that there is no god but Allah, One, with no partners; and I bear witness that Muhammad, Ibn-'Abd Allah, is the Prophet (and Messenger) of Allah. May Allah's praise be upon him, and upon his *ahl* (people), and his (immediate) companions, and his wives, and upon all who follow the guidance, (all of them) together until the day of reckoning; Amin.[22]

Allah, *ta'ala* says in the Qur'an, "Oh you who securely believe! If you hear the call to the *salah* on the day of the communal gathering (*al-jumu'ah*), hurry to the remembrance of Allah and leave aside your selling. That is better for you if you but knew (62:9).[23]

"Allah, there is no god but the God, (and) He/She/It is," the Ever-Living, the Self-Subsistent Fount of All Being. Neither slumber over takes Him, nor sleep. His is all that is in the heavens and all that is on earth. Who is there that could intercede with Him, unless it be by His leave? He knows all the lies open before [human beings] and all that is hidden from them, whereas they cannot attain to aught of His knowledge save that which He wills [them to attain]. His eternal power overspreads the heavens and the earth, and their upholding wearies Him not. And He alone is truly Exalted, Tremendous[24] *(ayat al-kursi,* 2:255).

Surely the men who surrender and the women who surrender, and the men who believe and the women who believe, and the men who obey and the women who obey, and the men who speak the truth and the women who speak the truth, and the men and the women who are patiently steadfast, and the men who are humble and the women who are humble, and the men who give in alms and the women who give in alms, and the men who fast and the women who fast, and the men who guard their private parts and the women who guard their private parts, and the men who guard their private parts and the women who [guard their private parts], and the men who remember Allah abundantly and the women who remember – Allah has prepared for them forgiveness and a vast reward (33:35).[25]

I stand before you in all my imperfections and weaknesses confessing that I bear sincere love of Allah and love for all of Her *ayat*/signs. These signs are everywhere. The buds of many colors, including green, are now being born in my yard from trees and bushes; and early flowers like crocuses and daffodils follow the birth of the buds. These are part of Allah's infinite mercy and their beauty reflects Allah's Self-Disclosure.

Allah pre-existed the creation of this world and as Creator, according to the Qur'an, promised that guidance would come in countless forms for humankind – if we but think and reflect.

The greatest mercy and guidance in the form of Allah's Self-Disclosure is, without a doubt, the gift of revelation. Revelation or *wahy,* to actual human beings, some of whom were chosen as messengers, holding the responsibility to convey those messages to all of humanity. There is no one chosen people, exclusive members of one of the world's many religions – some no longer in existence – some so widespread by numbers and powers that they look upon themselves as exclusively "the chosen." The "chosen" are all of humanity. Anyone (and everyone) – whether existing before the lifetime of the Prophet Muhammad (saw) or existing now, with no (direct or immediate) access to the special mission of the Prophet (as) as *khitmat-ul-anbiya,* seal of the prophets – is also chosen by the very gift of life that Allah has granted from three pronouns for God are indeed intentional of Its mercy and wisdom.

As Muslims we are fortunate to have Allah's generosity in the form of the last known effort of revelation as Self-Disclosure (in words), the Qur'an al-Karim. So let us build upon that gift today. (Read in Arabic first: (Among His signs is that He)) has created you from a single *nafs* and created from it, its mate: and spread from the two, countless men and women (4:1). This unity of origin, I would say, reflects two important implications, both extensions of the fundamental principle, *tawhid*: (1) of course Allah is One, Allah is Unique, Allah is united and Allah unifies (all things in creation); (2) no human being is ever the same as Allah, able to know or understand all of Allah's intention for the creation of humans, or the entire cosmos. Yet all human beings have been granted the potential to experience at-one-ment with Allah for fleeting moments in the creation, and eternally *fi-l-akhirah* (in the Ultimate and Permanent End)

Since humans, created from a single soul, by a single Lord of love, mercy and power, one dimension of experiencing that one-ness is by living before, in surrender to, Allah *ta'ala*, to practice the unity of human beings. *Tawhid* is the foundation of Muslim unity. Let us look at this *tawhidic* paradigm, as it relates to all human actions and interactions as well as to our gathering here today.

(Here I provided a succinct explanation of the *tawhidic* paradigm and horizontal reciprocity between any two humans, especially emphasizing between male and female humans, as detailed in chapter 1. The remainder of the *khutbah* was in Arabic, with the following English translations.[26])

Unto such of them as may [yet] attain faith and do righteous deeds, Allah has promised forgiveness and a reward supreme. We seek forgiveness from Allah and we ask of Her special blessing and mercy and forgiveness. Oh you who believe, seek forgiveness from Him, the Forgiver, the Bounteous. Our Lord, indeed I have wronged my soul a grave wrong and none forgives except You, so forgive me in this and in all things.

(Here, I sat sideways on the prayer mat and continued some personal remembrance, seeking more forgiveness and asking for guidance.)

The second and last part of the *khutbah* continued in Arabic and was delivered with the following translations:

Ya sin is our roof and ceiling. *Kaf Ha Ya 'Ayn Sad* are sufficient for us; *Ha Mim 'Ayn Sin Qaf* are our supporters or advocates. Allah will make you sufficient unto them all, and He is the All-Hearer, the All-Knower. The covering of the Divine Throne has come down upon us, and the Eye of Allah is watching us. With the Power of Allah, no one has power against us or over us.

Allah is enough for me! There is no deity save Him. In Him have I placed my trust, for He is the Sustainer, in awesome almightiness enthroned. In the Name of Allah, with Whose Name nothing on the earth and in the heaven can harm: and He is All-Hearing and All-Knowing. And there is no strength nor power save in Allah, the Sublime, the Tremendous. Limitless in His glory is the Sustainer, the Lord of Almightiness, [exalted] above anything that [human beings] may devise by way of definition. And Peace be upon all His message-bearers! And all praise is due to Allah alone, the Sustainer of all the worlds. And May Allah send blessings on our master, Muhammad, and on his family and people and companions and also peace.

In the Name of Allah, the Most Gracious, the Dispenser of Grace. O Allah, O Light, O Truth, O Obvious Manifest, shower me with Thy Light and teach me of Thy Knowledge, and make me understand of Thee, and make me hear Thee, and make me see Thee. Thou art Powerful over everything.

O Existent One, O Thou who art Present in all difficulties, O Thou of Hidden Kindness, of Subtle Making, O Gentle one, Who does not hasten, fulfill my need, with Thy Mercy, O Most Merciful of the Mercifuls. Glory be to Thee on Thy Grace, after Thy Knowledge. Glory be to Thee on Thy Forgiveness, after Thy Power. But if those [who are bent on denying the truth] turn away, say: Allah is enough for me! There is no deity save Her. In Him have I placed my trust for It is the Sustainer, in awesome almightiness enthroned. There is none like Him, and He is the Hearer, the Knower.

Amin.

Please join me in reciting al-Fatihah, the Opening chapter of the Qur'an.

Then I asked for the *iqamah*, immediate call preceding the prayer itself. I turned for the first time to face the *qiblah*, direction for prayer, toward the Ka'abah in Makkah, and I made my silent prayer of intention and raised my head with my hands at the sides of my face to recite "*Allahu Akbar,*" God is greatest. I was shocked to find cameras and journalists directly in front of me! This was *not* where I wanted to direct my prayer. This was not something I had given consent to. As I struggled with this surprising distraction while continuing with the long-ago-memorized portions of the prayer, I finally stumbled over the last few lines of the *surah* I had selected for the first unit of the prayer. This was the same *surah* I used for leading large congregations approximately 90% of the time I would accept this role as prayer leader. This *surah* was also part the sermon I had given in Cape

Town more than a decade before. *Surah Inshirah*, the 94th chapter, is my reminder that difficulty in life comes with ease in life. A few members from the congregation offered the requisite reminder of the portions over which I lost my flow of thoughts and memory. It reminded me of the difficulty before me: I was not facing the media, they were inappropriately located in the direction of prayer, as the organizers later told me, because they could not be controlled.

I was facing the reality that Allah is present in all ways, at all times, and in all places, and all I needed to do was to look with the eyes of my heart and turn my prayer back on track: an act of worship toward Allah. When those who claim a tradition of authority to prevent women from standing in front of men because the men might get distracted, it is the responsibility of the men, prior to the prayer, to consent and then to respond through consciousness of the act of worship and not the incidents of form. So, despite my lack of consent, I took self-responsibility at that moment to remember *what the prayer represents*: an act of devotion to That which is beyond our eyes' vision, as could be disturbed by the weakness of our hearts. If we settle our hearts back to Allah, then and only then can we hope to complete the worship as intended. That is what I did. The cameras and the media disappeared before my heart and no longer presented a distraction to my eyes.

Finally, I must acknowledge with gratitude those about whom I had the most knowledge of in organizing this event: Ahmad Naseef, Asra Normani, and Saleemah Abdul-Ghafur. Many others were involved but I never spoke with them directly. May Allah bless us all in this one moment in the timelessness of the cosmic order and important events in the gender *jihad* for justice and reform in Islam.

Conclusion

Why Fight the Gender *Jihad*?

I don't care who's wrong or right
I don't really wanna fight no more.
– Tina Turner[1]

Introduction

There have been multiple reasons for fighting the gender *jihad*, many of them so intimately connected to the question of my own well-being that I scarcely know where to start. However, there is enough evidence in this book that such a *jihad* was absolutely necessary for survival. The few thoughts I include here by way of conclusion are not a summary of the book. There are a few reiterations, but in the final analysis, this is really the place where I hope the preceding pages can come to some concluding words and purposeful closure.

On Being Female

God created women fully human. Anything, anyone, or any system that treats them privately or in public as anything less than that is destroying the potential harmony of the entire universe. "No person is your friend (or kin) who demands your silence or denies your right to grow and be perceived as fully blossomed as you were intended. Or who belittles in any fashion the gifts you labor so to bring into the world."[2] That such treatment of women and women's gifts has been justified by religious and secular discourse, interpretation, and action is an overt historical reality. It is my deepest desire to correct this flaw for all human beings, but especially to encourage women to affirm the reality of our full humanity by any means necessary. An Islamic studies professor recently told me that, by focusing so much of my time, research, and energy on gender, I run the risk of being a "gender fundamentalist." I accept that label, since working to dismantle the historical paradox of the utility of women without equal affirmations of their intrinsic worth, being, and agency, he claimed, "reduces (me) to being a female . . . and *nothing else.*" This makes me and my work the axis of female "dehumanization" as he called it. This blatant erasure of my whole integrity as a person because of my personal and professional focus on gender is fundamental to that intrinsic significance and worth of the very work that I have been doing. *To be female is to be human.* Those who act like I must be something else in order to merit full human status implicate themselves by implying that "man" is actually the same as human, such that being female is *de*humanizing. Women have consistently shown the moral fortitude to live *as Muslims* despite the absence of recognition of our full humanity in Islamic thought and practice. I have fought in the gender *jihad* to affirm both for myself and for other females, that being who we are is exactly what we were created to be. I could not be more or less than female. That *is* my humanity.

Patriarchal control over what it means to be human robs females of their God-given agency and full humanity. In this book, I have contributed some stories, some personal examples, and some intellectual considerations, in an effort to tell *a part of the grand story* including the dehumanization for female identity throughout Islamic thought, practice, and the basic con-structions of meanings of Allah and Islam, which have reduced femaleness to deviant in whatever ways women are like or unlike men, as subjects or utilities of or for male intellectual, social, political, sexual, spiritual, and historical analysis and experience. I have exposed my own location in the many ways that female dehumanization occurs and is often rewarded through the near male monopoly of determining the meaning of the divine, not only for their own self-aggrandizement as male – hence masculine-God identified – and for determining applications, uses, and abuses of "Islam," but also for denying women's "gifts" except as benefits of male public and private utility. When women sanctioned their own dehumanization, in part by attempting to be care-givers for themselves and others – even their patri-archal fathers, brothers, husbands, sons, colleagues, and friends – it is easy to see how constructs of gender relations are both problematic and essential to being human. Men have so much more to learn about the truth of women's full humanity – especially about the female potential to maintain wholeness despite entrenched practices contributing to this dehumanization, often from the very ones whom they have loved and cared for. Provided male chauvinism can be recognized as obsolete, even the most macho of men can learn by the historical and current examples of the female human as care-workers in a manner befitting and benefiting the divine status of both males and females.

The intrinsic nature of being human is not exemplified by patriarchal manipulation of the gifts females have been acculturated to practice in order to better the quality of life for all humanity. It is time for what it means to be female to become more than a utility of men's searching for self-affirmation and identity. It is time for men to be *empowered with* and not to exert power over female identity and contributions. It is time for women and men to accept the full humanity of women by removing the veils put over women being female. It will prove to be the only way to save the planet from more public and private violence, to end war and the preparation for war, and to become citizens of care and compassion. Those "manly" traits, which perhaps once helped the whole human race to move out of subjectivity to the vicissitudes of nature's unpredictability, have long outstripped their merits. The Qur'an says, "We have made (what is in) the earth subservient to you (human beings)" (22:65). Now that we have reached the epitome of our expressions and practices of *dominion over*, we must all take care to become servants of the earth's salvation. To continue on this macho trajectory only builds further destruction. The female humans who have participated in the continuity of human well-being are the ones with the longest and strongest history of performing the role of care-givers. Their newly forming leadership, without the assumption of the master tools or the limitations of male human standards of power over, will help dismantle this dangerous trajectory by teaching all who dare to listen how to assume the responsibility and facility of preserving that which is not only sacred, but also ordinary – peaceful co-existence with differences. Audre Lorde says,[3]

> Difference must be not merely tolerated, but seen as a fund of necessary polarities between which our creativity can spark like a dialectic. Only then does the necessity for interdependence become unthreatening. Only within that interdependency of different strengths, acknowledged and equal, can the power to seek new ways of being in the world generate, as well as the courage and sustenance to act where there are no charters.

Fully Claiming my Past and Heritage as a Transitioning African-American Muslim

I am my father's daughter. He was a devoted man of God. He felt called to God at the age of fifteen, while walking in the red Georgia dirt and hot lush fields. He gave his life, the next thirty years, to that call. He never achieved worldly success, neither in his ministry nor in terms of wage earning. He never wavered from his role as believer while becoming a husband, father, and man of the world. Although raised in and a practitioner of corporal punishment, he never hit his female children or his wife, and only disciplined his sons after due explanation of his expectations, and the ways he considered they had failed to meet them. I have five brothers, most married and/or fathers. None of my brothers has ever beaten a woman.

I am my mother's daughter. She was a full-figured African-American woman, extremely comfortable in her embodiment, highly sexual, and a living example of the best of southern hospitality. When I brought friends home, I told them her first or second question would always be, "Are you hungry?" or "Did you-all have something to eat?" It was always so. She suffered from undiagnosed depression. She hit only in anger – me, my sister, my brothers, and my father. She was pampered to imprisonment by my father's goal of being the protector and provider. She rebelled until he died. Then she transformed and became a competent human agent in the form of an independent woman. Despite my childhood inability to understand her, my female adulthood confirmed over and over again that she was the glue that kept our family together.

My childhood was full of paradox, sometimes conflictual, sometimes transformative, but always within a confirmation that humanity was a manifestation of the divine potential. Each of us could either rise to the highest level or indulge to the lowest level (95:5). I was raised on the idea that the Sacred is a constant – the only constant. I was raised on the idea that God was love. Of course my transition into Islam was influenced by my upbringing. I chose the name Wadud in its *indefinite* form to affirm the pervasiveness of God's love and not simply to admit my servitude by attaching '*abd* to the definite form, al-Wadud. The divide between the sacred and the mundane was no paradox: it was an illusion.

I have fought the gender *jihad* to remove the blinkers that see only the illusion of fragmentation and then build structures and formulate systems to sustain the perception that it is real; and then to give divine sanction to the illusion of human independence from transcendent peace and unity, and to pretend the practices, codifications, and systems constructed to sustain the illusion are divinely ordained. In doing this, no one can perform as *'abd/ khalifah*, servant/agent of Allah. Instead one must consider oneself Allah, granting rights to all others as if their status is inferior to self or deviant from the norm. Yet "the rain does not fall on only one man's house." There is no such divine arbitrariness toward humankind.

Early in my studies of Islamic thought I fell in awe of Sufi "saints and mystics," particularly Rabi'ah al-Adawiyah. I have relished the legacy and writings of Sufism until I hoped to one day reach such a devoted status. When I eventually committed myself to the practices of my teacher, Shaykh Ahmad Abdur-Rashid, head of several Sufi *tariqahs* or orders, I was still embroiled in the conflict between being a divinely ordained human being while being a female, and an African-American in transition. After spending thirty years, more than the number of years that Muhammad ibn-'Abd-Allah had spent in his divine commission as Prophet and Messenger of Allah, I considered myself equal to anyone on the earth and certainly equal to any who struggles in Islam, however understood or practiced. I was also transformed to realize the essential component of faithful actions, *al-'amal al salihah*, in completing my identity as servant. I wrote the following short essay as a personal journal entry. It was originally written over a decade ago and is only slightly edited here. This is a third and more significant reason for fighting the gender *jihad*.

The Active Principle of Islam, or, Activating Islamic Principles

There are no two ways about it, to understand the significance of this title requires some self-disclosure. Since the Islamic intellectual discourse has such a poor historical record of women's self-disclosure *in the name of Islam*, it is even more appropriate to admit to the personal as political.

In my return to the U.S.A. after three years in Malaysia, where I was given the opportunity to link my theories about Islamic theology with active social involvement *in the name of Islam*, I encountered the bleakest circumstances. The pervasive, systematic oppression and resulting spiritual strain in the lives of ordinary people – causing most to live in utter disregard for their fellow human – I found unbearable. I sought answers and resolutions to this dilemma by reading every kind of source material I could. There was little consolation. At each juncture, I continued to find more literature focusing on the extent of the problems, psychological, physical, social, economic, or political.

In the face of such massive problems, I have felt utter despair. How can I despair, I thought? I have faith in Allah. When I encountered literature from the world's religious experts, I was profoundly affected by the writings of Paul Tillich.[4] "For in these days the foundations of the earth *do* shake. May we *not* turn our eyes away; may we not close our ears and our mouths! But may we rather see, through the crumbling of the world, the rock of eternity and the salvation which has no end!" He cited the worldview of the prophets and holy men and women as expressions of the certainty of belonging "within the two spheres, the changeable *and* the unchangeable . . . Because, beyond the sphere of destruction, they saw the sphere of salvation; because in the doom of the temporal, they saw the manifestation of the Eternal" (emphasis in the original).[5]

I was indebted to these insights from a modern Christian thinker. I dove again into Islamic literature about the status of the soul. I was working from the conviction that I would find a more cogent and viable spiritual system that had been worked out in detail by great Islamic intellectuals and mystical geniuses. Yet finding the *link* between these mystical and intellectual musings was hopelessly insufficient for what I was experiencing as a daily reality.

The significance of Tillich's work was simply that it expressed itself explicitly in response to the moral–spiritual dilemmas of modern circumstances. I ran up against a scarcity of information in response to such dilemmas from modern Muslim thinkers. They were obsessed with the *réalité politique* (everything was power, authority, and control) through the medium of legal operations. I feel little hope for the future of Islam when only articulated in terms of Muslims seizing global control, instead of the dominating superpower. Such an outcome, fantastic as it really is, would still leave a tremendous spiritual void.

I have little confidence that Muslims gaining more political power to control the world would really make a better life for all the oppressed and exploited people of the world. I see very little from our current political leaders that would give me such confidence. What little I do see is marginalized by those who are wielding the greatest power. One reason for my lack of confidence is simply that the agendas expressed by Muslim political and intellectual elites are primarily top-down operations. They seem more focused on the role of legalized authority to assert unilateral power and control over the will and status of the people at the bottom. This removal from the masses, in all their diversity, speaks little toward my hope of the common human well-being.

At the level of a mass movement, we surely need new voices and agendas.

When re-reading the inspirational words of past Muslim mystics, I encountered beautiful discourses on the qualities of spiritual realization. Sadly, I found no social reality expressed as a component of that realization. Does this mean that a spiritually qualitative life is unconnected to social realities? I am reminded of Fazlur Rahman's critique of the quietism in early Sufi movements, while "what Islam generally inculcated among its early followers, in varying degrees, was a grave sense of responsibility before the justice of God which raised their behaviour from the realm of worldliness and mechanical obedience to the law to a plan of moral activity."[6] It cannot be that one is meant to feel connected to the Creator with no creature-to-creature interaction in activating that connection.

I see too few viable examples of spiritual motivation for social and political action, the actual *sunnah* of the Prophet, as also exemplified in the life and continued transformation in the transitions to Islam for Malcolm X. Yet there is overwhelming consensus that Islam is *din*, a living reality on the basis of one's connection to the Divine principles, not just a personal feeling of faith.

A New Future (Journal Continued)

A new impetus must be generated that applies the Islamic spiritual paradigms as forces of social movements. The consequences of this are a new world order that incorporates the meaningfulness of the lives of everyday citizens, be they Muslim or not. This impetus has few exemplaries visible among those who are projected as Muslim leaders most dedicated to Islam. This reflects that elitist–mass level dichotomy. The elites are preoccupied with more authoritative manipulation over the masses – while neglecting the mass level input. The masses act with a totally unviable sense of reality, including those who presume the spiritual worth of Islam is only in the mosque or *halaqah* as they continue to act with a world in such bleak disarray. If the world itself is going to hell in a rowboat, the best we can do is focus on saving our own souls for a glorious afterlife. Again, I find this arrangement untenable. If Islam is not generated as a human level concern and a mode of daily operations for the overall improvement of the quality of all aspects of life on the planet, then we will all go to hell in the same rowboat with the rest of the world. It's as simple as that.

As 'abd, obedient servant of Allah, the goal of the traditional ascetic mystic, we attain the level of active participants, fully agent, *khalifah only* in coordinating worldly affairs. The formulation of a thought system meant to enhance the overall quality of everyday life for all of God's creatures must become the immediate articulation for a long-term goal. It cannot and will not be done by taking recluse in the mosques as a spiritual consolation from the status of a beleaguered world. I cannot adhere to or even believe that Islam was intended for such a dichotomy.

Whoever wishes to add their voices to this new agenda must learn to speak aloud and to proliferate literature that addresses this need for greater spiritual and political synthesis. Muslims must consciously move out of the mosque recluse and onto the streets with the message actually revealed to and actualized by the Prophet. We surely will not do this simply by carrying the tag "Muslim" and taking more control and political power. We need a detailed system of interactions on a citizen-to-citizen basis, with the citizens all members of the human race, and then give allegiance only to those leaders who give meaningful help to coordinate authority in the name of the people.[7]

However, when people are unaware and unmoved by the relationship of the Islamic worldview to the whole world, as it actually exists now, and are equally insufficient to take up the task of a new world order premised by the essence of the spiritual center with its resulting manifest ethical principles, then hope is lost. *Khilafah* is a personal/private and public duty for every Muslim. We must begin preparation for the comprehensive fulfillment of this duty. Citizens should no longer acquiesce to systems of oppression because they will ultimately be held accountable for their actions as well as their lack of actions. Political and intellectual elites will no longer be able to gain or keep power until and unless they are full embodiments of the basic principles of Islam as *din*, the living reality of a spiritually qualitative interaction in the name of absolute certainty of belief in the mercy and grace of Allah. (*end journal*)

Reflections on the Journal
While rewriting my journal notes from over a decade ago, I am first struck by the simplicity and naivety of belief in such a possibility as inspired by my own vision of "Islam." I am also still struck by the lingering thoughts of the imagination expressed concerning the long-term goal of activating the spiritual core at the level of policy and social affairs. I have admittedly continued to transition within Islam – as only the historical and cultural patterns of Muslims – and gained a more pluralistic perspective of Islam, focused on human relations to sacred ultimate principles. I filter the terms of my humanism through the stark reality of being a Muslim female while gender remains excluded not only from its *fundamental* status as a category of thought, but also as a powerful example toward practicing care work for the sake of self and others as an example of one's humanity in agency *with*

the Ultimate, applying the divine principles. I am still hoping our examples, as women, will become representatives for achieving a new world order removed from the entrenched patterns and diverse forms of patriarchy.

Conclusion: The Final Reason for Fighting the Gender Jihad

Ultimately, I want to live and to share the experience of life with all who care to put down the weapons of *jihad*, and take up the tools of wholesome reconstruction. I have lived inside the gender *jihad* long enough to know that I had to take it up. It was my only means to survive. Now, I want to see and bring about the end of the necessity for *jihad*. The *only* reason I have been engaged in the *jihad*, struggle for gender justice, is because that justice and full human dignity granted to us by Allah has been ignored or abused. The history of nearly exclusive male and androcentric Islamic interpretation and codification has not nearly recognized the importance of women's contributions from their specific experience of being female and fully human with the intellectual capacity to contribute to a holistic under-standing of what it means to have a relationship with both the divine and other humans, while they have consistently shown the spiritual fortitude to live as Muslims despite that recognition. The spaces for women to demon-strate both their self-identification as female and their full humanity are not reserved for only those women whom elite male scholars and laypersons have already manipulated in mind and body, but belong to all women who have endeavored to sustain their roles as women and Muslims despite silence, separation, violence and invisibility. Still, too few women are recog-nized for their capacity to lead by example, not by asserting power over, but by representing power with, all others.

Notes

Notes to the Introduction

1 Amina Wadud, "Preface," in *Qur'an and Woman: Rereading the Sacred Text from a Woman's Perspective* (New York: Oxford University Press, 1999), p. xi.

2 Dr. Aminah McCloud, Professor and Founder, Director of The Islamic World Studies Program (2005) at DePaul University, made a very coherent argument against the overuse of the term "conversion." It implies completely leaving one's personal past, or severing oneself from that past, in order to enter something completely new and, by implication, unique or even at odds with one's past. Her research provides clear evidence that when non-Muslim Americans enter Islam, as also demonstrated by other communities throughout the spread of Islam historically, they often do so as part of a *continual* process of spiritual, moral, and symbolic progression already in motion prior to acceptance of or conformity with Islamic particulars. She prefers the term "transition" to indicate not only particular aspects of one's past as integral to their entry into Islam but also to indicate that once they enter, they neither exclude their past, nor are completed. I will use "transition" and "transformation" interchangeably to determine that Islam does not start or stop with the *shahadah*, declaration of faith.

3 Despite categorization of the Western feminist movement into stages – first wave, second wave, etc. – there is an internal critique if these stages are consistent with the work women have been doing for centuries to challenge male hegemony, privilege, and authority. I use "second-wave feminist movement" in the West, circa 1960, as one of the self-identifying terms of Western feminist thinkers, activists, and scholarship. The "first-wave feminist movement," circa 1860, was, in part, the product of the women's suffrage movement.

4 The etymological origin of the word oppressions lies in the Latin for "press down" or "oppress against." The root suggests that people who are oppressed suffer from some kind of restriction on their freedom. Not all restrictions on people's freedom, however, are oppressive. People are not oppressed by simple natural phenomena, such as the gravitational forces. "Instead, oppression is the result of human agency, human imposed restrictions of people's freedom. Not all humanly imposed limitations on people's freedom are oppressive, however. *Oppression must also be unjust*" (emphasis mine). Alison M. Jaggar, *Feminist Politics and Human Nature*, reprinted (Totowa, N.J.: Rowman & Littlefield, 1988), pp. 5-6.

5 I.M.L.C. was held in Kuala Lumpur, Malaysia, in May 2003. A fuller rendition of that event is described in chapter 6.

6 I include the full story of my choice to wear yet religiously disregard this head covering as a

principle to Islam, despite its symbolic intensity and my own transformations in wearing it, in chapter 6.

7 As will be elaborated in chapter 1.

8 I am particularly indebted to Sharon Welch's book, *Towards a Feminist Ethics of Risk* (Minneapolis: Augsburg Fortress, 1990), in reaching this conclusion.

9 The juxtaposition of a few male scholars against a reduction of "Muslim feminist" methodologies is explicit in Ebrahim Moosa's "The Debts and Burdens of Critical Islam" in *Progressive Muslims: On Justice, Gender and Pluralism*, ed. Omid Safi (Oxford: Oneworld Publications, 2003), pp. 111–127.

10 Detailed analysis between what is now seen as a Muslim feminist movement and preceding actions and articulations of Muslim women's rights and their historical struggles against patriarchal silences and marginalizations shows the multiple complexities of these historical struggles and the most recent prevalence of Islamic theory as the fundamental basis for the struggle of women's full humanity. See works by Margot Badran, Deniz Kandiyoti, Azza Karam, Afsenah Najmabadi, Ziba Mir-Husseini, and Azizah al Hibri, among others.

11 Khaled Abou El Fadl, *Speaking in God's Name: Islamic Law, Authority and Women* (Oxford: Oneworld Publications, 2001).

12 Amina Wadud, "On Belonging as a Muslim Woman," in *My Soul is a Witness: African-American Women's Spirituality*, ed. Gloria Wade-Gayles (Boston: Beacon Press, 1995), pp. 253–265.

13 I am indebted to Na'eem Jeenah for helping me trace the origins of this phrase to Rashied Omar, who used it along with "economic *jihad*" in the context of the post-Apartheid rethinking agenda. A reference to Farid Esack, *Qur'an, Liberation and Pluralism* (Oxford: Oneworld Publications, 1997), pp. 239–248, was included.

14 Huston Smith in the *Worlds of Faith* documentary series with Bill Moyers is one simple source, but extensive discourse followed the September 11 event.

Notes to Chapter 1

1 Amina Wadud, "On Belonging as a Muslim Woman," in *My Soul is a Witness: African-American Women's Spirituality*, ed. Gloria Wade-Gayles (Boston: Beacon Press, 1995), p. 256.

2 Fazlur Rahman, *Major Themes of the Qur'an*, 2nd edn (Minneapolis: Bibliotheca Islamica, 1994), p. 37.

3 Ibid.

4 As discussed in detail in chapter 3, "Muslim Women's Collectives, Organizations and Islamic Reform."

5 Toshihiko Izutsu, *God and Man in the Koran* (New Hampshire: Ayer Company Publishers, 1987), pp. 18–19.

6 Khaled Abou El Fadl, *Speaking in God's Name: Islamic Law, Authority and Women* (Oxford: Oneworld Publications, 2001), p. 3. As the title of this book suggests, it is all about the authoritarian practices of speaking *for* God. My very succinct references here and elsewhere should entice others to read the book in its entirety as one of the most precise articulations in our time on legal reductionism that inhibits progressive discourse and women's liberative resistance.

7 Fatima Mernissi, *Beyond the Veil: Male–Female Dynamics in Modern Muslim Society*

(London: Al Saqi Books, 1985), p. 17. Also note that her title could mistakenly suggest that her particular case study of Morocco is representative of the whole of *Modern Muslim Society*, rather than one of many.

8 Leila Ahmed, *A Border Passage: From Cairo to America – A Woman's Journey* (New York: Farrar, Straus and Giroux, 1999).

9 The limitations of the source texts themselves, and their authority as a concrete linguistic act, will be looked at below in more detail in chapter 6, "Qur'an, Gender, and Interpretive Possibilities." Here the emphasis is on interpreting and effective implementation of those sources, since they have so much authority.

10 Fazlur Rahman, "Approaches to Islam in Religious Studies: Review Essay," in *Approaches to Islam in Religious Studies*, ed. Richard Martin (Oxford: Oneworld Publications, 2001), pp. 189–202.

11 I will discuss this at some length in chapter 6, "Qur'an, Gender, and Interpretive Possibilities."

12 Rahman, "Approaches," in *Approaches to Islam in Religious Studies*.

13 Carolyn Rouse published a book in 2004 about African-American Muslim women with the title *Engaged Surrender* (University of California Press). Although not developed in the substance of her book, she attributes her introduction to this phrase to a lecture I gave in Southern California during the time of her data collection among Muslims in the area. This phrase is undefined in her book and given no direct corollary to her case studies. Furthermore, although I owe the phrase originally to numerous discussions on its meanings and applications with Dr. Alan Godlas from the University of Georgia, I take sole responsibility for how I use it here, with the hope that I have done justice to our discussions.

14 This dynamic between Allah, as disclosed through text, human agency, and interpretation, requires further discussion, which I provide in chapter 6, "Qur'an, Gender, and Interpretive Possibilities."

15 Wadud, *Qur'an and Woman*, pp. 56–69.

16 I will argue below against this inequality and restrict it to a specific cultural context at the time of revelation in chapter 4, "A New Hajar Paradigm: Motherhood and Family."

17 The term "Islamist" has been used recently to refer to the neo-traditionalist, neo-conservative return to the *shari'ah* as distinct in the role of politics. Islamist hope is to re-establish traditional *shari'ah* as the means for returning to an imagined pristine Islam perfectly attained at the time of the Prophet.

18 I will elaborate in quite some detail on double-talk, as it confirms a double bind for women, in chapter 4, "A New Hajar Paradigm: Motherhood and Family."

19 See, for example, Ali Shariati, "The World-View of Tauhid," in his book, *Sociology of Islam* (Berkeley: Mirzan Press, 1979).

20 For example, Zia-din Sardar, Mohammad Arkoun, Azizah al Hibri, Ismail Faruqi, and Fazlur Rahman.

21 As emphasized in the Christian tradition: "Do unto to others what you would have them do unto you."

22 See Sachiho Murata, "Introduction," in *The Tao of Islam* (New York: State University of New York Press, 1992) for further discussion of these *Jalal* and *Jamal* attributes or what she calls the "two hands of God" from which the human has been created.

23 My translation intentionally removes gender symmetry from its literal translation "one of you does not believe until *he* loves for his brother" in order to stress the meaning of the statement in accordance with the gender-inclusive perspective and pluralistic goals of this

book. *An-Nawawi's Forty Hadith*, trans. Ezzeddin Ibrahim and Denys Johnson-Davies (Damascus: The Holy Koran Publishing House, 1979) p. 56.

24 Murata, *The Tao of Islam*, pp. 49–80.

25 Quoted by Ali Shariati in "Tauhid," 1979, p. 83.

26 Martin Buber, *I and Thou*, 2nd edn., trans. Ronald Gregory Smith (New York: Collier Books, Macmillan, 1958).

27 Amina Wadud, "An Islamic Perspective on Civil Rights Issues," in *Religion, Race, and Justice in a Changing America*, eds. Gar Orfield, Holly Lebowitz (New York: A Century Foundation Book, 1999), p. 157.

28 *Inni jaa'ilun fi-l-'ardi khalifah*: another translation will be referenced in the footnotes below. It falls in the context of a lengthy Qur'anic quotation. Two words differ. The first is *jaa'ilun*, the active participle of 'the One who 'makes' or 'creates'." I have chosen "create" following my discussions in *Qur'an and Woman*, p. 18. The other difference is *khalifah*, the key term discussed, translated, and interpreted in detail in this chapter.

29 Wadud, *Qur'an and Woman*, pp. 16–17.

30 Ibid., pp. 17–23, indicating how the above cited statement means duality was pre-intentional to the cosmological process. "[T]he Qur'an establishes that humankind was created in the male/female pair," p. 21. So male and female are equally essential to what it means to be human created from a single soul (*nafs*).

31 Amina Wadud, "Faith and Citizenship," in *Women and Citizenship*, ed. Marilyn Friedman (New York: Oxford University Press, 2005), pp. 170–187.

32 Note the two terms are extremely close in transliteration: *khalifah* is the agent, while *khilafah* is agency.

33 Rahman, *Major Themes*, p. 12.

34 Wadud, "Faith and Citizenship" also discusses citizen, civil society and *khalifah*.

35 "Truly We offered the Trust (*amanah*) to the heavens and the earth and the mountains, but they declined to bear it, and the human being undertook it. But he has been and oppressor [of himself and others] and ignorant" (33:72).

36 7:169, 13:19–25, 57:5–9, Coincidently this next reference precedes the Qur'anic reference to the creation of the *khalifah*, and is therefore significant enough to be quoted in full. 2:26–30 "Truly Allah does not disdain to set forth an example [even of] a gnat or something bigger. And as for those who believe, they know that the Truth is from their Lord. As for those who cover up [the Truth], they say, 'What does Allah want [to teach us] by this example?' Thereby He misleads many and thereby He guides many. And thereby he misleads only the dissolute – those who break the covenant (*mithaq*) with Allah after confirming it [in their beings], and cut what Allah has ordered to be joined, and who corrupt the earth [thereby]. It is these who are the loser. How can you cover up [the Truth] about Allah when you were dead and He made you alive? Then He will make you dead, then make you alive [again], then to Him you shall return. It is He Who created for you all that is on the earth [and] regulated the heavens – fashioning seven heavenly realms – and He has knowledge of all things. And when you Lord said to the angels, 'I shall place upon the earth an emissary,' they said, 'will you place upon it [one] who will corrupt it and shed blood, [while] it is we who hymn Your praise and sanctify You?' He said, 'Truly, I know what you know not.'"

37 "There is no power except in Allah" (18:39).

38 This dual relationship – agency and service (*khilafah* and *'ibadah*) – has a powerful symbolical demonstrated in Islam's major liturgical practice, *salah*, the five-times daily worship or prayer. The worshipper takes the standing position at the opening of the prayer

and follows with bowing, repeats standing until assuming the pose of full prostration. Thus the positions of the body juxtapose the stand as Allah's agent with the prostration as Allah's servant.

39 Neither the consideration of slavery as inhumane nor the inequalities of the inheritance shares are critically examined here. Both examples, directly from the Qur'an, indicate real social practice in seventh-century Arabia, the time and circumstances of revelation. They are mentioned here as a utility showing literal textual support for the idea of relative responsibility. The text acknowledges the social reality of that time when some humans functioned on unequal terms. However, this book refutes both slavery and subjugated wives through later discussions on interpretation to render these literal examples obsolete. Primarily, this is done by distinguishing between limitation in social function and full human agency.

40 Both children and people with certain handicaps are fully human but their capacity in fulfilling some responsibilities requires assistance, so that their humanity is functionally complete.

41 Majid Fakhry, *Ethical Theories in Islam* (Leiden: E.J. Brill, 1991).

42 Ibid.

43 Ibid.

44 Ibid.

45 Ibid.

46 Ibid.

47 Seyyed H. Nasr, "Music and Dance," in *Islamic Spirituality II: Manifestations*, ed. Seyyed Hossein Nasr (New York: Crossroad, 1991) p. 478.

48 Susan Moller Okin calls this "false gender neutrality" in her book *Justice, Gender and the Family* (New York: Basic Books, 1989) p. 11.

49 Rahman, *Major Themes*, p. 28.

50 This will be dealt with in greater detail in chapter 4, "A New Hajar Paradigm: Motherhood and Family." The institutions and politics not imbued with Islamic morality but with patriarchal codes, legitimated by the use of authoritative Islamic semantics, deny the woman who speaks out her identity as a true Muslim. Silence and invisibility becomes her only guards against any offences to her honor.

51 This will be discussed at full length in chapter 4, "A New Hajar Paradigm: Motherhood and Family."

52 Rahman, *Major Themes*, p. 37.

53 Alison Jaggar, *Feminist Politics and Human Nature* (Totowa, N.J.: Rowman & Littlefield, 1993).

54 Tariq Ramadan and others refer to it with the phrase "*al-fiqh al-waqiyah*," the jurisprudence of current realities.

55 According to the U.N.D.P. Human development report, Oxford, 1998, the richest fifth of the world's population consumes and wastes "86% of total private consumption expenditure," while the poorest fifth "a minuscule 1.3%." We have the means to not only eradicate poverty but also to do so without depriving the well to do from experiencing extreme luxury and privilege.

56 Joan C. Tronto, *Moral Boundaries: A Political Argument for an Ethic of Care* (New York: Routledge, 1993).

57 Terri Apter, *Working Women don't have Wives* (New York: St. Martin's Griffin, 1993), p. 1.

58 Tronto, *Moral Boundaries*.

59 Sharon D. Welch, *A Feminist Ethic of Risk* (Minneapolis: Fortress Press, 1990).

60 Welch, *Ethic of Risk*, p. 23.

61 Ibid., p. 3

62 Ibid., p. 4.

63 Ibid., p. 5.

64 Ibid., p. 6.

65 Eckhart Tolle, *Practicing the Power of Now: Essential Teachings, Meditation, and Exercises from the Power of Now* (Novato, CA: New World Library, 2001), p. 44.

66 Diana L. Eck, *Encountering God: A Spiritual Journey from Bozeman to Banaras* (Boston: Beacon Press, 1993), pp. 222–223.

67 In chapter 4, "A New Hajar Paradigm: Motherhood and Family," I give detailed consideration of the advantages and disadvantages or shortcomings along the lines of this mutuality as a matter of communal concern and not merely in nuclear or extended kinship.

68 Thomas Sowell, *The Quest for Cosmic Justice* (New York: The Free Press, 1999), p. 9. It is worth reviewing his full chapter with the same title as the book. pp. 1–48.

69 Ezzeddin Ibrahim, and Deny Johnson-Davies, transl., *An-Nawawi's Forty Hadith* (Damascus: The Holy Koran Publishing House, 1976), p. 26. Translation as included in this text is my own. Readings looking for a reference to authenticate the *hadith* can use an-Naawwi, which includes the original Arabic.

70 The human body has nine or ten openings. Nothing about the number of bodily orifices predetermines moral agency.

71 Fakhry, *Justice*, p. 24.

72 Abdullahi Ahmed An-Na'im, *Toward an Islamic Reformation: Civil Liberties, Human Rights and International Law* (New York: Syracuse University Press, 1990), pp. 86–91.

73 As quoted by Ebrahim Moosa in his "Dilemma of Islamic Rights Schemes," *Journal of Law and Religion*, XV (2000–2001), pp. 209–210.

74 Ziba Mir Hosseini, "The Construction of Gender in Islamic Legal Thought and Strategies of Reform," *Hawwa: Journal of Women in the Near East and the Islamic World*, 1.1 (2003), 1–28, at p. 2.

75 Feisal Abdul Rauf, *Islam: A Sacred Law: What Every Muslim Should Know About Shariah* (Brattleboro, VT: Qiblah Books, 2000), p. 72.

76 Ebrahim Moosa, *Law and Religion*, pp. 209–210

77 An-Na'im, *Islamic Reformation*.

78 Feisel Abdul Rauf, *Islam: A Sacred Law*, p. 110.

79 Ibid., p. 15.

80 *Gender in Islamic Legal Thought*, p. 3.

81 RichardValantasis, "Constructions of Power and Asceticism", *Journal of the American Academy of Religion*, 63.4 (1995), pp. 775–821.

Notes to Chapter 2

1 Murata Sachiko, *The Tao of Islam: A Sourcebook on Gender Relations in Islamic Thought* (New York: State University of New York Press, 1999), p. 2.

2 See chapter 3, "Muslim Women's Collectives, Organizations, and Islamic Reform," especially on the relationship between theory and practice.

3 The significance of diversity, coherence, and hegemony in definitions of the term "Islam"

itself has been discussed extensively in chapter 1, "What's in a Name?" It is continually used to grant authority and legitimacy to the user.

4   Lee Wigle Artz and Mark A. Pollock, "Limiting the Options: Anti-Arab Images in U.S. Media Coverage of the Persian Gulf Crisis," in *The U.S. Media and the Middle East: Image and Perception*, ed. Yahya R. Kamalipour (Westport, CT: Greenwood Press, 1994), pp. 119–132.

5   See endnote 3 in the Introduction for a full explanation.

6   See "Paradise Lies at the Feet of the Mother" in chapter 4, "A New Hajar Paradigm: Motherhood and Family."

7   See Nasr Abu Zaid with Esther Nelson, *Voice of an Exile: Reflections on Islam* (Westport, CT and London: Praeger, 2004), pp. 121–125: "We separated, but continued to live in the same apartment . . . In the Arab world, it is easy to live separately, but together – all the while *giving the appearance* to your family, your friends, and your colleagues *of a happily married couple*," p. 123 (emphasis mine).

8   In chapter 4, "A New Hajar Paradigm: Motherhood and Family," I deal extensively with this illusion and the enhanced burden it causes for single female heads of household. I also give related discussions about notions of family, the birthplace of gender relations, and of the domestic sphere that nurtures patriarchy and female abuse.

9   The theory–practice relationship is a thread that runs throughout this book. In the previous chapter, "What's in a Name?," the issue of authority granted by abusing of the word "Islam" is discussed at length. This chapter concludes with some issues of obstruction in the section on "Toward an Islamic Feminist Theory in Muslim Women's Studies," while chapter 3, "Muslim Women's Collectives, Organizations, and Islamic Reform," provides a section, "The Relationship between Theory and Practice," and chapter 6, "Qur'an, Gender, and Interpretive Possibilities," specifically details the authoritative patriarchal control over interpreting the primary sources.

10 Chapter 7, "Stories from the Trenches," provides a complete discussion of Islamic dress, specifically the *hijab*.

11 Artz and Pollock, "Anti-Arab Images," in *The U.S. Media and the Middle East*, p. 121.

12 p. 54.

13 Ada Maria Isasi-Diaz, *Mujerista Theology: A Theology for the Twenty-first Century* (Maryknoll, N.Y.: Orbis Books, 1966), p. 79.

14 p. 56.

15 Ibid., pp. 51–57.

16 Amina Wadud, "Teaching Afro-Centric Islam in the White Christian South," in *Black Women in the Academy: Promises and Perils*, ed. Lois Benjamin (Gainesville: University Press of Florida, 1997), pp. 134–144.

17 This term has been increasingly used to refer to Islamic studies scholars. It may eventually become standard, but because of its proximity to the term "Islamist," referring to one of the neo-conservative Muslim groups responding to Islam and modernity, it may cause some confusion.

18 Gisela Webb (ed.), *Windows of Faith: Muslim Women Scholar-Activists in North America* (New York: Syracuse University Press, 2000). Webb identifies two important sessions at the Middle East Studies Associate meeting and at the American Academy of Religion in 1995 as the origins for a "particular sense of urgency," which needed to be collected for publication, and was the coordinator of a unique published contribution on Muslim women scholars and activism moved "by the spirit of solidarity" to collect some of their individual

work for publication in response to the "urgency of the audiences present at those two meetings", Introduction, pp. xiv–xv.

19   V.C.U. summer workshop, "Survival in the Electronic Classroom," sponsored by the Office of the Provost and the Office of Instructional Development, August 7–17 2000.

20   The final version of that paper is presented as chapter 5, "Public Ritual Leadership and Gender Inclusiveness."

21   The *Journal of Feminist Studies in Religion*, 16(2), 73–131, dedicated its round table discussion to just the topic "Feminist Theology and Religious Diversity," with some similar issues raised and other problems repeated.

22   In 1997, Michelle Kimbell and Barbara von Schlegell wrote a bibliography, *Muslim Women Throughout the World* (Boulder, CO and London: Lynn Rienner) with an annotated section "which were selected on a national survey of scholar's choices of the most highly recommended books and articles on Muslim women, and for their originality, perceptive commentaries, and reflection of increasing awareness on the subject," p. viii. An updated version or new addition of such a bibliography would be an asset in organizing the publications in this last decade.

23   Fazlur Rahman, "Approaches to Islam in Religious Studies: Review Essay," in *Islam in Religious Studies*, ed. Richard Martin, especially pp. 195–196.

24   At a historical level, Islam is also an amalgam of how Muslims have understood and lived it.

25   Abou-el-Fadl, *Speaking in the Name of God.*

26   Gita Sen with Caren Crown, *Development, Crisis, and Alternative Vision: Third World Women's Perspectives* (India: the Development Alternatives with Women for a New Era [D.A.W.N.] project, June 1985): "For many women in the world, problems of nationality, class and race [and here I would insert religion, especially, Islam] are inextricably linked to their specific oppression as women. The definition of feminism to the struggle against all forms of oppression is legitimate and necessary. In many instances gender equality must be accompanied by change on these other fronts. But at the same time, the struggle against gender subordination cannot be compromised in the struggle against other forms of oppression, or relegated to a future when they may be wiped out" (p. 13).

27   From a hand-out "Why Gender Mainstreaming," generated as part of the workshop documents created by the Office of the Special Adviser on Gender Issues, Department of Economic and Social Affairs, U.N.D.P., Two United Nations Plaza, 12th Floor, New York, N.Y. 10017.

28   Simone De Beauvoir, *The Second Sex*, translated by H. M. Parshley (London: Penguin, 1972).

29   Chapter 1, "What's in a Name?"

30   Rita Gross, p. 141.

31   Shulamit Reinharz, with the assistance of Lynn Davidman, *Feminist Methods in Social Research* (New York: Oxford University Press, 1992), p. 4.

32   Audre Lorde, "The Master's Tools Will Never Dismantle the Master's House," in *Sister Outsider: Essays and Speeches by Audre Lorde* (Freedom, CA: The Crossing Press, 2001), p. 110

33   Azza Karam, *Women, Islamisms and State: Contemporary Feminisms in Egypt* (London: Palgrave Macmillan, 1997).

34   Margot Badran and Nikki Keddie, "Islamic Feminism: What's in a Name?" in *Al-Haram Weekly On-line*, http://www.ahram.org.ef/weekly/2002/569/cu1.htm, January 17–23, 2002.

35   Rosalind Delmar, "What is Feminism?" in *Theorizing Feminism: Parallel Trends in the*

Humanities and Social Sciences, eds Anne C. Herrmann and Abigail J. Stewart (Boulder, CO: Westview Press, 1994), p. 5.

36 For example, the nearly unprecedented article by Scott Kugle, "Sexuality, Diversity, and Ethics in the Agenda of Progressive Muslims," in *Progressive Muslims*, ed. Omid Safi (Oxford: Oneworld Publications, 2003) challenges patriarchal heterosexual privilege while rescripting the privilege of male sexuality.

Notes to Chapter 3

1 In another sense, an "idea" does not occur in a vacuum. It flows from influences in one's context.

2 Audre Lorde, *Sister Outsider: Essays and Speeches by Audre Lorde* (Freedom, CA: The Crossing Press, 2001), pp. 110–113.

3 Here, the words "it has been said" refer to human speculation, not to Qur'anic articulation or mandate. This is not an attempt to redefine the Qur'anic story of creation or to ascribe error to Allah. I simply point to how human speculation on transcendent ideas, like cosmology, are embedded in communal discussions whether or not they have explicit textual references from particular scholars within Islamic sciences or other religious discourse.

4 *"innama al-a'malu bi al-niyyah,"* al-Nawawi, *Forty Hadiths.*

5 This will be reiterated in chapter 7 within the section "H.I.V./A.I.D.S. and Vulnerability," when I state that "Islam cannot cure A.I.D.S."

6 See chapter 1 for a detailed consideration of this term.

7 Although I will argue at length in chapter 5, "Public Ritual Leadership and Gender Inclusiveness," that rituals, equally incumbent upon women and men in Islam, do not rule out considerations of reform in public Islamic rituals and leadership.

8 *Inna li-rabbika 'alayka haqqan, wa li-'ahlika 'alayka haqqan, wa li-nafsika 'alayka haqqan. Fa'ti kulla dhi haqqan haqqahu.*

9 Elisabeth Schussler-Fiorenza, *Bread Not Stone: The Challenge of Feminist Biblical Interpretation* (Boston: Beacon Hill Press, 1984), p. xiv.

10 *Women and Citizenship*, ed. Marilyn Freidman (New York: Oxford University Press, 2005) provides some interesting articles interrogating concepts of citizenship, creating new ones, and investigating the relationship between various concepts of citizen and the workings of the nation-state. See especially the chapter, "Arenas of Citizenship: Civil Society, the State, and the Global Order," where Alison Jaggar interrogates the newly formed shift in emphasis between civil society and the state. Where some have attempted to apply a more inclusive definition of civil society to integrate work contributed in previously divided public and private space, she avoids the dichotomy. Care work is not relegated to the private sector of society. Work in the public sphere is neither more important essentially nor inherently immoral, despite the exploitive tendencies of state governments. Contributing to the civil society and contributing to the state are both potential arenas for ethical change and development. This radical inclusive perspective has the potential not only to raise the citizen status of all women, but also to increase women's empowerment and access to rights.

11 Although I cannot date the origins of racial oppression, the origin of the mainstream "civil rights movement" in America is circa 1950.

12 C.A.I.R. study.

13 Joan Tronto, "Care As the Work of Citizens: A Modest Proposal," in *Women and Citizenship*, ed. Marilyn Friedman (New York: Oxford University Press, 2005), pp. 130–131.

14 Names are used by permission and to explicitly draw attention to the inspiration I have drawn from these two women. My small contribution to them is a necessary part of shining light through public recognition of their services, faith, and care.

15 Lorde, *Sister Outsider*, p. 111.

16 Qasim Amin was one of the first writers in early modern period to prioritize Muslim women's rights in his book, *Tahrir al-Mar'ah*. However, his goals were borrowed wholesale from Western secular paradigms.

Notes to Chapter 4

1   A revised version of this poem will appear in Mohja Kahf, *The Hajar Poems*, forthcoming. An later version of this poem has appeared on the Muslim Wake Up website (15 January 2005): www.muslimwakeup.com/main/archives/2005/ 01/the_fire_of_haj.php. Dr. Kahf is a poet who works as Associate Professor of Comparative Literature at the University of Arkansas in the Middle East and Islamic Studies Program. She is author of *The Girl in the Tangerine Scarf* (New York: Caroll and Graf, 2006), among other titles.

2   For example, *Daughters of Abraham: Feminist Thought in Judaism, Christianity and Islam*, eds. Yvonne Yazbeck and John L. Esposito (Gainesville: University Press of Florida, 2002) was the result of an earlier conference with the same theme at Georgetown University.

3   Sylviane Diouf, *Servants of Allah: African Muslims Enslaved in the America* (New York: New York University Press, 2000).

4   Nabia Abbott, *Two Queens of Baghdad, Mother and Wife of Harun al-Rashid* (Chicago: University of Chicago Press, 1979).

5   Audre Lorde, *Sister Outsider: Essays and Speeches* (Freedom, CA: The Crossing Press, 1984), p. 111.

6   One notable exception is Khaled Abu Fadl's *In the Name of God*.

7   Clarissa Atkinson, *The Oldest Vocation: Christian Motherhood in the Middle Ages* (Ithaca, N.Y.: Cornell University Press, 1991), p. 243.

8   Ibid., p. 5.

9   Ibid.

10 Ibid., p. 27.

11 Aliah Schleifer, *Motherhood in Islam* (The Islamic Texts Society, 1996).

12 This is an excellent book. My concern here is only about the use of the sacrifice and martyrdom paradigm mentioned. I do not think the evidence she chose makes a clear a case, but that she read this image into it.

13 Atkinson, p. 241.

14 Ibid., p. 246.

15 Ibid.

16 Ibid., p. 243.

17 This section of the chapter is dedicated to my mother, whose death at the end of a research leave to work on this very topic at the Harvard Divinity School's Research on Women and Religion Program in 1996 reminded me of the frailty of mothers against such constructs. An extended version of this work was first presented in 1999 for a workshop on Islam,

Reproductive Health and Women's Rights, organized by Sisters in Islam, Malaysia, who published it in a book by the same name in 2000.

18 One abuse resulting from unexamined notions of family is dealt with in my discussion on H.I.V./A.I.D.S. and vulnerability in chapter 7, "Stories from the Trenches."

19 W. Robertson Smith, *Kinship and Marriage in Early Arabia*, c. 1903 (reprinted by Boston: Beacon Press, n.d.). He states, "the object of the present volume – to collect and discuss the available evidence as to the genesis of the system of male kinship, with the corresponding laws of marriage and tribal organization, which prevailed in Arabia at the time of Mohammed; the general result is that male kinship had been preceded by kinship through women only." He indicates that "the steps of the social evolution in which the change in kinship law is the central feature" led to the male kinship model. He builds "a self-contained argument on the Arabian facts alone" (pp. xix–xx).

20 Ibid., p. iv.

21 Ibid.

22 Clarissa Atkinson, *The Oldest Vocation: Christian Motherhood in the Middle Ages* (Cornell University Press, 1991), p. 24. This book outlines some of the changes in human knowledge and the effects these changes have on what we know about physiological mothering, let alone ideological, social, cultural, or religious mothering.

23 Ibid., p. 243.

24 Smith, *Kinship and Marriage*, p. 203.

25 Shere Hite, "Bringing Democracy Home," *MS Magazine*, March/April, 1995, p. 57.

26 Smith, *Kinship and Marriage*, p. 27.

27 Ibid., p. 50.

28 Ibid., p. 53.

29 Ibid., p. 52.

30 Ibid., pp. 66–67.

31 Ibid., p. 65.

32 Ibid., p. 69.

33 Atkinson, *Oldest Vocation*. "It is also a historical construction – embattled, vulnerable, requiring recreation in each generation. To recognize its historicity is to begin to assume responsibility for the character of its reconstruction."

34 An-Naim, *Towards an Islamic Reformation*; Asifah Qureshi, "Her Honor: An Islamic Critique of the Rape Laws of Pakistan from a Woman-sensitive Perspective," in *Windows of Faith: Muslim Women Scholar-Activists in North America*, ed. Gisela Webb (New York: Syracuse University Press, 2000), chapter 5.

35 Based on the U.N.D.P. Human Development Report, Oxford, 1998.

36 Atkinson, *Oldest Vocation*, p. 242.

37 Lorde, *Sister Outsider*, p. 111.

38 Nimat Barangzangi, *Women's Identity and the Qur'an: A New Reading* (Gainesville: University Press of Florida, 2004) goes so far as to erroneously refer to this financial role as biological. In addition, she says, "all men are financially responsible toward the women in their household" (p. 74).

39 Nurturing and care-taking are learned traits, not exclusive to one gender. An Islamic scholar of *'usul al-fiqh* from Sarajevo was emphatic that he *could not* do his wife's job of taking care of children. It was against his natural disposition. It is easy to see that more men need to learn these skills as well, instead of abdicating them to some biological predisposition. Otherwise women will continually be presumed to be predisposed for them, rather than acknowledged as exercising their agency in service to others.

40 Suad Joseph, "The Kin Contract and Citizenship in the Middle East," in *Women and Citizen* (New York: Oxford University Press, 2005), p. 151.

41 Ibid.

42 Ibid., p. 157.

43 Ibid., p. 159.

44 Patricia Hills-Collins, "Work, Family and Black Women's Oppression", in her book *Black Feminist Thought* (Boston: Unwin Hyman, 1990), p. 44.

45 See two explicit examples in chapter 3, "Muslim Women's Collectives, Organizations, and Islamic Reform."

46 Niara Sudarkasa, *The Strength of Our Mothers: African and African-American Women and Families: Essays and Speeches* (Trenton, N.J.: Africa World Press, 1996), p. xvii.

47 Carolyn Moxley Rouse, *Engaged Surrender: African American Women and Islam* (Berkeley: University of California Press, 2004), p. 51.

48 Ibid.

49 Amina Wadud, *Qur'an and Woman: Re-reading the Sacred Text from a Woman's Perspective* (Oxford: Oxford University Press, 1999), pp. 1–3, 5–10, and 99–104.

50 Hite Report, p. 57.

51 Elisabeth Schussler-Fiorenza, *Bread not Stone: The Challenge of Feminist Biblical Interpretation* (Boston: Beacon Press, 1984), p. 5.

52 Carol Tarvis, *The Mismeasure of Women* (New York: Simon & Schuster, 1992), p. 17.

Notes to Chapter 5

1 A formula of remembrance of God.

2 The word for chapter of the Qur'an.

3 The Merciful and the Mercy-Giver.

4 Marriage agreement.

5 Way of life, religion.

6 Personal prayer or supplication.

7 I am very grateful the late South African activist, Soraya Bosch, from the Muslim Youth Movement Gender Desk in South Africa, who transcribed the presentation from a video recording made that day. I am also grateful to the editor, Na'eem Jeenah, and to the staff from *The Call*, a progressive Muslim newspaper for publishing the entire lecture.

8 It made little difference that one of the organizers was female. As a non-Muslim scholar of Islam, at that time Muslim female identity was apparently not an issue of concern for her.

9 They were unable to secure funds at that time, but since the conference organizers were paying for my airfare, they could take advantage of my presence in the country to set up their own program.

10 I wrote many journal entries after my visit, including the following account of meeting Shamima: "As I entered the place for the workshop I was met by a young *Muslimah* of Indian descent. She greeted me with a handshake and quick embrace: starting on the left side. We almost bumped heads as I headed for the right: the protocol of the Arab world, Asia and the U.S. Despite almost kissing a total stranger in the mouth, I liked her right away: she had no airs; no fan fares, no feminine vanities. She impressed me as a person who worked with a cause, and found meaning in doing: I liked her right away."

11 One evening during the conference, I attended an awards ceremony for President Mandela with Bishop Desmond Tutu as the keynote speaker and awards presenter.

12 Throughout this chapter, as elsewhere in this book, I refer to some individuals, real people with real-life expectations and capacities. I mention them only to facilitate my construction of a narrative, even while acknowledging that no one is reduced to a mere facility in my construction in real terms. I also realize that my reference to them is not even-handed: some are only mentioned in passing, while others feature more significantly in my narration and interpretation of the event. It is especially important how a prism of paradoxes bounce between my own intentions and outcome, and these various characters. That they configure differently, in my telling of the story, than they may configure in another telling, leads to two inevitable hermeneutical considerations: whose version of this story is true? Or, how are *all* versions of this story true?

13 See discussion below on the significance of embracing between Muslims.

14 See the full details of the *tawhidic* paradigm in chapter 2. Here I will provide succinct reiterations as they bear on gender equality in public ritual leadership.

15 A body of (usually all) men attached to particular Islamic community associations in or to decide on matters of significance to the community and Islam.

16 Lucinda Joy Peach, *Women and World Religions* (Englewood Cliffs, N.J.: Prentice Hall, 2002), especially the brief preface, pp. xi–xii.

17 Once the public frenzy over the March 18 congregational prayer in New York was in full thrust, I also remained silent. By this time, I had experienced enough public controversy to learn one lesson very well. To react to the sensationalist nature of the immediate discussions will have little or no effect on disentangling the substantive issues from the immediate sensationalism.

18 On the one hand many people would openly discuss that I had a personal desire to be leader, which, according to some traditions, would render me unworthy of leadership. On the other end, one progressive, Ebrahim Moosa, told me, this event had *nothing* to do with me.

19 As discussed in chapter 3, "Muslim Women's Collectives, Organizations, and Islamic Reform." I will return to this in chapter 7, "Stories from the Trenches."

20 Farid Esack, *Qur'an Liberation and Pluralism: An Islamic Perspective on Interreligious Solidarity against Oppression* (Oxford: Oneworld Publications, 1997), pp. 38–42 and 179–206. "In South Africa those who identified with the oppressed similarly refused to distinguish between their commitment to Islam and their commitment to the liberation struggle. Instead, they viewed both commitments as strands in a single tapestry" (p. 199).

21 That thought will prove to be a litmus test in these deliberations.

22 A complete discussion on the *hijab* is included in chapter 7, "Stories from the Trenches."

23 Member of my marital or blood relations.

24 Barbara Metcalf, ed., *Making Muslim Space: In North America and Europe* (California: University of California Press, 1996), pp. 31–64.

25 *The Call.*

26 A lengthy discussion of *hijab* is given in chapter 7, "Stories from the Trenches."

27 Most female Muslim academics in North America do not and will not wear *hijab*, especially in Islamic studies. It is as if being an academic and progressive demands the removal of all external symbolisms as well, as discussed in chapter 2, "The Challenges of Teaching and Learning in the Creation of Muslim Women's Studies."

28 Leia Ahmed, *Women and Gender in Islam* (New Haven and London: Yale University Press, 1992), p. 61.

29 See Abdulkader Tayob, "The pre-khutbah, khutbah and Islamic change," in *The Call* (August 1994), p.15, where he commented on this rhetorical irony.

30 *The Call*, August and September 1994.

31 This question will be answered in chapter 7, "Stories from the Trenches," where I give a brief discussion on the March 18 congregational prayer in New York City in 2005.

32 Esack, *Qur'an, Pluralism and Liberation*, p. 247.

33 It is also worth noting that Esack is the founder of "Positive Muslims," an organization that addresses H.I.V./A.I.D.S. and Muslims directly.

34 At the Second Muslim Leader Conference on H.I.V./A.I.D.S. in Malaysia in 2002 I learned that Sitty Dhiffy had died from A.I.D.S. I will discuss gender and the H.I.V./A.I.D.S. issue at greater length in chapter 7, "Stories from the Trenches."

35 As discussed at length in chapter 1, "What's in a Name?"

36 Discussed in full in chapter 7.

37 Notably, Chandra Muzaffer and Hasan Hanafi.

38 I once attended an *'Id al-Adha* celebration where the *khutbah* focused on what type of man Abraham must have been to circumcise himself without anesthesia, to demonstrate his obedience to Allah. Such a reference cannot have the same meaning for women as it must have for circumcised men. Clearly, exclusive male experiences are deemed the highest. In addition, although the sacrifice of the son is part of this occasion, we are rarely reminded of Hajar, the mother, who was abandoned in the desert by that very same man. See chapter 4, "A New Hajar Paradigm: Motherhood and Family."

39 Martha Minnow, *Not only for Myself: Identity, Politics and the Law* (New York, the New Press, 1997).

40 Ibid., p. 26.

41 This may be one explanation why so many modern writers point to *hadith* collections and *sirah* literature that includes women in acts of war; as if the particular violent form of heroism is the litmus test for full humanity!

42 Ali Shariati, "The World-View of Tauhid," in *Sociology of Islam* (Berkeley: Mirzan Press, 1979).

Notes to Chapter 6

1 Ebrahim Moosa, "The Debt and Burden of Critical Islam," in *Progressive Muslims: On Justice, Gender and Pluralism*, ed. Omid Safi (Oxford: Oneworld Publications, 2003), p. 125.

2 Ibid., p. 126.

3 Ibid., p. 125.

4 Ebrahim Moosa, *Ghazali & the Poetics of Imagination* (Chapel Hill: University of North Carolina Press, 2005), Acknowledgements, p. xi.

5 Carol Tarvis, *The Mismeasure of Women* (New York: Simon & Schuster, 1992), p. 17.

6 Especially useful in my research in this are two works, that of Khaled Abou El-Fadl, *Speaking in God's Name: Islamic Law, Authority and Women*, and the work of Alison Jaggar, *Feminist Politics and Human Nature*.

7 Fatnah Sabbah, *Women in the Muslim Unconscious*, trans. from the French, *La Femmedans L'inconscient Musulman* (New York: Pergamon Press, 1984).

8 As explained in details about linguistic construction in Chapter 1, "What's in a Name?"

9 See chapter 4, "A New Hajar Paradigm: Motherhood and Family."

10 Amina Wadud, *Qur'an and Woman: Re-Reading the Sacred Text from a Woman's*

Perspective (Oxford: Oxford University Press, 1999), pp. 15–16; inclusive of Kenneth Burke, *The Rhetoric of Religion* (Boston: Beacon Press, 1961), footnote, p. 14.

11   As cited by Abou El-Fadl, *Speaking in God's Name*, p. 24.

12   Jaggar, *Feminist Politics*, p. 125.

13   Wadud, *Qur'an and Woman*, pp. 94–95.

14   Ibid., p. 70.

15   Abou El-Fadl, *Speaking in God's Name*, p. 33.

16   Ibid., p. 213.

17   Ibid., pp. 93–94. See also Mary Daly and conceptions of God and patriarchy.

18   Ibid., p. 213.

19   In *Qur'an and Woman*, I have already argued that the Qur'an proposes three recommendations in response to marital disruption, which should be applied in the order in which they were articulated. Unless each method has been fully exhausted, the next cannot be applied. The first recommendation in verse 4:34 is mutual consultation between husband and wife. Another verse suggests more extensive consultation with others (members of the extended family, or professional counselors as arbitrators). The second suggestion is a separation between the marital partners. I assert that the fullest application of such a separation could suggest the permanent separation of divorce. These two would prevent any access to the third, daraba. The Qur'an gives evidence of the extended separation through a prophetic example. In reality, men and women who respond violently to a disruption with their spouse, or any other member of the family, do so as their primary response. This abuse is not a reflection of the Qur'an, no matter how many post-event justifications abusers try to associate with the text.

20   Abou El-Fadl, *Speaking in God's Name*, p. 93.

21   Furthermore the Qur'an exhorts, "*fa hal 'ala al-rasul illa balaaghan mubin*, So is it [the responsibility, capacity] on the Prophet [to report anything] except rhetorical clarity?" (16:35).

22   Wadud, *Qur'an and Woman*, pp. xii–xv, 3–9.

23   Ibid., pp. 81–91, 100–104.

Notes to Chapter 7

1   Amina Wadud, "Preface," in *Qur'an and Woman: Rereading the Sacred Text from a Woman's Perspective* (New York: Oxford University Press, 1999), pp. xviii–ix.

2   In 1992, Merryl Wyn Davies, an intellectual Muslim commentator, and I coined this sixth pillar designation of *hijab* as it is always discussed despite its triviality to the principles of Islam.

3   In addressing the issue of sexuality and Islamic history and practice later in this chapter, I will provide further elaboration not appropriate at this point in the discussion. In addition, the reduction of women to their sexuality will be addressed further vis-à-vis the issue of women as *imams*.

4   See chapter 5, "Public Ritual Leadership and Gender Inclusiveness," for details particular to that event.

5   I have already provided the details of my authentic surrender to the call of Islam in the Introduction. The most significant impetus for my surrender was reading the Qur'an, which the brothers who gave me the *shahadah* never even mentioned.

6   See Mohja Kahf, *Western Representations of the Muslim Women: From Termagant to*

Odalisque (Austin: University of Texas Press, 1999) for other false images and representations. Also see "Harem Literature, 1763–1914: Tradition and Innovation," in Billie Melman, *Women's Orients: English Women and the Middle East 1718–1918* (Ann Arbor, The University of Michigan Press), pp. 59–76.

7   See 'Erasure' below in this same chapter.

8   Discussed in more detail in this chapter.

9   Discussed below in this chapter in more detail.

10   www.womensenews.org.

11   Noor al-Deen Atabek, "The Modernist Approach to Hadith Studies" at Islam-on-Line, 9/19/2004; www.islamonline.net/english/Contemporary/ 2004/ 09/ Article03.shtml.

12   Sandra Lee Bartky, "Feminine Masochism and the Politics of Personal Transformation," in *Living With Contradictions: Controversies in Feminist Social Ethics*," ed. Alison M. Jaggar (Boulder: Westview Press, 1999), p. 519.

13   Scott Kugle (Siraj al-Haqq),"Sexuality, Diversity, and Ethics in the Agenda of Progressive Muslims," in *Progressive Muslims* (Oxford: Oneworld Publication, 2003).

14   Ibid., p. 191.

15   A more detailed consideration of these three verses and their interpretations, especially on the verse about post-menopausal women, is included in chapter 6, "Qur'an, Gender, and Interpretive Possibilities."

16   Fact sheet no. 242, June 2000, Women and H.I.V./A.I.D.S., www.who.int/inf-fs/en/ fact242.html.

17   Fact sheet, Gender and H.I.V./A.I.D.S., December 2001, http://www.hivnet.ch:8000/ topics/gender-aids/views.

18   Or shouted in their face. Indeed, this statement was prophetic to the exact response that disrupted the I.M.L.C. proceedings. The direct attack on my status as a Muslim woman was the charge, because I expressly challenged the inadequacy of the normative neo-conservative discourse and strategies vis-à-vis the spread of H.I.V./A.I.D.S. and its consequence on women and children's vulnerability. In all the commentaries that occurred throughout the consultation and those that followed for several months thereafter, the major concern was misdirected at discrediting my "Islam." Consequently, little or nothing was offered to address the insufficiency of the dominant theological paradigm, *laa taqrabuna al-zinaa*, and the total failure of that agenda regarding protection for those most vulnerable to H.I.V./A.I.D.S.

19   Faisal Abdul-Rauf, *Islam: A Sacred Law: What Every Muslim Should Know about shari'ah* (Brattleboro, VT: Qiblah Books, 2000).

20   *Muslim Wake Up* is an Internet publication, with a large readership, that promotes consideration of progressive perspectives and their opposition. This particular article was published in its February 11, 2005 edition.

21   I will no longer self-identify as a progressive Muslim or as a participant in progressive Islam after my experiences this past year, and in light of the comments I have made in this book about the male elitism that still characterizes the movements and discourses under this name. However, I will undoubtedly still be characterized under this name or as a member of these discourses. The same is true of Islamic or Muslim feminism. I have never self-identified as a Muslim feminist and wrote extensively about this in the new preface in the U.S. edition of *Qur'an and Woman*, 1999. I have also continued (and will probably still continue) to be identified as such. Because no one form, format, or formula will resolve the multi-leveled complexities of Islamic growth and development at this point in history, these

overlaps and distinctions only reiterate the need I have stressed for multiple strategies for real reform.

22 Translation my own.

23 Translation taken from A. Nooruddeen Durkee, translator and transliterator, *Tajwidi Qur'an*, English edited by Hajjah Noura Durkee (Charlottesville, VA: un-Noor Foundation, publisher and distributor, and@noor.net, 2003), p. 887.

24 Shaykh Ahmed, compilation of *Hizb-ul-Bahr: The Orison of The Sea* with the permission of Shaykh-ul-Tariqa Al Hajj Azad Rasool (Alexandria, VA.: The Circle Group, 2000), pp. 4–5 (with the exception of my own translation for portions in quotation).

25 Durkee, *Tajwidi Qur'an*, pp. 673–674.

26 All of them taken from translations in Abdur-Rashid, Hizb-ul-Bahr; pp. 14, 20–21, 28, 30–32, 34–34; except for the prayer for forgiveness taken as *du'a* from my own memory of various sources.

Notes to the Conclusion

1 Turner, Tina, "I Don't Wanna Fight" (lyrics © S. Duberry, Lulu and B. Lawrie) from the album *What's Love Got To Do With It?* (1993).

2 Alice Walker, *In Search of Our Mothers' Gardens* (San Diego: Harcourt Brace Jovanovich, 1983), p. 36.

3 Audre Lorde, *Sister Outsider* (Berkeley: The Crossing Press, 1984), p. 111.

4 Especially Paul Tillich, *The Shaking of the Foundations* (New York: Charles Scribner, 1978).

5 Ibid., p 11.

6 Fazlur Rahman, *Islam*, 2nd edn. (Chicago and London: University of Chicago Press, 1979), p. 129.

7 This was the original intent in developing *fiqh* and *shari'ah*. Both are still important positive mechanisms, as long as the will of the people in our current reality is integral to reforms in the traditional codes.

Index

Locators in brackets refer to notes